WHO ARE THE CRIMINALS?

WHO ARE THE CRIMINALS?

———————— The Politics of Crime Policy ————————
from the Age of Roosevelt to the Age of Reagan

John Hagan

Princeton University Press • Princeton and Oxford

Library of Congress Cataloging-in-Publication Data
Hagan, John, 1946–
Who are the criminals? : the politics of crime policy from the age of
Roosevelt to the age of Reagan / John Hagan.
p.   cm.
Includes bibliographical references and index.
ISBN 978-0-691-14838-0 (hbk. : alk. paper)   1. Crime—Government policy—
United States.   2. Crime—United States.   3. Criminal justice, Administration
of —United States.   I. Title.
HV6789.H24 2010
364.97309′045—dc22   2010018663

British Library Cataloging-in-Publication Data is available

This book has been composed in Palatino
Printed on acid-free paper. ∞
Printed in the United States of America
1 3 5 7 9 10 8 6 4 2

To the extended Hagan family,
with love and appreciation

||||||||||

When the capital development of a country
becomes a by-product of the activities of a casino,
the job is likely to be ill-done.

—*John Maynard Keynes, 1936*

You can't go forward if you don't know where you've been.

—*Hank Williams, 1952*

CONTENTS

||||||||||

ILLUSTRATIONS

|||||||||||

Figures

Tables

Map

WHO ARE THE CRIMINALS?

Prologue
Washington Crime Stories

I̶т̶ ̶ᴡᴀꜱ ᴍᴏʀᴇ ᴛʜᴀɴ "a beer at the White House" moment when President Barack Obama rolled up his sleeves and sat down with Henry "Skip" Gates and James Crowley in the back garden. Gates was the president's African American friend from Harvard arrested a few weeks earlier on his own front porch in Cambridge, and Crowley was the white arresting officer from the Cambridge Police Department. The White House invitation was atonement for the president, in a rare moment of recklessness, remarking to the press that the Cambridge police had behaved "stupidly." The meticulously scripted and flawlessly staged photo opportunity, with its soothing message of reconciliation dubbed in advance the "beer summit," displayed in a politely confected way just how highly politicized the joined issues of race, class, crime, and punishment have become in America. The parties agreed before meeting that the event would be entirely social, although Gates and Crowley promised there would be substantive conversations to follow.

Their plan seemed worthy, perhaps even more so if going forward it had included the president. There is much yet to learn about the politics of crime. This book aspires to advance the way politicians engage with citizens, academics, and policymakers to shape our thoughts about crime and its control. In it I develop three thematic arguments about crime in America that will take more than a few shared beers to consider.

My first argument is that an ongoing interaction of politics and ideas determines crime policies in America. During the age of Roosevelt (ca. 1933–73) and the age of Reagan (ca. 1974–2008), politicians, academic criminologists, and criminal justice practitioners developed mutual understandings of crime and connected policies that they expected could reduce crime. Crime policy-making became an increasingly politicized process, with leaders often advocating and implementing definitions of crime and causal arguments to suit ideological preferences, placate fears, and serve electoral needs. Over time, and with the transition from one era to the next, we came to fear the city streets too much and the corporate suites too little. As a result, in the age of Reagan public concerns and resources were pushed in directions with counterproductive consequences for controlling the types of crimes that do the most harm to the most citizens.

Second, I develop a class and race inequality argument about the different emphases on common crimes of the streets and financial crimes of the suites during the Roosevelt and Reagan eras. The politics of the age of Roosevelt, flowing from the Great Depression and in the aftermath of World War II, sought partly to make the lax prosecution of suite crimes more comparable to the harsh response to street crimes. However, in the age of Reagan politics reversed course, demanding increased imprisonment of street criminals and a reduced scrutiny and enforcement in the financial sector. The age of Reagan mobilized economic rhetoric about free markets and deregulation in ways that rationalized and enabled white-collar crime as acceptable and expected in the life of a market. Age of Reagan politics treated financial crimes more like suite misdemeanors, wrongly touting the financial sector as self-controlled and self-correcting.

Third, I argue that the massive growth and overpopulation of U.S. prisons has *combined* with the deregulation and collapse of the U.S. economy in the age of Reagan to impose unsustainable costs. As we move beyond the age of Reagan, we will need to redistribute the risks and punishments of street and suite crimes in America. The street- and suite-linked patterns of over- and undercontrol that I emphasize are not uniquely American, but they have become uniquely prominent in the United States during the age of Reagan. Furthermore, our politicized domestic crime wars feed into our policies on war crimes and state crimes in international conflict zones as far removed as Darfur and Iraq, adding global dimensions to our national crime politics.

An unlikely combination of Barack Obama and Edwin Meese led me to write this book about Ronald Reagan and crime in America. Barack Obama started it with his comments in January 2008 to the editorial board of the *Reno Gazette-Journal*. Obama was deep into the presidential primaries, and the field was narrowing to a contest with Hillary Clinton. He explained to the board members,

> I don't want to present myself as some sort of singular figure. I think part of what is different is the times. I do think that, for example, the 1980 election was different. I think Ronald Reagan changed the trajectory of America in a way that Richard Nixon did not and in a way that Bill Clinton did not. He put us on a fundamentally different path because the country was ready for it. They felt like with all the excesses of the 60s and the 70s and government had grown and grown but there wasn't much sense of accountability in terms of how it was operating. I think he tapped into what people were already feeling. Which is we want clarity, we want optimism, we want a return to that sense of dynamism and entrepreneurship that had been missing.

Obama's view that Ronald Reagan rather than Bill Clinton "put us on a fundamentally different path" caused considerable consternation among many Democrats. The implication was that Reagan's influence extended well beyond the partisan dimensions of his own personality and party. Indeed, Barack Obama implied that Bill Clinton as well as George W. Bush positioned themselves within a trajectory that Ronald Reagan had established. I shared Obama's estimation of Reagan's influence with regard to crime policies.

Of course, it was unlikely that Obama was thinking about crime, and this was also true of Sean Wilentz, the Princeton historian whose book, *The Age of Reagan*, also appeared in 2008 and gave little attention to crime. Nonetheless, Reagan's presidency radically influenced domestic policy about crime in the streets as well as in the suites. For me, Obama and Wilentz simply placed this influence in a broader frame of reference. Within this broad sweep of domestic and foreign policy, it is possible to underestimate and neglect the specific importance of Reagan to crime, and of crime to Reagan. Yet this oversight is misleading.

Less than a year after Obama's remarks, I was asked to serve on a National Academy of Sciences panel to set a research agenda for the National Institute of Justice. The invited members included a famous political ally of Ronald Reagan. When I learned that Reagan's former chief of staff and attorney general, Edwin Meese, would serve on the panel, I leapt at the opportunity to get an inside look at a living partner in a political alliance that had shaped the recent history of crime in America.

I learned a lot by watching and listening to Edwin Meese during the panel's work. Although now in his eighties, Reagan's former ally was an energetic and fully engaged participant on the panel. He reliably attended meetings, he often came to dinner afterward, and he shared many amusing anecdotes as well as fascinating stories about the Reagan years. I distrusted many of the stories, but they were always interesting and often revealing. As an example, I offer a story he told one evening while we were walking back to our hotel after a dinner in a downtown Washington restaurant.

Meese began by explaining that in the spring of 1968, Reagan, who was then governor of California, had agreed to give a speech in Washington. On the evening of the speech, the nation learned that Martin Luther King had been shot and killed on a motel balcony in Memphis. King had been in Memphis to support striking garbage workers. Reagan delivered his speech and then prepared to return to the Mayflower Hotel, where he planned to spend the night. However, riots had broken out in several ghetto neighborhoods around Washington, and traffic was at a standstill. Reagan's driver could not return him to his hotel by car.

Reagan was undeterred. He insisted he knew the city well and could simply walk the several blocks to the Mayflower. However, Reagan's security team was concerned he would be recognized, and they insisted he at least put on a pair of sunglasses. Reagan donned the dark glasses and set off with Meese and others on the walk to the hotel. He soon encountered a tall African American man leaving an appliance store with a large box apparently containing a television.

The man did a double-take when he spotted Governor Reagan—the dark glasses were insufficient disguise—and quickly placed the box on the ground beside him. "Governor Reagan!" he exclaimed. "Can I get your autograph?" By this point in Meese's telling of the story, our small group was chuckling and we were approaching our own hotel. We would have to guess the rest of the tale. Did the governor give the autograph? Did he comment on the large box? Did the autograph seeker thank the governor? We will never know.

It was impossible not to laugh along with the others, but I was full of skepticism and growing dismay by the time I reached my hotel room. It seemed unlikely there would have been any television appliance stores along the path that Reagan would have walked on that fateful night forty years ago. Despite our laughter, the story seemed on reflection almost certainly false, and it contained a number of disturbing elements.

Indeed, the story contained many characteristics of the kinds of tall tales often attributed to the "Great Communicator."

The entire episode also suggested insights into the relationship between Edwin Meese and Ronald Reagan. In particular, the two seemed quite similar in their carefully crafted capacities for affably framed aggression. Edwin Meese is an extremely amiable, even avuncular personality. My sense was that these many years later, with Meese now an octogenarian, I had witnessed the long-practiced performance of one of the former president's still masterful messengers.

Consider several aspects of this Washington crime story. The account underlines Governor Reagan's celebrity while placing the assassination of Martin Luther King in a secondary role and locating the governor at the center of events. The story also underlines the property crime of an African American man who was presumably taking material advantage of a time of national tragedy. Finally, the tale draws a direct connection between this brazen theft for apparent personal gain and the rebellion of the nation's black ghettos against the injustice of the assassination of our still best-remembered black civil rights leader. The account makes an implicit case for the punishment of criminal insurrection while simultaneously softening the image of the governing figure, namely, Ronald Reagan, through which this case is made. The story has all the elements of an urban social legend created for punitive political advantage.

In sociological terms, the story was a framing device to deliver a political message about race and street crime in America. I draw on a critical collective framing theory in this book to explain how elites and elite organizations manage images of the kind conveyed in Ronald Reagan's story to influence crime policy and practices. At the heart of the Reagan era, there was a strong political imperative to frame a message about increasing the control of crime on America's city streets. The age of Reagan featured a parallel imperative to reduce control of the nation's business suites through a reframing process that led to decriminalizing and deregulating important financial practices. I emphasize the redistribution of control involved in the linkage between these street and suite framing processes.

My time on the National Academy panel with Edwin Meese revealed at least one more story about how framing processes are undertaken but also sometimes fail. This second story involved the suppression of a presidential crime report during Reagan's first term in office. I learned the story early in the work of the panel, and I retell it in detail in the first chapter of this book.

The key to the story is that that the administration blocked a presidential advisory board, appointed amid controversy before holding meetings all over the country, from distributing its completed report and delivering its final recommendations. A hired pen and now widely read writer, Joseph Persico, wrote the report, which he titled "Too Much Crime . . . Too Little Justice." When I heard about the report, I recognized the name of its author.

Persico's work includes a book about Nuremberg that was also the basis of a made-for-television movie featuring Alec Baldwin as the tribunal's famous American prosecutor, and more recently he co-authored Colin Powell's best-selling personal and political memoir. More relevant to this book, however, when Persico was hired to redraft the advisory board's report he had already written a well-received book about his time as Nelson Rockefeller's personal speechwriter. In his book, Persico had written about the development of Rockefeller's highly punitive drug policies as governor of New York State.

I developed my account of "the president's secret crime report" after interviewing Persico about his involvement as the ghostwriter and after visiting his archive at the State University at Albany. The first chapter of this book explains how and why the president's crime report was ultimately a failed exercise in political frame construction. The report did not effectively convey the message the Reagan administration wanted to tell. Put simply, the report did not make a persuasive case for the punitive policy on street crime that the administration would soon put in place. Persico's principal challenge in rewriting the report was that crime actually declined in the early 1980s during Reagan's first term as president. This undercut the administration's push for more punitive policies, one result of which was a spike in mass incarceration, in which the United States now leads the world.

After reviewing the circumstances surrounding the failed report, in chapter 2 I place the Reagan administration's failed experience with the advisory board in context by explaining how criminologists "know what we know" about the occurrence and distribution of crime. Chapter 3 examines American criminologists' classical explanations of crime in the immediately preceding period, which Arthur Schlesinger called the Age of Roosevelt and which I believe persisted through the late 1960s and into the 1970s. In chapter 4 I describe how a new cohort of criminologists reconfigured the field with explanations of crime in the age of Reagan, an age whose influence has lasted at least to the time of this writing.

Chapters 5 and 6 explore in considerably more detail how the age of Reagan exerted its influence in response to the very different problems posed by crime in America's city streets and the nation's business suites. The account of street crime in the age of Reagan focuses on drug crime and the massive increase in imprisonment. The account of suite crime focuses on financial crime and the precursors of the banking and credit crises underlying the recent Great Recession.

Finally, chapter 7 looks beyond the borders of the United States to consider the problems of torture and sexual violence at Abu Ghraib prison in postinvasion Iraq, and to what I refer to as "state rape" in Darfur and pre-invasion Iraq. We live in a time of expanding awareness of war crimes, although the level of this attention is still far from what it should be. Turning to the Obama presidency in the epilogue, I am skeptical that we are on the cusp of a new era. The influence of the age of Reagan is far from finished.

The question that worries me most is whether we will be able to move beyond the age of Reagan in our politics of crime. My goal is to engage citizens and criminologists alike—whether Republican, Democrat, or independent—in a process of change. America's punitive images of crime run deep, and they are highly resistant to change.

The age of Reagan involved a sweeping reframing of the American political imagination with regard to the punishment of street crime and the deregulation of business. This reframing could not have achieved the breadth and depth it did without the consent of both major political parties. I document this point with regard to street crime in tracking the major roles that Democratic senators Ted Kennedy and Joe Biden played, along with Republican senator Strom Thurmond, in the 1980s reconfiguration of sentencing policies leading to the escalation of imprisonment to world-leading levels. I similarly trace the role that the Democratic Speaker of the House James Wright played in the savings and loan scandals that set the foundation for the subsequent subprime mortgage collapse.

The Clinton and Bush administrations extended important policies of the age of Reagan with regard to both the streets and the suites. The age of Reagan gained surprising forms of bipartisan support through the frame realignments it brought to American politics. The age of Reagan may be even longer-lasting and therefore more consequential than previously imagined.

Chapter 1
The President's Secret Crime Report

||||||||||

Ronald Reagan was elected president in November 1980 with an agenda that included making the country safer from violent forms of street crime. This goal seemed quite sensible to most voters at the time. The Reagan administration promised a "get tough" approach to the punishment of crime. There would be reasons for questions later, especially about the very punitive response to crack cocaine, the drug whose epidemic use spread rapidly through America's racial ghettos and spiked a fearful, massive, and enormously expensive growth in American reliance on imprisonment that has lasted for more than a quarter century.

But there was steadfast agreement in the innermost circle surrounding President Reagan in 1980, a circle that included his personal lawyer, William French Smith, who became attorney general, and Reagan's closest political adviser, Edwin Meese, who succeeded as attorney general when Smith returned to his California law practice. Both Smith and Meese believed it was time to lift what a presidential board soon called "the veil of fear over crime." *Fear* of crime was the administration's overriding concern.

||||||||||

Early in his administration Ronald Reagan appointed a presidential advisory board with the mandate to, in conjunction with the National Institute of Justice, recommend justice system policies and research priorities. The appointees were replacements for board members selected by Jimmy Carter before he left office, some of whom filed lawsuits about their removal. The nineteen Reagan appointees consisted of a former speechwriter, campaign contributors, and criminal justice officials, as well as enduring political figures such as Mitch McConnell, presently the U.S. Senate minority leader from Kentucky. The board held hearings in Los Angeles, Atlanta, New Orleans, and Nashville, and met with police chiefs from all over the country. The experience of the board offers instructive insights into how crime policies and priorities are often advanced in America.

The president's advisory board reported finding great fear of crime wherever the members went. The board chairman reported that Attorney General Smith had walked the streets of Newark and "talked with residents and shopkeepers and heard their daily concerns about the peril in their community and threats to their lives and property." Board members visited high-crime areas of Los Angeles, where they "saw the barred windows, locked storefronts, graffiti-ridden buildings, a walled-in shopping center and felt the apprehension of the people on their streets." They found that homicide was the leading cause of death in Los Angeles, with some 1,700 criminal assaults occurring daily.

The advisory board members were convinced that fear of crime was growing and that the president urgently needed their input. They wanted to give clear voice to their concerns and recommendations. They took as the subtitle of their report "The Police, Court, and Correctional Officials Who Administer America's Criminal Justice System Speak Out for Change."

A Hired Pen

Given the gravity of the topic and the circumstances, the board was determined to write a persuasive report with recommendations that would "strengthen the hand of the law in the contest with the lawless." The board took this commitment so seriously that it decided to hire a professional writer to sharpen their message and the power of their recommendations. Their choice was Joseph Persico.

The board's choice of Persico was somewhat surprising in that he came to the task with a measure of skepticism based on his firsthand experience with Nelson Rockefeller's passage of drug laws in the state of New York. Persico later would write award-winning books about Franklin Roosevelt and the Nuremberg Trials, and he co-authored Colin Powell's autobiography. He had already displayed a capacity to write nonfiction with a best-selling biography of Nelson Rockefeller that included a chapter titled "The Imperial Governor." Persico was in an ideal position to write about Rockefeller because he had been his principal speechwriter for more than a decade and had observed firsthand the development of New York State's drug laws.

New York's drug laws were among the most punitive ever passed in the United States and have only recently been moderated. New York's laws foreshadowed Reagan's war on drugs, as reflected in an anecdote told by Persico. He recalled that Rockefeller was warned about the consequences of his punitive proposals by an adviser who presciently predicted that "the jails could not hold all the prisoners that this law would generate, and that pushers would recruit minors to carry their dope" (Persico 1982:146). I will have reason to return to this prediction later in the book. At the time, this advice had already led Persico (148) to wonder about the role of research in the development of crime policy: "Where did Nelson Rockefeller get this idea? Had penologists and jurists (like the President's Advisory Board) urged him along this course? Was it the product of professional investigation and research?"

The answer was perhaps surprising. Rockefeller had simply heard from an interested family friend about low rates of drug addiction in Japan and the use of life sentences for drug pushers in that country. The friend was William Fine, president of the Bonwit Teller department store, who had a drug-addicted son and who chaired a city drug rehabilitation program. Rockefeller later attended a party at which Reagan asked Fine for further information about Japan's drug laws. Worried about his reputation as a liberal and his limited credentials as a crime fighter, Rockefeller diverted Reagan's request and moved swiftly ahead with his own severe state drug legislation. This gave Persico an answer to his question about the role of research in Rockefeller's crime policy: "the law under which thousands of narcotics cases would be tried in the courts of a great state had been . . . improvisation without the deadening hand of oversophisticated professionals" (Persico 1982:148).

So Persico approached the president's crime report with the skepticism of a hired pen and a disillusioned political speechwriter, yet he also brought a notable writing talent to the task of drafting a presidential report. He crafted an interesting title, "Too Much Crime . . . Too Little Justice," and introduced the then innovative technique of interposing provocative quotations from members of the board as bolded sidebars throughout the report.

The recurring theme of the report was captured in a quotation from the president of the National Organization for Victims Assistance, who ominously remarked that "If there is any problem as destructive as crime, it is the fear of crime" (National Institute of Justice [NIJ] 1984:5). James K. "Skip" Stewart, the director of the National Institute of Justice, noted in his preface to the report two research literatures that channeled this fear: (1) data revealing that the majority of crimes were committed by a small minority of highly active offenders, and (2) studies challenging the value of indeterminate sentences in reducing criminal behavior. Chapter 4 shows just how important these two research sources were to a "developmental criminology" that set a foundation for crime policy during the age of Reagan. Indeed, much that has gone wrong in American criminology, and the role it has played in the formation of national crime policy, may be traced to the misguided influence of the above two areas of research.

Yet these research lines were not what focused Persico's drafting of the report to the president. Rather, the very first highlighted quotation, from Houston's police chief, in the opening chapter of the report reflected a sense of uncertainty in Persico's approach, perhaps resulting from his past experience with Rockefeller. He chose to lead in bold lettering on the first page of the report with the following overview by Houston police chief Lee Brown of the advisory board's work: "We have looked at the causation of crime from perspectives ranging from economic factors and phases of the moon to biological phenomena. . . . Do we know what we need to know? Are we asking the right questions? I am afraid at the present time we are not" (NIJ 1984:4).

The Reagan administration never allowed "Too Much Crime . . . Too Little Justice" to see the public light of day. Although the Institute used its own budget to print more than a thousand copies of the report, which were dramatically bound in a dark, blood red cover, these copies of the report never left the loading dock for distribution. At the last moment, someone in the Department of Justice halted the release of the report. The only bound copy I was able to find is preserved in the collected papers of Joseph Persico at the State University of Albany Library. The board quietly went out of existence when the Reagan administration passed the Anti-Drug Abuse Act of 1986.

Too Much Crime . . . Too Little Justice

Why would the work of nineteen prominent Americans and a talented professional writer on a topic as important as serious and violent crime have been suppressed when the work was already completed and the report was bound and ready for public distribution? Joseph Persico's answer is perhaps discernible from his reaction to his own exposure to Governor Nelson Rockefeller's earlier development of drug enforcement policy. Persico (1982:149) writes:

I never fully understood the psychological milieu in which the chain of errors in Vietnam was forged until I became involved in the Rockefeller drug proposal. This experience brought to life with stunning palpability psychologist Irving Janis' description of group think: "the concurrence-seeking tendency which fosters over-optimism, lack of vigilance and sloganistic thinking about the weakness and immorality of outgroups."

It may have been the déjà vu nature of this experience that framed Persico's writing of the president's report. It was probably the uncertain tone and content of the report that caused Reagan's Justice Department to block its distribution.

In bold contrast to the report, there was stirring certainty to Ronald Reagan's message to the voting public about crime. Reagan voiced a strong conviction that there was altogether Too Much Crime, just as the title of the report indicated. But the subtitle, "Too Little Justice," sounded a note of fatal ambiguity. Was there too little justice for the victims? Or was it also, or alternatively, too little justice for the defendants accused of the crimes? Or was the problem the taxes paid by the public for the justice system? The report signaled uncertainty from the outset, admitting that "traditional approaches—the addition of more police, detective work, more judges, probation, parole and rehabilitation—as commonly practiced—have not been proven substantially effective in preventing crimes, solving crimes or weaning repeat offenders from a life of crime" (NIJ 1984:4).

Furthermore, the report acknowledged that U.S. prisons were already extremely costly and overcrowded. The number of Americans imprisoned had more than doubled over the previous decade, and the report lauded certain jurisdictions in which "prison crowding [had been] reduced through research-inspired management innovations." The advisory board probably could not have imagined that the number of Americans in prison would more than quadruple over the next several decades, but the board members were already worried about the financial if not human costs of a growing reliance on imprisonment. The report was fundamentally uncertain about what to do about this situation. This uncertainty undermined the administration's strong views and "can do" message about crime control.

The report looked to further research for its answers to the crime problem and placed its greatest emphasis on the work of Alfred Blumstein, who would later become president of the American Society of Criminology. Blumstein became the age of Reagan's most influential criminologist, but he also later became one of the most quoted critics of the policies of this era. Blumstein was an operations researcher with a background in the use of engineering principles to organize and conduct major social and governmental programs. He had worked on planning for the Vietnam War and had played a prominent scientific advisory role in the earlier Johnson administration's presidential commission, named for its topic, The Challenge of Crime in a Free Society. I briefly introduce Blumstein's approach here and then discuss it more fully in later chapters.

The aspect of Alfred Blumstein's research agenda (Blumstein, Cohen, and Nagin 1978; Blumstein et al. 1986) that captured the advisory board's hopes involved the concept of the "career criminal" and Blumstein's broader interest in the study of criminal careers. The board was encouraged but also frustrated by the perceived promise of this research agenda. It found that

> We are presently refining, through research, possibly the best crime-fighting tool available—a capacity to identify the minority of career criminals who commit the majority of crimes. Yet, too many police forces, prosecutors, judges and parole authorities still lack the resources to put this tool to work and thus concentrate on these one-person crime waves. (NIJ 1984:4)

The board blamed the unrealized potential of career criminal research to reduce crime on poor coordination in the justice system. The board saw the losers in this situation as the victims of crime who were "pawns of the judicial process" and whose rights "are subordinated to the rights—even the convenience—of their victimizers."

All of this led the board members to an uncomfortably ambiguous conclusion. They were painfully aware of prison overcrowding and escalating costs. They also knew that crime rates in the early 1980s were not actually increasing. In fact, from 1980 until 1985, American rates of serious and violent crimes declined from their previous peak level. This was the longest sustained break in rising crime rates from the early 1960s to the early 1990s. So, despite the Reagan administration's concern about crime victims, serious and violent victimization actually decreased during this president's first term in office.

Notwithstanding this period of declining street crime and a much longer and more sustained decline beginning in the early 1990s, however, rates of imprisonment in the United States uniformly and unrelentingly increased. When Joseph Persico linked his earlier experience with the Rockefeller drug laws to the present downturn in serious violent crime, he must have realized that he was a hired pen caught in a potentially contradictory predicament.

The advisory board and its writer came to a meeting of minds by placing the emphasis of the report on fear of crime rather than on crime itself. They fudged the facts by claiming crime rates were steady when they were actually falling, and they reasoned that even steady crime rates at an unacceptably high level were a source of damaging fear. Rather than use the crime decline to reduce the fear of crime, they emphasized what they discerned as a fearful spiral of community decline:

> Fear of crime continues to rise even though actual crime rates have tended to be steady (at unacceptable levels). This fear by itself has produced tangible negative economic

and social costs particularly for our inner cities. Crime-wary residents and business people make decisions about where and when they will work, shop, locate, open and close stores which can hasten a declining neighborhood's descent into decay. (NIJ 1984:5)

The board worried that "despair has begun to set in that any-thing can be done about this condition." The report tried to argue that a reasoned pursuit of research-led innovations could prospectively show a way to more hopeful solutions. However, for political advisors in the Reagan administration, such as Edwin Meese, this conclusion must have sounded like *Waiting for Godot*. The report never left the loading dock and has remained an essentially secret document for the past third of a century.

I argue in this book that the suppression of President Reagan's secret crime report coincided with a missed opportunity. The missed opportunity was the rationale that the downturn in crime could have provided for shifting resources away from the rapidly rising reliance on imprisonment that was still gaining momentum. However, this policy option was the "path not taken" throughout the last quarter of the twentieth century, when imprisonment increased to historically massive levels. To understand this outcome requires a better understanding of the politics of crime in America.

From Roosevelt to Reagan and Beyond

There was a time when it was thought that presidential politics had little to do with crime in America. Most crimes were prosecuted under state laws and in state and municipal courts, with those convicted of the crimes then sent to local and state jails. However, Jonathan Simon (2007) argues that this began to change during the Great Depression and with the election of Franklin Roosevelt. Even earlier, perhaps beginning most obviously with the national passage of Prohibition nearly a century ago, crime became an increasingly important focus of federal as well as local politics.

In his book, *Governing Through Crime* (2007), Simon argues that crime, and even more so the fear of crime, is today the defining problem of government. Indeed, Simon goes so far as to say that the federal role of the U.S. attorney and his leadership of the Department of Justice has become the late modern equivalent of what the Department of Defense was during the cold war: "the agency within . . . the federal government that most naturally provided a dominant rationale of government through which other efforts must be articulated and coordinated" (45).

As I show in this book, the scholarly understanding of crime is closely tied to the politics of crime in the two respectively progressive and more conservative eras that I call the age of Roosevelt (1933–73) and the age of Reagan (1974–). The modern classical theories of crime, which I take up in chapter 3, mostly evolved during the rather persistently progressive age of Roosevelt, while a more recent and dominant form of "developmental criminology," discussed in chapter 4, emerged during the more conservative age of Reagan. To be sure, there are preludes and postludes to both of these eras, and our categorization runs some risks of overgeneralization. Still, there is considerable value in organizing our understanding of the evolution of modern American criminology over much of the past century along this political fault line.

The Age of Roosevelt

I will have more to say in this book about the age of Reagan than the age of Roosevelt, but it is important to understand the earlier period too, in part because Ronald Reagan began his own political life in the movie industry's union politics of the late Roosevelt era. In chapter 2, I discuss the major increase in the national government role with regard to crime control that began in response to immigration during the Prohibition era.

Then as now, immigration was an important "hot button" issue that was linked in the public mind and in stereotypes with crime. Here it is enough to say that Prohibition unlocked a door that Franklin Roosevelt opened more widely with his New Deal agenda during the Great Depression.

Roosevelt's first attorney general, Hommer Cummings, played a major role that began with a crime conference in 1934. Roosevelt (1934:17–18) may have been the first president to use the "war on crime" metaphor at this conference. He asked the participants to help mount a "major offensive" in "our constant struggle to safeguard ourselves against the attacks of the lawless and the criminal elements of our population."

Roosevelt was signaling his willingness to use law enforcement and the justice system as part of his economic recovery effort. He saw that the law itself could be a valuable weapon, to be used against the "banksters" in the suites as well as against the "gangsters" on the streets. (I discuss the use of framed images in apposition in chapters 5 and 6.) Roosevelt encouraged Attorney General Cummings to use the law both as a symbol and as an instrument for change, the latter use manifested in the Securities Act of 1933, the Glass-Steagall Act of 1933, and the Securities Exchange Act of 1934. Roosevelt also worked closely with Cummings to pack the Supreme Court in defense of his New Deal legislation.

If Prohibition was the criminal law prelude to the age of Roosevelt, the role of Robert Kennedy as attorney general in the Kennedy and Johnson administrations was the postlude. The bold stroke with which John Kennedy would choose his brother as attorney general was itself an indication of the importance he assigned to this office. We will see in chapter 3 that Robert Kennedy's involvement in the Mobilization for Youth program was an outgrowth of a "differential opportunity theory of crime," and his advocacy of bail reform was a further building block in the War on Poverty, which focused many of the most progressive hopes of the Kennedy and Johnson administrations.

As attorney general, Robert Kennedy oversaw passage of the 1964 Criminal Justice Act and the establishment of an Office on Criminal Justice. This office was responsible for advancing fairness in the justice system and provided for a public defender system. Simon (2007:52) argues that more than any of his predecessors, notably beginning with Roosevelt and Cummings, "Kennedy made the attorney general 'America's prosecutor.'"

The Age of Reagan

Although Richard Nixon is the figure that overlaps and connects the ages of Roosevelt and Reagan, his importance pales in comparison with Ronald Reagan's. The Princeton historian Sean Wilentz (2008) is the source of the argument about the distinctiveness of Reagan and persuasive in regarding this expansive era as lasting from 1974 to 2008. Wilentz emphasizes the links that extend from Nixon through Reagan to the subsequent Bush father and son presidencies and even to Bill Clinton, but he also sees distinctions. As Wilentz remarks, "Reagan, a committed ideological conservative, attempted to push American government and politics in a more decisive direction than Nixon did—and far more so than his chief Republican rival in 1980, George H. W. Bush, would in later years" (5). Of course, Wilentz's point is that Ronald Reagan's influence was not only unique but also long-lasting.

The view that Wilentz further provides of the illegalities of the Reagan administration adds perspective to our argument that Reagan is a key figure in the U.S. crime experience. The importance Wilentz attaches to abuses of law in the age of Reagan stems from a worldview that stressed the political uses of threat, risk, and fear:

> The Reagan White House established a pattern of disregard for the law as anything other than an ideological or partisan tool. Laws that advanced the interests of the administration were passed and heeded; those that did not

> were ignored, undermined, or (if necessary) violated. The administration's sorry record of corruption, partisan favoritism, and influence peddling stemmed in part from the shabby venality that is inherent in human affairs. But it also stemmed from an arrogance born of the same ideological zealotry that propelled . . . the belief that, in a world eternally 'at risk,' the true believers must take matters into their own hands and execute. The rule of law, by those lights, would always be subordinated to, and as far as possible aligned with, the rule of politics. (286)

I spell out in chapter 5 the consequences of this worldview for more ordinary street crime, and then in chapter 6 for the interconnected crimes of financial and political elites. Thus, the age of Reagan was a turning point in how the United States regarded and punished crime that would prove costly for years to come.

Nixon's presidency was clearly a prelude to the age of Reagan. Nixon's attention to the crime issue is commonly seen as an example of "backlash" politics and an early part of the culture wars (see also Garland 2001). However, Vesla Weaver (2007) argues that the transition to a new era, especially in relation to crime control, actually began even earlier, in the Johnson administration's efforts to co-opt the angry responses of many increasingly conservative Americans to the black activism and ghetto rebellions of the late 1960s (see also Gottschalk 2006). Weaver calls this a "frontlash" stage in the changing politics of crime in the United States. A signal of this change was that although President Johnson began by supporting Robert Kennedy's reforms and making them integral to his War on Poverty, Johnson later launched his own more punitive War on Crime.

Johnson, ironically, was led to a punitive response to crime in the aftermath of his 1964 electoral victory over Barry Goldwater and Goldwater's "law and order" campaign (Beckett 1997). Johnson attempted to co-opt the law and order attack on his own presidency, which refused to disappear with Goldwater's defeat. The most important of Johnson's efforts was the creation of the Law Enforcement Assistance Administration (LEAA), which at least in part was also a response to a growing organized movement by and for crime victims in the United States (Gottschalk 2006).

Malcolm Feeley (2003; Feeley and Sarat 1980) explains that the importance of the LEAA was that it set the foundation for federal aid to state and local law enforcement, indirectly and dramatically expanding the federal role in crime control. The effect of this new federal program and the legal bureaucracy it created was to mute critics of Johnson's support for civil rights legislation. Critics claimed there were connections between this support for civil rights laws and the black power movement and ghetto riots, as well as links to increases in African American involvement in crime in the late 1960s. One quarter of the first year of funding from the LEAA was for state and local control of race-linked riots and civil disturbances, while the overall LEAA budget grew from about $100 million to nearly $700 million by 1972 (Schoenfeld 2009).

An irony of Johnson's War on Crime was its unanticipated effect on official crime rates and the following Nixon administration's attempts to pick up on the law and order theme. Nixon delivered strongly worded speeches on the topic of law and order during his 1968 presidential campaign. He attacked the progressive perspective on the root causes of crime in a "Freedom from Fear" position paper that argued, "we cannot explain away crime in this country by charging it off to poverty" (cited in Weaver 2007:259). Meanwhile, Johnson's new LEAA grants to states and local governments had created incentives for these governments to actually inflate their crime statistics in bolstering their claims for assistance.

A result of the new incentives was that official crime rates kept increasing when Richard Nixon was elected president. Nixon's attorney general, John Mitchell, eventually was forced to diffuse the law and order issue in the Nixon years by calling the increases a "paper crime wave." The fact was that crime rates were substantially higher when Nixon left office than when he entered. A further irony was that this was also true for Ronald Reagan, who left California and the nation with crime rates that were rising rather than falling.

Like Nelson Rockefeller, who entered political life as governor of New York, Ronald Reagan launched his career as governor of California. He arguably defeated the incumbent governor Pat Brown in 1966 with his stand in favor of the death penalty. Jonathan Simon (2007) speculates that a reason why governors have done so well recently in American presidential politics is the unique involvement they have in the use of the death penalty.

When the Supreme Court nullified all existing death penalties in the 1972 *Furman v. Georgia* case, state governors had the opportunity to become instrumental in passing and enforcing new state death penalty statutes. Pat Brown had imposed the death penalty in California but also opposed it on religious and moral grounds. Reagan responded that Brown was valuing cold-blooded killers' lives over their victims' lives. This may have been Reagan's first taste of the possibilities of what Simon calls "governing through crime," or more specifically governing through the fear of crime (see also Savelsberg, King, and Cleveland 2002; Scheingold 1984).

Reagan picked Edwin Meese, a California district attorney, first as his closest political adviser and later as his attorney general. Meese was already a veteran crime warrior when Reagan began to rely on his advice in California. His initial attraction for Reagan was his reputation in the 1960s for fighting University of California student radicals and ghetto activists. During Reagan's governorship, Meese helped shut down the work of radical scholars and students at the University of California's School of Criminology. During the Reagan presidency, Meese led fights against defendants' rights and successfully reduced constitutional protections for defendants. Meese also spearheaded legislation increasing the role of victims in the criminal justice system and focusing on organized crime.

Yet much of Reagan's approach to governing through crime was more subtle and covert than Meese's frontal assaults on the Supreme Court and the Constitution (Garland 2001). These efforts also involved Meese, for example, in the Iran–Contra arms affair, which entailed ignoring the smuggling of cocaine into the United States, and in the passage of criminal sentencing guidelines that mandated extreme penalties for the possession of crack cocaine, ratcheting up mass incarceration for years to follow.

The latter sentencing guidelines were part of an omnibus crime bill, passed in 1988, that included death sentences for murder resulting from large-scale illegal drug dealing. The law was expanded in 1994 during the Clinton administration to cover dozens more crimes, many of them drug-related or violent. The reach of these laws beyond Reagan's presidency, and the willingness of Clinton Democrats to govern through the death penalty, is consistent with Wilentz's argument that the age of Reagan lasted through both of the Bush and the Clinton presidencies and at least until 2008. Clinton so closely heeded lessons from the age of Reagan on crime and the death penalty that he famously interrupted the 1992 New Hampshire primary campaign and returned to Arkansas to oversee as governor the execution of a prisoner with diminished mental capacities for the murder of a policeman.

Another lesson from the age of Reagan is that the forces of popular outrage and moral panic, once unleashed, are hard to tame. Even politicians who might wish to contain and reduce the outrage and panic feel their self-fulfilling fury. President Reagan seemed bent on sustaining this fear even as he was leaving office, lamenting, "There can be no economic revival of the ghettoes when the most violent ones are allowed to roam free" (1985).

Savelsberg (1994) reminds criminologists that the government funding of research that began in earnest with the LEAA and continues today creates self-reinforcing tendencies. He reminds us that "public opinion polls and speeches of politicians reinforced each other once the punitive trend had gotten under way" (939) and that "when research is funded by political agencies, which to a large degree is the case in criminology and criminal justice studies, then it is rather likely that academically produced knowledge will follow political knowledge" (934). This point is explored further in chapter 4.

The links between and among public opinion, politics, and the funding of criminology in the United States are longlasting. The public hostility and fear that today still feed punitive penal policies spiked in the 1970s and have continued, with only a slight recent moderation that has not undone persistent support for the death penalty and the public sense often noted in opinion polls that "local courts are too lenient" (Savelsberg 1994). Neither politicians nor criminologists can ignore the recurring feedback effects of these punitive attitudes.

John Sutton (2000) has identified the distinctively American nature of our punitive politics. He notes that the United States has a highly fragmented and decentralized governing structure—a form of federalism that is intensely political, local, and particularistic. A salient manifestation of this structure is that local judges and prosecutors must constantly receive the renewed approval of voters, and this approval requires sensitivity to fearful and often panicked public responses to crime. One nationally famous American politician, Speaker of the House and Democratic congressman Tip O'Neill, made this truth iconic in his aptly titled memoir, *All Politics Is Local* (1994). O'Neill ratcheted up a longlasting national punitive response to crack cocaine with just such a localized response to the highly publicized death of a hometown Boston basketball player. Often local events resonate on a wider national stage and are a source of a broad moral consensus that responds to latent and more widely shared fears. The age of Reagan was an ongoing exercise in the recirculation of locally felt truths through more broadly projected symbols intended to recreate a sense of the "shining city on the hill" in our national life.

These were not new ideas: they date as far back as John Winthrop's God-inspired vision of building the "city on the hill" and Beaumont and Tocqueville's (1833) argument, in their observations on the American penitentiary system, that America's localized politics and its historical obsession with punishment were two sides of the same sword used to enforce these visions. Reagan himself insisted on this moral linkage between the local and the national in one of his most famous early speeches. His formula was not complicated: "There is a simple answer—not an easy answer—but simple: if you and I have the courage to tell our elected officials that we want our national policy based on what we know in our heart is morally right" (Reagan 1964).

What Presidents and the Public Need to Know

Ronald Reagan was not a man to allow factual ambiguities or uncertainties to interfere with the development of his artfully crafted rhetorical images. Instead, Reagan was preoccupied with the persuasive expression of the lofty images that he created. His gift was communicating inspirational messages. He was the "Great Communicator," best known for his mystical references to a "new morning in America" and to the ideal of America as the "shining city on the hill." Ideological purity and clarity took priority over factual accuracy or certainty.

For Reagan, too-close attention to the facts and their explanation could lead, for example, to the kind of "malaise" about energy conservation that contributed to the unpopularity of the prior Carter administration. Resistance to fact-based policymaking was a challenge for the board that President Reagan appointed to advise him about crime policy. The board's charge was to frame an overarching crime policy. It wound up posing questions about the kinds of policies that Ronald Reagan and Edwin Meese brought with them to the White House based on their prior experiences in California.

Most challenging for the advisory board was that crime unexpectedly began to decline even before the new administration took office. The result was that at a crucial moment in the age of Reagan, a presidential advisory board chose to ignore the fact of declining crime rates and to justify its policy pre-scriptions on a more ambiguous and uncertain *fear* of crime rather than on crime itself. The advisory board mimicked the fear-driven choices of the president, and with consequences that remain highly counterproductive for American society.

This book tells the story of how the age of Reagan led to a realignment of priorities from the age of Roosevelt, leading simultaneously to more severe punishment of street crime and deregulation of the financial sector. The result was a major re-distribution of risk and regulation in American life. American minorities and the poor lost in several ways: they were prose-cuted and incarcerated for street crimes at massively increased rates, and they were victimized by evolving forms of financial manipulation, including subprime mortgage lending and sim-ilar kinds of lending arrangements for credit cards, cars, and the like. The unsustainable subprime mortgage lending and resulting defaults and foreclosures disproportionately affected minority neighborhood homeowners and counteracted efforts to reduce street crime by stabilizing minority neighborhoods.

Policies of the age of Reagan imposed a fundamental realign-ment of conceptions of the "good" and the "bad" in American life. As this era, and more specifically the Reagan administra-tion, vilified risk-taking on our city streets, it simultaneously valorized risk-taking in our nation's financial suites. The con-sequences of these policies continue to unfold in growing evi-dence of carceral and community socioeconomic inequality. I argue that we need to more fully appraise and analyze the consequences of these policies in the streets and the suites in terms of their co-dependency, and that when we do this we can begin to see more fully the unequal redistributive effects of the age of Reagan in American life.

In the following chapters, I trace the political and racial roots of the realignment of the regulation of street and suite crimes to the early years of the age of Reagan and to the elec-tion campaign of Ronald Reagan as governor of California in

1966. I show that many policies and consequences of the age of Reagan that realigned the criminal control of city streets and simultaneously deregulated the financial suites remain in place today, and that the age of Reagan aroused perhaps surprisingly robust sources of bipartisan political support that have made the influence of this era longlasting.

My analysis poses questions about possibilities and responsibilities that extend beyond the age of Reagan. The age of Roosevelt challenged narrow ideas about street crime with broadened images of financial crimes and passage of legislation such as the Securities and Exchange Commission Act. We will see that the Congress of this era challenged bankers with hearings and legislation, and that many bankers faced both criminal and civil prosecutions when their banks failed.

It is still possible to reframe our understanding of the streets and the suites, and I argue that a key to doing so is to analyze and emphasize the link between the two. My argument is that a new cycle of reform can rebalance the ledgers of the twenty-first century by reconsidering our conceptions of the feared and the fearless in our city streets and corporate suites. I propose a critical collective framing perspective as an explanatory pathway toward this goal and toward a renewal of crime theory beyond the age of Reagan.

Crime policy often thrives on fear, and the focus of President Reagan's advisory board on the fear of crime therefore may have been predictable. Yet although the fear of crime is common and may even be inevitable, the costs of feeding this fear with steadily increasing reliance on imprisonment should by now be apparent to criminologists and citizens alike. President Reagan and his advisers already knew what they wanted to do when they assumed office. They wanted to attend to victims of street crimes, crack down on drugs and organized crime through more severe sentences, compel judges to restrict defendants' rights, and get on with their punishment. They did not need or want an overarching plan that raised as many questions as it answered. The president's crime report was dead even before its arrival. This book is about why the nation deserves better than it got from this board, and more broadly from the age of Reagan policies that persist in the United States.

Chapter 2
Street Crimes and Suite Misdemeanors

ONE OF THE LESSONS OF THE Reagan administration's suppression of the crime report is that the actual occurrence of crime and the fear of it can be quite distinct. Crime does not need to increase for the fear of crime to become prominent. More worrisome is that groundless fears about crime have a lot to do with what and whom a society calls criminal.

For example, in many parts of the world, including the United States, there are false fears that immigration causes crime. Sometimes the combined fears of immigration and crime are so great that immigration itself is treated as if it were criminal. A major challenge for criminology is to overcome such biases in developing meaningful definitions and measures for the study of crime. The fear that immigration causes crime is therefore a highly relevant place to begin thinking about how criminology can confront the challenges that the fear of crime presents. This chapter is about how fear plays a determining role in what we conceive and count as crime.

The Feared Casual Connection of Immigration with Crime

In response to public fears linking immigration to crime in the 1920s, the U.S. Congress passed major legislation to restrict immigration. The focus was then on South and East European immigrants, but there was also a broad, diffuse fear of the foreign-born. The public often vilified immigrants for their alleged alcohol and drug abuse, but also for their criminality more generally. The assumed linkage was clear and crude: the public believed that immigration caused crime (e.g., Immigration Commission 1911; Industrial Commission 1901). The public tendency was to regard immigrants as prospective criminals and to treat them as such. Much of this response to immigrants was mixed with a growing fear of the effects of alcohol and drugs.

The United States has experimented with prohibiting two kinds of chemical crimes: the use of alcohol and the use of narcotic drugs. These experiments mixed elements of fear and hostility with regard to groups Americans regarded as foreigners and outsiders. There is little doubt that narcotics legislation was partly an expression of hostile attitudes toward foreign and domestic minority groups associated with drug use. Musto (1973:5) observes that "in the nineteenth century addicts were identified with foreign groups and internal minorities who were already actively feared and the objects of elaborate and massive social and legal constraints." For example, the Chinese were associated with opium (Musto 1973; Reasons 1974), southern blacks with cocaine (Musto 1973), and Mexicans with marijuana (Bonnie and Whitebread 1974). By gradually persuading the public to associate narcotics use with disenfranchised foreign and domestic minorities, politicians and lobbyists laid the foundation for an enduring legislative prohibition.

The prohibition of alcohol differed in several ways from the outlawing of narcotics. Alcohol prohibition was aimed mainly at urban and European immigrants, who, although poor, ultimately were able to form an active and organized opposition to Prohibition through urban machine and union politics. Thus, Timberlake (1963:99) observes that although urban wage-earners were at first unable to thwart the enactment of temperance legislation, they eventually became strong enough through their union memberships and urban political machine connections to defeat and repeal the prohibition of alcohol.

At its height, Joseph Gusfield (1963) called the vilification of immigrants as drunken, drug-addicted, and criminal a "symbolic crusade." He argued that the arrival of record numbers of immigrants early in the twentieth century provoked the fears of U.S.-born, rural Protestants that they were at risk of losing their advantaged positions in American society to these newcomers.

A tide of immigration ominously symbolized to native-born groups the threatening forces of urbanization and industrialization that they saw restructuring American society around them. The national prohibition against alcohol and restrictive immigration laws symbolized their growing opposition to these feared forces of change. The politicians principally involved, whom Becker (1963) calls "moral entrepreneurs," seized the immigration and crime connection as a symbol for a moral crusade. While the prohibition against alcohol obviously failed, the prohibition against narcotic drugs prevailed.

Few challenged the assumption of this era that immigration caused serious forms of crime (see Tonry 1995), although new restrictions on immigration temporarily tempered these concerns. Thus, the contentious politics surrounding this issue subsided during the age of Roosevelt, from the mid-1930s through the mid-1960s. However, the fears and opposition of established native-born groups did not disappear altogether. They were simply subdued for the middle third of the twentieth century and remained relatively dormant in U.S. mass culture until the age of Reagan.

As with so much else in the United States, things changed in the late 1960s and 1970s. Between 1960 and 1990, both annual immigration into the United States and homicide rates nearly doubled (from 1.7 to 3.0 per thousand for immigration, and from 4.8 to 8.3 per hundred thousand persons for homicide). The new era of immigration renewed the relevance of Gusfield's symbolic crusade thesis, and the parallel rise in homicide as well as imprisonment brought crime back into the picture. Politicians drew more nuanced distinctions between legal and illegal or undocumented immigrants, but the re-newed fear causally connecting immigration to crime was again pervasive.

Crime ultimately and dramatically came back down in the 1990s and continued to decline in the new millennium, while immigration continued to grow (e.g., Rumbaut 1997). Mean-while, criminologists collected increasing evidence that the crime-immigration link was largely a myth (Hagan and Pal-loni 1990). Rumbaut and Ewing (2007) used the 2000 U.S. Cen-sus to show that the risk of conviction and imprisonment was lower for immigrant than for native-born Americans. Crime rates among immigrant groups typically increased only after they had spent time in the United States. For example, among Hispanic men, the incarceration rate was nearly three times higher for those individuals who had been in the country six-teen years or longer than for those who had been in the coun-try five years or less. Furthermore, even incarceration rates of Hispanic male immigrants who were in the United States the longest were lower than for the native-born in 2000.

The Harvard sociologist Robert Sampson (2006) published an opinion piece and accompanying graph in the *New York Times* demonstrating that over the preceding decade and a half, as immigration increased, crime actually declined (figure 2.1). On National Public Radio, Sampson spoke with a reporter while walking through a Chicago Latino neighborhood and explained that a positive effect of immigration likely followed from the strong community traditions and networks that the immigrants brought with them from their country of origins to their new neighborhoods.

Nonetheless, the old fears of urbanization and industriali-zation were now accompanied by new anxieties about globaliza-tion and technological change. Migration flows were an impor-tant component of this economic transition (Sassen 1999), and members of the public responded to jobs being outsourced from the United States as new immigrants, both legal and undocu-mented, were arriving. So, despite the actual reversal in evi-

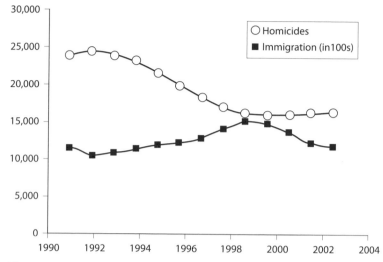

Figure 2.1 Immigration flows and homicide trends (U.S. totals in three-year averages). Source: Sampson (2006; data from Pew Hispanic Center and United States Department of Justice).

dence that now indicated immigration coincided with a *decline* in crime, new anxieties about globalization and technological change reignited old fears and led to a renewal of the old symbolic politics of status displacement.

Abdelmalek Sayad (2004) argues that these symbolic crusades cannot be blamed entirely on new status anxieties. Sayad argues that the official concept or category of the "immigrant" reflects how the laws of all nations discriminate between categories of residents, and observes that the simple presence of immigrants "disturbs the mythical purity or perfection of [the national] order" (280). He emphasizes that all states distinguish between nationals and non-nationals. This state- and law-based view of the immigrant, he notes, because it potentially upsets the national order, is a stubborn symbolic framework that further explains the strength and durability of public fears about immigrants (278–82).

It is in the area of crime and delinquency that we most clearly see the consequences of public fear and distrust of immigrants. According to Sayad, the very status of being an immigrant presents a situational form of delinquency, or an "initial sin," so that when an immigrant is charged with a crime, he or she is socially perceived as committing not one but two offences (282–83).

What Sayad is saying is that immigration itself is collectively perceived as a "latent, camouflaged offence," and that when an immigrant commits a legal offence, he or she is further "breaking the unwritten law" about how foreigners should act (282, 285). This has far-reaching implications when individual immigrants are charged with criminal offences: "any trial involving a delinquent immigrant puts the very process of immigration on trial, first as a form of delinquency and second as a source of delinquency" (282).

As a result, a close connection forms in the public mind between fears about crime and immigration. In Sayad's terms, "the case against immigration is always inseparable from the case made against the immigrant because of some offence, even a minor one that he has committed" (284). We see this kind of connection between crime and immigration represented in the cable television analysis of crusading political commentators such as Lou Dobbs and Patrick Buchanan.

These voices often articulate through the national media a broad base of nativist fear and opposition to immigration that echoes Gusfield's symbolic crusades. Buchanan based a 1996 presidential campaign around his promise to "stop illegal immigration cold by putting a double-linked security fence along the 200 miles of the border where millions pour in every year" (cited in Dillon 1997). Buchanan's campaign failed, but the fence building continues. The framing of the issue in terms of illegal immigration is easily mixed with fears of crime and the status displacement emphasized by Gusfield.

In the mid-1990s, a report by the U.S. Commission on Immigration Reform concluded that "many people believe that undocumented aliens are the source of the increase in serious crime . . . and that the increasing number of undocumented aliens is due to the U.S. Government's inability to control the border" (see Bean et al. 1994:3). Nearly three quarters of the National Opinion Research Center's General Social Survey respondents in 2000 agreed that it is "very likely" or "somewhat likely" that "more immigrants cause higher crime rates."

In 2006, a wave of city council ordinances copied a Hazleton, Pennsylvania, declaration that "illegal immigration leads to higher crime rates" (see Rumbaut and Ewing 2007). The National Conference of State Legislatures reports that lawmakers in 2008 submitted more than 1,400 immigration bills across the United States, and states enacted 170 of these bills.

A recent test of the link between illegal immigration and crime focused on deportable aliens in Los Angeles (Hickman and Suttorp 2008). The study compared 517 deportable and 780 nondeportable aliens for thirty days after their release from the Los Angeles County Jail. There were no significant differences in the rearrest patterns of the two groups. Nonetheless, nativism is a resilient force in U.S. politics, and it is highly resistant to social facts and evidence.

Such parochialism and nativism are not unique to the United States. The European Union is witnessing what Wacquant (2005:41) describes as a "criminalization of immigrants," with a dramatic increase over the past two decades in the percentage of foreigners and non-nationals being incarcerated. Wacquant notes that Europeans perceive foreigners as "darker skinned, uneducated, unattached and uncouth, prone to crime and violence," and therefore as "anti-persons" to be dealt with solely through the state's penal apparatus (46).

In the United States, Jonathan Simon (1998) provides parallel evidence of "immigration imprisonment." The result is a self-fulfilling prophecy of a crime-immigration connection (Wacquant 2005:41). In a symbolic crusade that threatened to become a moral panic, U.S. federal prosecutions nearly doubled from 2007 to 2008, reaching a level of more than 70,000 immigration prosecutions nationally (Moore 2009).

A recent and dramatic story of "immigration imprisonment" helps make the point that immigrants and their families can easily become the victims of crime control. A college-trained engineer, Jason Ng, died in a Rhode Island detention facility for immigrants that nearly doubled in size between 2007 and 2008. Jason was married and lived in New York for fifteen years with two young sons, both of whom and his wife are U.S. citizens. He had overstayed a visa date years earlier and was arrested when he was asked to report for his final 2007 interview for a green card at an immigration center in Manhattan. Jason Ng suffered in detention from undiagnosed cancer and was refused medical tests. He was shuttled through several detention centers. Weak and racked with pain, he was refused a wheelchair when he was taken to a 2008 hearing in shackles and pressured to withdraw his legal appeals and accept deportation. He died, untreated, in detention.

Defendants like Jason Ng, with no prior criminal record, make up a large category of immigration detainees. More than 100 deaths have occurred in detention since 2003, although government records on this are suspect and sketchy (Bernstein 2010). In 1996, Congress expanded the mandatory detention of charged immigrants, and in 2005 it doubled spending on detention spaces.

One Group's Fear, Another Group's Hope

The fearful public response to immigration contrasts with the seemingly paradoxical role of hope in the movement of peoples across borders. For many persons and groups, international as well as internal migration holds the hope of upward mobility. The United States is often called a nation of immigrants, and our history abounds with the stories of immigrants' successful accomplishments.

Yet it is also the case that for a small fraction of immigrants coming from particular places and settling in specific settings, life in America has sometimes begun with involvement in what at the time was defined as criminal. For example, the passage of Prohibition had the ironic effect of creating a new mobility route for some members of European groups who had legally produced as well as consumed alcohol as a part of the traditions of their countries of origin. Thus, Italian American involvement in organized crime grew during Prohibition, and when the act was repealed, some Italian Americans continued to pursue these and other illegal opportunities, sometimes called ethnic vice industries (Light 1977).

Overblown images of organized crime have distorted our national politics and the profession of criminology. A young Robert Kennedy wrote an overwrought book on organized crime titled *The Enemy Within* (1960), and the criminologist Donald Cressey added exaggeration in a book provocatively titled *Theft of a Nation* (1979). In absolute terms, the involvement of immigrant groups in organized crime has been small. A dramatic series of Hollywood movies has misled many Americans by encouraging ethnic stereotypes. The criminological concept of ethnic succession tells part of the story.

A sequential involvement of various groups in organized crime across waves of migration to America, including the movement of European groups to the New World, and within America, including the movement of rural southern blacks to the cities of the North, is referred to in the criminological literature as ethnic succession. This succession refers to the suggestion that, for lack of alternatives, first some Irish, then Jewish Americans, later Italians, and most recently African Americans and Hispanic Americans have sought to move upward in the social structure through organized crime activities (Ianni 1972, 1974). Popular films—about the Irish in *The Gangs of New York*, Jewish Americans in *Bugsby*, Italian Americans in the *Godfather* trilogy, Cuban Americans in *Scarface*, and African and Hispanic Americans in *American Gangster*—stereotype and exaggerate these ethnic patterns of involvement in organized crime.

Three crucial lessons emerge from the literature on criminal ethnic succession. The first lesson is that this process has never involved very large parts of any ethnic group in the United States. The second lesson is that even among those fractions of immigrant groups that may have pursued organized crime, the process of ethnic succession is marked by group members quickly making the intergenerational transition into conventional occupations (Ianni 1972). The third lesson is that the process of ethnic succession is showing signs of decline, if it ever very prominently existed, as a mobility route in American society. When Steffensmeier and Ulmer (2006) examined organized crime networks in two northeastern American cities, they found little evidence of the emergence of what Ianni (1974) called a new "black Mafia" that was taking over organized gambling from crime groups in these cities.

Nonetheless, where opportunities are scarce, hope still entices the poor and the jobless into the enduring vice industries of drugs, prostitution, and gambling—this despite evidence of escalating risks and limited financial rewards. Levitt and Venkatesh (2001) interviewed low-level drug dealers in Chicago and found that they earned little more than the minimum wage and regularly supplemented their incomes with legal earnings. They concluded that the riches of the ghetto gangster lifestyle were vastly overrated.

Yet both fear and hope endure, and Mercer Sullivan's (1989) account of New York City neighborhoods may best explain why. Lacking legitimate jobs and earnings, adolescents and young adults in low-income communities are drawn to the promise of drug dealing and related lines of activity. Sullivan (241) draws the connection to the earlier Prohibition era:

> The selling of illegal drugs functions much as did the selling of illegal alcohol beverages during Prohibition. Inner-city residents supply criminalized goods and services first to the local population and then to the wider community. . . . Inner-city entrepreneurs risk violence and stigmatization in their personal careers in return for

a flow of money back to them and into their neighbor-hoods. Respectability flows out and money flows back in.

The point is that while these activities bring much needed re-sources into the inner city, they also activate and exaggerate the general public's fears and anxieties, and they in turn rele-gate these ghettoized neighborhoods to the moral as well as physical periphery of the social and economic system.

Especially because of the punishments participants incur through the criminal justice system, as well as the threats of violence involved, America's ethnic vice industries are not the mobility ladders they might once have promised to be. The lesson is that fear trumps hope in the American crime equa-tion, and in particular it does so through its designations of crime and punishment, considered next.

The Changing Meanings of Crime

In a fast-changing world, not only do people and groups mi-grate, so also do the meanings attached to crime. We have seen that members of migrating groups are at heightened risk of being called criminal. A sociological and historically informed criminology recognizes this selective designation of criminals and both enumerates and explains it. However, we can suc-cessfully explain crime in America only if we first understand the persistent influence of fear in the changing meanings of crime.

A Futile Yet Revealing Search for Universal Conduct Norms

Thorsten Sellin, himself an immigrant to America in the first half of the twentieth century, first alerted criminologists to the necessity of understanding the variable nature of crime's meanings. Sellin, who saw himself as an early scientist of crime, questioned the assumption that law could reliably tell us what is criminal. He noted the variability in laws across nation-states, each of which possesses its own criminal code.

Sellin reasoned that a science of crime required a more universal definition of its subject matter. He is best remembered for this distinction between a scientific and legal approach to defining crime.

Every social and political group, Sellin observed, has its own standards of behavior. He called these group standards "conduct norms" and noted that they were not necessarily inscribed in law. His foundational premise was therefore that "For every person . . . there is from the point of view of a given group of which he is a member, a normal (right) and abnormal (wrong) way of reacting, the norm depending upon the social values of the group which formulated it" (Sellin 1938:30).

Yet Sellin also believed there are normative proscriptions that are invariant across cultural groupings, and he argued that these invariant or universal conduct norms are what criminologists should study. He therefore urged that "such study would involve the isolation and classification of norms into universal categories transcending political and other boundaries, a necessity imposed by the logic of science."

Sellin's solution to the scientific problem failed because he could not ultimately specify what these universal conduct norms were. Law provides little guidance in this regard because it is so variable. Anthropology does no better, conversely informing about remarkable diversity in cultural norms. Even the law of murder proves problematic. Exculpating claims of self-defense can be enormously complicated and contentious. Killing in war is rarely prosecuted as murder. Mass murder, which can extend to genocidal killing sprees, provokes remarkable disagreement. Later in this book I discuss the killing of 200,000–400,000 Africans in Darfur. Although the United States calls this mass murder genocide, a UN commission of inquiry for Darfur could not agree that genocide had occurred.

If there are universals of human behavior, such as the wrongfulness of incest, they are few and far between. In the end, Sellin could not enumerate conduct norms that were both nontrivial and universal. His importance to criminology instead

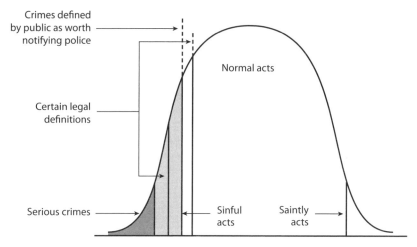

Figure 2.2 A statistical approach to the definitions of crime and disrepute. Source: Wilkins (1964:47).

lies in his emphasis on the inadequacy of official criminal codes to define the subject matter. So we must look elsewhere.

A Science of Normative Statistics

Leslie Wilkins (1964) agreed with Sellin's diagnosis of our dilemma. However, Wilkins chose to further emphasize the importance of the regularity or frequency with which behaviors do and do not occur in any particular society. He visualized a continuum of behaviors shaped like the normal curve we learn about in basic statistics. On this continuum, he noted, high-frequency behaviors are considered normal and low-frequency behaviors are inferred to be deviant, in both normative and statistical terms. Wilkins (47) then reasoned in relation to figure 2.2 that "the model given by the normal frequency distribution shown in this chart represents the distribution of ethical content of human action."

The references to sins and saints in the diagram seem oddly moralistic for a scientific exercise, but the point is well made by Wilkins's figure that serious crimes constitute an extreme normative category that is narrower than legally defined crimes, which category in turn is narrower than the category of crimes defined by the public as encouraging police notification. This range from criminality to legality is an important focus of our attention.

A detraction of Wilkins's statistical approach is that it makes the designation of our subject matter seem simpler than it is. There is no clear role in this diagram for the influence of politics and interest groups in determining which infrequent behaviors will be responded to by law. How do fears of specific acts among the public influence which and how many acts will result in criminal punishment? To explain the levels of mass incarceration reached in America in the new millennium requires the addition of analytical content to this numerically grounded framework.

A Conceptual Continuum of Crime

To understand the continuum approach to defining our criminal subject matter that I use in this book, it is useful to first consider the concept of white-collar crime that Edwin Sutherland (1949) introduced in the middle of the twentieth century. Today this concept is one of the most common sociological contributions to legal and public discourse, which is a way of saying that prior to Sutherland, the behaviors we now call white-collar crime were too seldom recognized as crimes. Sutherland insisted that the concept of white-collar crime included a range of unethical business practices that often were handled in civil courts as civil infractions. Today Sutherland would treat as white-collar crimes many lending practices leading individuals to take on subprime mortgages they can never hope to pay. Sutherland's point was to include a range of unethical business practices that might be handled in the civil courts but that are nonetheless regarded as socially injurious and legally penalized. He argued that it is the latter two criteria, injury and penalty, that make white-collar infractions criminal for social scientific purposes.

The continuum approach I propose similarly includes not only behaviors considered criminal by law but also behaviors that may vary in their treatment but nonetheless are crimes for many practical purposes. In this conception, if a police officer is prosecuted in a federal court for violating the civil rights of a minority suspect he has beaten, he is categorized as having committed a crime, just as he would be if he was being prosecuted for assault causing bodily harm. That is, the continuum approach considers behaviors that are both potentially and actually liable to criminal punishment. This is consistent with Sellin's injunction to not allow nonscientists—such as legislators or prosecutors—to determine the terms and boundaries for the scientific study of crime.

A continuum approach conceives the subject matter for study as a subset of the larger range of behavior sociologists call deviance, which is defined as variations from social norms. My further premise is that the driving influence of fear guides which kinds of deviance are selected for criminal sanctions. This fear underwrites three dimensions of judgment determining locations of persons and their behaviors on the pyramid-shaped representation in figure 2.3.

The first dimension involves the degree of agreement about whether a behavior is wrong. The second dimension involves the severity of the punishment prescribed for the behavior. The third dimension involves a judgment about the harmfulness of the behavior. Once a behavior is located on these dimensions, it becomes possible to consider its placement within one of four categories: consensus crimes, conflict crimes, social deviance, and social diversions. All of the dimensions and the categories are prominently influenced by fear of the behavior involved.

Agreement about the norm: The public is sometimes ambivalent about what to call criminal; however, the public is more engaged when it is fearful of the behaviors involved. For example, fear is a source of rising agreement in recent years

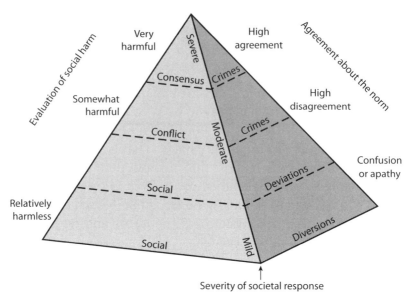

Figure 2.3 Kinds of crime and disrepute.

about the wrongfulness of the commission of crimes with handguns. We are more likely to agree about defining as morally wrong the behaviors that we fear the most. So agreement about the wrongfulness of an act can range from amusement and disinterest, through degrees of dispute, to circumstances of general agreement.

Severity of societal response: We also want to punish most severely the behaviors we fear most. This tendency is a major source of the stubborn reliance of Americans on imprisonment and the death penalty. Fear drives our incarceration of more than two million Americans, or one in every hundred adults, and helps to account for our execution of more than two Americans every week. We reserve these desperate punishments for the behaviors we fear the most. More broadly, our range of social penalties is inventive, extending from feigned or real indifference and avoidance to public humiliations, torture, and executions, with responses like ostracism, derision, and ridicule in between. This variety is disturbingly imaginative. But there is order to this literal madness: it is strongly driven by fear, with numerical (e.g., years of imprisonment) and finite (e.g., life and death) precision.

Societal evaluation of harm: Crime includes behaviors that range from those considered victimless to those thought to be massively victimizing. Perceptions that guide the evaluation of harmfulness are based in subjective as well as objective dimensions of fearfulness. What we fear most we perceive as most harmful, either to ourselves or to others. When the harm is nearly entirely personal, we may fear less for others around us and even consider the behaviors involved "victimless." As examples, acts such as gambling, drug use, and prostitution may seem largely personal in their consequences and are sometimes therefore called "victimless." This viewpoint argues that these behaviors are only indirectly harmful to others, especially when compared to acts of direct interpersonal confrontation, such as robbery, assault, and murder. The latter acts tend to be feared for self and others as well, and they therefore are generally considered more harmful, although sometimes such judgments are clouded by determinations of who had first access to the more lethal weapon. The fear that drives the evaluation of harmfulness has objective and subjective components.

A pyramidal conception of crime: The fear that drives the above three distinct but related and overlapping dimensions of crime also tightly connects them. This fear explains why the same acts that provoke broad agreement as to wrongfulness also tend to provoke strong penalties and to be regarded as very harmful. The acts that rank highest on all three of these dimensions are feared most and are therefore most likely to be called criminal. Yet this strong intercorrelation is not a source of full determination. With movement away from the acts that are feared most and ranked highest on these dimensions, there is considerable disagreement about wrongfulness, more equivocation in the severity of societal response, and less certainty about perceived harmfulness. This variability—the possibility and indeed certainty that behaviors across times and places will vary in where they fall on these dimensions—is precisely what a continuum approach to the definition of our subject matter emphasizes.

Thus, the behaviors that are most driven by public fear and most consistently defined as crimes are concentrated at the top of the pyramid-shaped conceptualization in figure 2.3, while the least feared behaviors fall toward the base. The bottom-heavy shape of this figure is intended, like Wilkins's normative statistics, to indicate that the behaviors clustered at the top are actually relatively infrequent in society, while those at the bottom are much more frequent. A key aspect of the pyramid is that it contains four categories that are separated by broken lines. The broken lines reflect the porous quality of the divisions between the categories, which are thought of as not only impermanent but even constant in their openness to change. The overarching division in the pyramid is between behaviors considered criminal and noncriminal, with further subdivisions between consensus and conflict crimes, on the one hand, and social deviations and diversion on the other. This representation is intended to capture dynamic changes in the meanings of crime.

From Torturous Deviance to War Crimes

The following discussion of the categories in the pyramid moves from the least feared to the most feared behaviors. I emphasize that this ordering of our subject matter is neither objective nor moral in its sequence. The point instead is that the public fears driving the categorizations are open to political and other sources of manipulation that by some measures seem clearly misguided. For example, although alcohol use is noncriminal and narcotic use is criminal, alcohol may actually be the more dangerous chemical of choice. Criminologists similarly emphasize that unpunished but highly unethical and nonetheless noncriminal business practices can be much more harmful in financial terms than many more familiar and perhaps therefore more widely feared and criminalized forms of theft. In fact, a point implicit in this continuum is that fear may often make fools of us all.

An example of particular concern is the legal authorization of methods of interrogation in the war on terror by President Bush (see also Hagan, Ferrales, and Jasso 2008). The president and his supporters apparently did not fear the use of these methods as much as they feared the threat they believed was posed by those who were tortured. The former president has said he authorized harsh interrogation practices (such as water-boarding) by the agents of the U.S. government on the basis of legal advice from his Department of Justice.

The president was apparently referring to an infamous memo issued on August 1, 2002, by the Office of Legal Counsel (OLC). The OLC offers legal opinions to the president and others for the Department of Justice, and in this instance it issued a memorandum entitled "Standards of Conduct for Interrogation," which is now commonly known as the torture memo. Assistant Attorney General Jay Bybee and John Choon Yoo drafted the opinion to explain the restrictions imposed by the Convention Against Torture and Other Cruel, Inhuman or Degrading Treatment, known as the CAT, as implemented in U.S. law. The memo greatly broadened the actions and circumstances that would allow interrogation techniques to avoid being classified as crimes of torture.

The torture memo did this in several ways, including defining torture as "only those interrogation techniques that inflict pain akin in severity to death or organ failure." In the event this first interpretation failed, the memo went on to claim that the president of the United States furthermore has constitutional authority to determine which interrogation techniques shall be used as a matter of national necessity and self-defense against further al Qaeda attacks. Finally, the memo argued for a legal distinction between protected prisoners of war and unlawful enemy combatants to justify the use of torture.

At the beginning of 2002, John Yoo publicly opined that "treaties do not protect Al Qaeda," Donald Rumsfeld stated that "unlawful combatants do not have any rights under the Geneva Convention," and Alberto Gonzales observed that "this new paradigm renders obsolete Geneva's strict limitations." These pronouncements sought to redefine criminal as legal behavior (cited in Hagan, Ferrales, and Jasso 2010).

Jack Goldsmith, Yoo's successor at the OLC, later acted to rescind the torture memo and argued for doing so on the following basis:

> The message of the August 2, 2002, OLC opinion was indeed clear: violent acts aren't necessarily torture; if you do torture, you probably have a defense; and even if you don't have a defense, the torture law doesn't apply if you act under the color of presidential authority. CIA interrogators and their supervisors, under pressure to get information about the next attack, viewed the opinion as a golden shield, as one CIA official later called it, that provided enormous comfort. (2007:144)

A former White House lawyer has suggested that "if you line up 1,000 law professors, only six or seven would sign up to [the torture memo's argument]" (Hatfield 2006:516).

The torture memo and the administration's policies regarding the legality of torture generally undermined the scope and force of the Geneva Conventions and placed the final authority in the hands of the U.S. president to determine what torture meant more broadly, and specifically in the context of al Qaeda. On the one hand, articles of the United Nations International Covenant on Civil and Political Rights, which Iraq and the United States have both ratified, specifically prohibit the torture of war criminals. On the other hand, following the terrorist attacks on September 11, coercive interrogation techniques were authorized at the highest levels of the administration, legally certified by attorneys in the White House and Department of Justice, conveyed to the Pentagon and Central Intelligence Agency, and presumably passed down the chain of command to prison guards and interrogators in Iraq and elsewhere.

The bottom line is that the Bush administration treated harsh interrogation techniques as legal rather than criminal. The columnist Andrew Sullivan (2009:86) wrote in an open letter to President Bush that "no previous American President has imported the tools of torture into the very heart of the American system of government as you did." The program authorized and operated by the Justice Department and the CIA began with an "attention slap" and, for some, ended with waterboarding. The Supreme Court ruled in 2006 in *Hamdi v. Rumsfeld* that prisoners suspected to be al Qaeda were entitled to Geneva Convention protections. Most would agree that the Bush administration's contrary and tendentious interpretation of torture law was driven by the fear generated by the 9/11 attacks.

Many in the U.S. military leadership feared that abandoning standing interpretations of torture as criminal would be counterproductive in reducing the threat of terrorism and would have the effect of making U.S. military forces more vulnerable to torture. The latter fears of the counterproductive effects of torture prevailed when President Obama's new attorney general, Eric Holder, testified in his confirmation hearing that waterboarding and related practices were torture. This may have begun a process of redefining waterboarding and other techniques of torture as criminal. This important episode in American history underlines how prominent the role of fear is in definitions of crime and how variable the influence of this fear can be in determining what is called criminal.

From Social Diversion to Deviance

Before turning to criminal forms of deviance, it is important to acknowledge the range of behaviors at the bottom of the conceptual pyramid that are typically not considered criminal but are still subject to official control, such as those proscribed under alcohol and liquor control acts, juvenile delinquency legislation, statutes defining mental illness, and numerous civil statutes that attempt to control various forms of professional and business activities. At the bottom of the pyramid approach, these behaviors include what I call the social deviations and diversions. Probably the most notable of these diversions involves the previously criminally prohibited consumption of alcohol.

The legalization of alcohol production and consumption in the United States represents a classic illustration of the point that the range from fearful to fearless responses of the public to behaviors often does not coincide with the dangers presented by these behaviors. Excessive alcohol consumption is the third leading preventable cause of death in the United States. To analyze alcohol-related health impacts, the Centers for Disease Control (CDC) estimated the number of deaths attributable to alcohol and years of potential life lost in the United States during 2001.

The CDC's calculations indicated that approximately 75,766 deaths and thirty years of life lost per death were attributable to excessive alcohol use in 2001. The CDC concluded that these results confirmed the importance of adopting effective strategies to reduce excessive drinking. The strategies they recommended did not include criminalization but instead increasing taxes on alcohol and screening for alcohol misuse in clinical settings. The point is not that CDC is wrong about these recommendations but rather that the level of fear of many behaviors does not correspond well to their dangers, and therefore that fear can be a highly fallible foundation for criminalization.

Conflict Crimes

Yet some behaviors that are the subject of much conflict and often morally manipulated fear do get treated as crimes. Legal philosophers consider such behaviors as "wrong by prohibition," or *mala prohibita*. These behaviors are defined by law as criminal even though the public is uncertain and divided in its thinking about them, with opposing groups strongly supporting or resisting this criminalization. The contesting groups often counter one another's views by seeking to incite or temper public fears about the behaviors involved. As we have already seen, in American history this kind of conflict has often surrounded alcohol and drugs.

It is impossible to enumerate all of the conflict crimes and their comings and goings from official criminal codes. Some of the most notable examples, in addition to the chemical crimes (alcohol and narcotic offenses), include public order offenses (malicious mischief, vagrancy, and creating a public disturbance), political crimes (treason, sedition, sabotage, espionage, and conspiracy), minor property offenses (petty theft, shoplifting, and vandalism), and the so-called right-to-life offenses (abortion and euthanasia). Some of these debates are seemingly endless, as in the case of abortion. There is good reason for this: there is no agreement on the underlying issues, such as the permissible perimeters of political protest, the dimensions of public disorder, the consumption of comforting chemicals, the protection of public property, and the limits of living and dying. In the absence of agreement, dissent often rules through the definition of these behaviors as conflict crimes.

Perhaps the most important examples of conflict crimes in our recent domestic history involve heroin and cocaine, which have played large roles in the rise and fall in arrest and incarceration rates considered in this book. It made little difference—in the United States, Canada, and Great Britain, as well as other countries—that addicts were predominantly members of the upper and middle classes in the first decades of the twentieth century. Until the early twentieth century in America, many patent medicines that could be bought in stores or by mail order contained morphine, cocaine, and heroin. The manufacturers of these products fought off criminalization, while the middle classes freely consumed the products with a sense that their use was medicinal.

The class character of this situation and its shift from medical to criminal meaning began to change radically with the passage of the Harrison Act in 1914. Thus, "by 1920, medical journals could speak of the 'overwhelming majority [of drug addicts]' from the 'unrespectable parts' of society" (Duster 1970:11). The Harrison Act was originally a tax measure, but law enforcement moral entrepreneurs, such as Harry Anslinger, then director of the Bureau of Narcotics, established in 1930 in the Treasury Department, shifted the focus from taxing a medical drug to punishing a feared source of criminal violence. Lobbyists like Anslinger increasingly associated the newly criminalized behaviors with immigrants and internal minorities, and he soon added marijuana to the mix by supporting new and extended state laws.

Anslinger attracted national attention with his crusade against the "marijuana menace." He wrote a widely read *American Magazine* article titled "Marijuana: Assassin of Youth" and attracted the support of the national Hearst newspaper chain. His attacks were ethnically and racially incendiary, featuring charges that "fifty percent of the violent crimes committed in districts occupied by Mexicans, Greeks, Turks, Filipinos, Spaniards, Latin Americans, and Negroes may be traced to the abuse of Marijuana" (cited in Bonnie and Whitebread 1974:146).

Similarly, narcotics legislation had its roots in a wave of fear and hostility directed against isolated immigrant and internal minorities, particularly Chinese, African, and Mexican Americans. Bonnie and Whitebread (1974:17) write that "a consensus had emerged: the non-medical use of 'narcotics' was a cancer which had to be removed entirely from the social organism." The media continued to play an important role in stoking these fears, making marijuana and other drugs classified as narcotics perhaps the single most historically important source of conflict in crime enforcement in America.

Consensus Crimes

The crimes that most Americans fear the most are known to legal philosophers as *mala en se*, or "bad in themselves." Even though it is easy to exaggerate how much of this crime there might be, there is a select group of human behaviors that for centuries and across many countries have been so consistently treated as seriously criminal as to earn the status of consensus crimes. Among these behaviors are common law crimes of premeditated murder, forcible sexual assault or rape, armed robbery, and kidnapping. When members of the public are asked to rank the seriousness of crimes, such behaviors are consistently and persistently ranked highly.

Thus a pioneering study asked judges, police, and college students in Philadelphia to rank the seriousness of a long list of crimes, and found great agreement within and across groups (Sellin and Wolfgang 1964). When researchers in subsequent studies asked subjects in a variety of international cultural settings to engage in this same task, they again found widespread similarity in rankings (Newman 1976). There were some notable caveats to this consensus: less-educated respondents disagreed more about violence between individuals who knew one another (Rossi et al. 1974). The problematic distinction between consensus and conflict crimes also became apparent when forms of organizational and white-collar crime (see Schrager and Short 1978) were included in the rankings and produced higher scores when information about physical harm to victims was noted (e.g., in car design decisions and dangerous work conditions).

Two considerations most clearly distinguish consensus and conflict crimes. Consensus can be said to exist when a population is widely agreed in attitudes about behaviors and these attitudes are unrelated or only weakly related to group memberships. In contrast, conflict can be said to exist when attitudinal agreement is lower in a population or attitudes are related more strongly to group membership. Using these criteria, criminal behaviors can be located relative to one another and with reference to an overall continuum of attitudes toward criminal behaviors. Consensus crimes are located toward one end of this continuum, while conflict crimes are located toward the other.

Still, the bottom line to this discussion is that even the consensus crimes are neither immutably nor permanently criminal. The distinction nonetheless can be useful. For example, this distinction helps to account for the different purposes involved in trying to explain why some people violate laws (especially consensus crimes), on the one hand, versus why some groups and societies resort to the use of criminal law to punish other violations (especially conflict crimes) on the other.

An extremely important and recent example of the changeable meaning of behaviors is the sudden and fearful use of imprisonment in response to crack cocaine violations as if they were consensus crimes. The effect of smoking or injecting crack is faster and stronger than the effect of snorting powdered cocaine, less crack than powdered cocaine is required to get the first strong effect, and the smaller amounts of crack are relatively inexpensive. As a result, in the 1980s crack rapidly became a drug of choice in open-air street corner ghetto drug markets. Meanwhile, many white Americans continued to be ambivalent about the seriousness of powdered cocaine use, which became relatively frequent on college campuses. The response to crack cocaine was far more fearful, and on a scale that suggested a new consensus crime had emerged in America.

As crack use spread across U.S. cities during Reagan's second term, the administration passed federal sentencing guidelines that established especially long mandatory sentences for crack cocaine possession and trafficking. The disparate sentences rapidly increased the presence of black offenders in U.S. prisons, but Congress refused to change the guidelines. Crack cocaine finally began to be more widely recognized as a conflict crime when the Supreme Court ruled in 2007 that the guidelines for cocaine were only advisory. Chapter 5 discusses the evolution of U.S. sentencing guidelines and their role in the escalation of imprisonment rates during the age of Reagan.

The Accounting of Crime

The last topic of this chapter shifts from questions about what is crime to equally basic uncertainties about how much crime is there, and where do we find it. More specifically, we ask, are there measurable trends in crime? Are Americans uniquely criminal? And are some groups of Americans uniquely vulnerable to crime and punishment? Fortunately, criminologists have developed meaningful measures of crime which can reduce uncertainties about the answers to these questions.

Long-Term Crime Trends

Despite the fears widely shared by Americans about crime, there is near- and long-term evidence that our crime problems could be, and indeed have been, far worse. This is consistent with the fact that although most Americans have never been victims of serious predatory forms of crime, we nonetheless tend to be very fearful of crime.

In the relatively near term, which includes the last half century, rates of crime in the United States increased in the 1960s and 1970s. Crime rates then declined notably for the first half decade of the 1980s, increased sharply for the next five to ten years (i.e., from the mid-1980s to the early to mid-1990s), and thereafter declined for a decade and a half. Since this is a decidedly up-and-down pattern in the near term, it is of interest to first consider if there is a longer-term trend.

Criminologists have established that other than for homicide, long-term data on crime are nearly useless. Especially as we move backward in time, there is vast variation in how much crime is recorded in official crime statistics. Criminologists confirmed the extent of this long-suspected problem in official crime data by asking respondents in contemporary community "victimization surveys" to report experiences of crime by members of their households (Biderman 1967). The results revealed vast amounts of officially unrecorded crime. Other than homicide, where people go missing and bodies are hard to hide, victim-reported crimes in surveys often triple the number of officially recorded crimes (Skogan 1986).

Yet criminologists have documented the relatively unique validity of homicide statistics in two ways: by comparisons with the kind of victimization surveys just described and by comparisons with health statistics gathered from medical sources. Early comparisons of police-based homicide rates with victimization surveys (Ennis 1967) and health surveys (Hindelang 1974) found that these unofficial and official data sources yielded nearly identical trends. This validation of homicide statistics allows us to consider some fascinating long-term trends that go beyond the history of the United States.

The most prominent of these trends is a long and predominantly downward but also slightly U-shaped curve in English rates of homicide from the Middle Ages to the current century, shown in figure 2.4. Although most associated with Ted Robert Gurr (1979, 1981), this pattern is also emphasized in the work of Monkkonen (1981, 2006), Lane (1980:36), and Gillis (1989). Similar to the findings about immigration discussed earlier in this chapter, the downward slope in figure 2.4 contradicts the belief that urbanization and industrialization increased crime. Lane concludes that rates of violence were apparently far higher in medieval and early modern England than in the twentieth century—as much as ten to twenty times higher—notwithstanding increases in the latter part of the twentieth century.

Nearer-Term American Crime Trends

Even though medieval England's criminal violence rates may have exceeded anything reported for several centuries in the United States, the near-term U.S. experience is nonetheless unusually violent. Monkkonen (2006) separated all of U.S. and European history, summarized in table 2.1, into two eras divided at about 1850, to capture the onset and development of modern consumer capitalism. He then compared homicide data from New York City with data from Europe. Before 1850, New York City had a murder rate double the average European rates. However, after 1850 the New York City rate increased from about five to ten homicides per hundred thousand, while the European rate declined from about 2.7 to 2.1. Monkkonen concluded that United States has become increasingly plagued

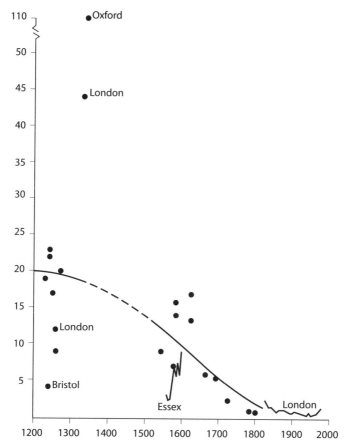

Figure 2.4 Homicide rates per 100,000 population in English counties and cities, 1200–1970. After Gurr (1981:313).

with murders, while Europe has continued its centuries-long decline, with many nations stabilizing at around one murder per hundred thousand population. The country most comparable to the United States is in many ways Canada, but Canada too has a much lower homicide rate, less than two per hundred thousand.

It is important to emphasize that the homicide rate in the United States has risen and fallen several times over the past century and is now at about the same level as it was half a century ago. Thus, the homicide rate reached near-term peaks

TABLE 2.1
Estimates of European and American Murder Rates

Place	Pre-1850	1850–2000
New York City murder rate	5	10
European murder rate	2.7	2.1

Source: Monkkonen (2006).

in 1930, 1980, and 1991. The century-long low of 4.0 occurred in the late 1950s, and the rate is currently nearly back to the 1960s level of 5.6. Homicides nationwide fell 10 percent in the first half of 2009 compared to the same period in 2008. They peaked in New York City at 2,245 deaths in 1991 and hit a record low of 461 in 2009. As mentioned throughout this book, the age of Reagan was a period of notable variation in homicide rates. The homicide rate stood at 10.2 at the beginning of the Reagan administration in 1980, dropped to 7.9 by the end of Reagan's first term in 1984–5, and then climbed again to 9.8 near the conclusion of the successive Reagan-Bush administrations. Since then the homicide rate has dropped by nearly half, which leaves the United States with homicide rates about five times higher than most of Europe but still about one quarter those of medieval England.

American Disproportionality and Exceptionality

The United States is more exceptional in its disproportional and selective incarceration trends than in its crime trends. These trends have produced a "mass incarceration" (Garland 2001) that is distinguished not only by its overall scale but also by its selective focus on drug offenders and it impact on less educated black American males and, increasingly, females.

Contemporary mass incarceration in America is made more striking by a long-term trend toward what Alfred Blumstein and Jacqueline Cohen (1973) called the "stability of punishment" just before the use of imprisonment began its explosive

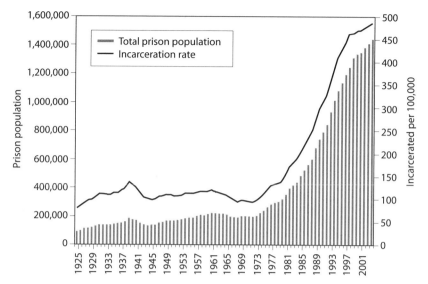

Figure 2.5 Imprisonment in the United States, 1925–2002. Source: *Sourcebook of Criminal Justice Statistics Online* (http://www.albany.edu/source book/pdf/t6282004.pdf), table 6.28.2004. Note: Data do not include local jail population.

upward climb in the United States. This stability is evident in figure 2.5. Each year from about 1925 to 1975, about one-tenth of 1 percent of Americans were imprisoned. However, from 1975 on, each year the numbers of imprisoned increased, so that by the early years of the twenty-first century about seven-tenths of 1 percent of Americans were imprisoned (Western 2006:13). The American incarceration rate quadrupled, producing a prison population of 2.4 million in the United States by the beginning of 2009. We incarcerate more people and more women than any other country, and more than 150 percent more than Russia, our nearest competitor in this regard (National Council on Crime and Delinquency [NCCD] 2006).

The trajectory of incarceration turned notably upward with the election of Ronald Reagan in 1980. The source of this rise began with the increase in drug arrests of black adults, which gained momentum in 1985 after Reagan's reelection to a second term. Figure 2.6 uses black and white drug arrests to show

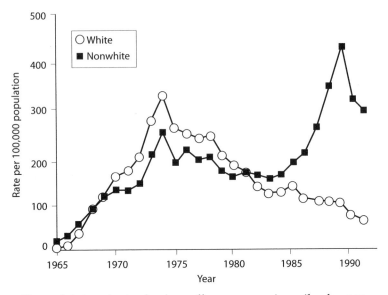

Figure 2.6 Arrest rates for drug offenses among juveniles, by race, 1965–1991. After Blumstein (1993:3).

that this upturn increasingly reflected the incarceration of black juveniles after 1985. The intensity of this upturn from 1985 on coincided with the law enforcement crackdown on the crack cocaine epidemic in American black communities.

Earlier I noted that crime rates in the United States declined more generally during the first Reagan term in the early 1980s, increased from 1985 through the early 1990s, and then began a longer-term decline. Because imprisonment increased throughout this period, from 1975 on, rising crime rates cannot in any simple way explain the increasing imprisonment. Crime was markedly declining at the same time that incarceration rates were increasing from 1980 to 1985, and crime has further declined since the early 1990s.

This disjunction between index crime rates and incarceration rates is clear in much of figure 2.7. While this figure shows that crime increased along with imprisonment from 1970 to 1980, things changed with the election of Ronald Reagan. Beginning with the Reagan administration, imprisonment unre-

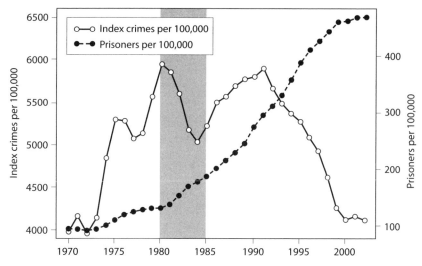

Figure 2.7 Trends in index crime rate and imprisonment. After Western (2006:39).

mittingly increased despite the period from 1980 to 1985, when crime rates declined.

Two trends drove the increase in imprisonment during the Reagan administration and especially during Reagan's second term. We have already seen that the first of these trends involved the increase in drug arrests of young black males. The second trend was handgun violence involving youth associated with the drug trade. The latter trend is shown in figure 2.8. This figure shows the escalating rates of handgun homicides in three age groups. It is especially in the youngest age group, those age seventeen and younger, that the handgun murder rate spiked from about 1987 to 1994.

Handgun murders by juveniles alone could not alone explain the rise in imprisonment that gained speed from the mid-1980s on. Yet Alfred Blumstein and Joel Wallman (2006) convincingly argue that this gun violence is an important part of a larger explanation elaborated by Bruce Western (2006). This explanation is that the jump in the arrests of adult drug offenders not only accounted for much of the rise in imprisonment but also created "vacancy chains" in the drug trade that

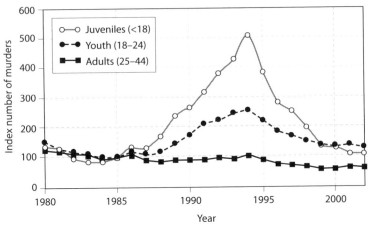

Figure 2.8 Use of handguns in murder by three age groups (indexed, 1985 = 100). After Blumstein and Wallman (2006:324).

were filled by youth who gained access to handguns and who were more impulsive in using guns in drug-connected disputes. These youth in turn were also highly vulnerable to imprisonment for their involvement in this kind of violence most feared and severely punished in the courts.

Disproportionality in Black Drug Arrests

Two potentially overlapping assumptions bear on the racial disproportionality in drug arrests. The first assumption is that adverse class and minority group circumstances resulting from limited resources and opportunities make drug crime more visible and conspicuous in minority neighborhoods. The second is that prejudicial and discriminatory laws and law enforcement make minority group members more vulnerable to drug arrests and imprisonment.

It seems likely that a subtle mixture of these socioeconomic and discriminatory sources of disproportionality explains the overrepresentation of persons of color and disadvantaged circumstances in drug law enforcement. The arrival of the cheaper and more powerfully addictive crack cocaine in the mid-1980s was obviously economically attractive in impoverished black communities, while the more expensive and less addictive powder cocaine remained a party drug of choice for more advantaged college and business-class users. The limited private spaces in poor black neighborhoods pushed the crack drug trade into the public "open air" market spaces of the street corners, while college and business-class users of powder cocaine were able to take advantage of the private spaces provided, for example, by college residences and hotel suites.

The resulting differentials in police surveillance and enforcement combined with the disparity in sentencing guidelines for crack and powder cocaine to create huge differences in racial vulnerabilities to arrest and imprisonment. The combination of these factors and patterns makes official crime statistics an unlikely reflection of the true distribution of drug use and abuse in America. Sociologists began to develop research methods to address biases in official crime statistics more than half a century ago.

Thus, when sociologists began to doubt the meaning of official crime statistics in the late 1950s, they started to do school-based "self-report" surveys to study juvenile delinquency (Nye and Short 1957). Self-report surveys initially used paper-and-pencil instruments and more recently have used computers to allow respondents to anonymously report their involvements in youth crime. Self-report studies have often revealed no relationship, or only a weak one, between parents' socioeconomic status and the delinquency of their teenage children, leading to the suggestion that this relationship may be a myth (Tittle and Meier 1990; Tittle, Villemez, and Smith 1978).

There is a concern that self-report studies often tend to focus on minor forms of delinquency (Braithwaite 1981; Hindelang, Hirschi, and Weiss 1981) and that some of the most seriously delinquent youth are not in school to respond to such surveys (Hagan and McCarthy 1997). When these surveys pay closer attention to serious forms of delinquency and include homeless street youth as well students in schools, the results of self-report studies are somewhat more consistent with the official

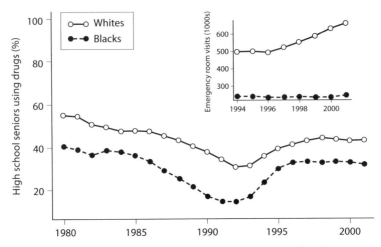

Figure 2.9 High school seniors reporting drug use. After Western (2006:47).

data (Elliott and Ageton 1980; Hagan and McCarthy 1997; Johnson 1980; Thornberry and Farnsworth 1982). As noted earlier, official crime data are probably most meaningful when they focus on the most serious behaviors, such as homicide. There is reason to accept the indication of these data, for example, that rates of black homicide have ranged from six to seven times those for whites for much of the last half century (Hawkins 1986; Rose and McClain 1990).

Still, there is equal reason to believe that the official crime statistics on drug abuse are highly biased and misleading. Bruce Western (2006:47) persuasively makes this point by comparing data gathered in the Monitoring the Future self-report survey of high school youth with a Drug Abuse Warning Network report of drug-related emergency room visits. The latter should reflect more serious drug problems. These sources are summarized in figure 2.9. The high school self-report survey revealed that (1) teenage drug use declined significantly over the past twenty years, (2) black and white youth had similar levels of use, and (3) white youth actually reported slightly higher drug use than black youth. Surveys of adults yielded similar results. The reports based on emergency rooms also revealed more white than black visits for drug problems. Western concluded that "there is little evidence that mounting drug use or relatively high rates of drug use among blacks fueled the increase in drug arrests in the 1990s" (48).

Fear of Crime in the Age of Reagan

Several conclusions emerge from this chapter. A first conclusion is that fear of crime is a driving force in public conflict and consensus about what and whom we define as criminal. A second conclusion is that a fear of crack cocaine emerged as the leading edge in the punitive definition and response to crime in the age of Reagan. A third conclusion is that this fear of drug-related crime led to a massive increase in the imprisonment of African American males in America.

There are many different ways to make the point that U.S. drug policies are punitive and discriminatory. An ominous note is sounded by Harry Levine (2007:1), who testified that "Although almost nobody knows this, in the last ten years New York City has arrested and jailed more people for possessing marijuana than any city in the world." Levine reports that for a decade, police in New York City have each day arrested about 100 mostly young people, approximately 85 percent black or Latino, even though self-report studies indicate that marijuana use is likely lower among these groups than among whites. The *New York Times* columnist Bob Herbert (2010) calls this radically disparate treatment of black and white suspects "Jim Crow policing." Official crime statistics indicate that per 100,000 persons in each group, there are 124 white, 430 Hispanic, and 975 black marijuana arrests. In a decade, New York City police have arrested and kept in jail for at least one day on marijuana possession charges nearly 200,000 blacks, more than 100,000 Latinos, and 50,000 whites.

American fears about crime have involved dubious beliefs about links between and among immigration, minority groups, drugs, and crime. As these connected fears have intensified, the explanations offered by criminologists for crime have also changed. I make this point in the next two chapters by considering how classical explanations of crime first emerged in the age of Roosevelt and were then reconfigured during the age of Reagan.

Chapter 3
Explaining Crime in the Age of Roosevelt
||||||||||

THE CLASSICAL THEORIES of crime in America developed over a lengthy period, from the Great Depression and the age of Roosevelt to the age of Reagan. Viewed broadly, the age of Roosevelt spans forty years, from about 1933 to 1973. The classical explanations of crime reflected in many ways the progressive politics of this era, in contrast to the more conservative politics of the age of Reagan.

My dating of the eras of Roosevelt and Reagan includes preludes and postludes, and this categorization admittedly involves risks of overgeneralization. Still, for the reasons indicated in chapter 1, there is considerable value in organizing our understanding of the evolution of modern American criminology along a political fault line that divides the influences of the Roosevelt and Reagan eras in American life.

||||||||||

Three distinguishable traditions of social theory—structural functionalism, symbolic interactionism, and conflict theory—organize the classical explanations of crime from the age of Roosevelt. The influences of these three traditions are clear and continuing, although in some instances the connections within these traditions are tentative, and other categorizations of the theories are plausible (see, e.g., Kornhauser 1978). Regardless, it is impossible to study crime today without considering what I call the classical theories of the age of Roosevelt and some of their most prominent derivations and applications.

There is a notable progression in the criminal subject matter explained by these theories, from the early nearly exclusive attention to common law street crimes such as murder and robbery and common forms of juvenile delinquency to the later broadened focus that included the perhaps less frequent but more lucrative white-collar and political crimes. This shift in focus of classical crime theories during the age of Roosevelt reflected the anger in populist and progressive politics with the upperworld crimes of business people and bankers. It further reflected a growing sensitivity to the role of more powerful groups in defining the behaviors of other, less powerful groups as criminal rather than the behavior of their own groups.

The Structural Functionalist Theories

The structural functionalist theories have continued to play a significant role in our understanding of crime, even though the roots of these theories in American criminology are during the period of the Great Depression that marked the onset of the age of Roosevelt. The Depression posed devastating challenges to the United States and its major institutions. So it is not surprising that the structural functional theories tend to see crime and other forms of disreputable behavior as resulting from a breakdown of or strain in major social institutions and processes that otherwise produce conformity in American life.

The focus of the structural functional theories is on institutions, such as the family and school, that socialize individuals to conform in their behaviors to the core values of the surrounding society. The particular concern is with the ways in which these institutions can fail in their socialization mission. Wide agreement or consensus is assumed by this approach about the core socioeconomic values of society—about what people want from their lives and how they are expected to behave in achieving these goals.

Structural functionalist theories explain why some individuals, through their criminal behavior, come to challenge such a consensus. The question asked by this group of theories therefore is, why do some individuals come to violate the conforming values that nearly all of us are assumed to hold in common? Specific answers emerge from anomie, subcultural difference, differential opportunity, social disorganization, control, and social learning theories of crime. Some of these answers focus on broad class- and group-level processes while others focus more specifically on individuals. Over time, the emphasis in this theoretical tradition has shifted from the group to the individual, a shift that intensified after the age of Roosevelt and in the early age of Reagan.

Anomie Theory

The roots of functional theory lie in Émile Durkheim's (1951 [1897]) concept of anomie. Durkheim defined anomie in terms of lack of social regulation, and this concept is usually translated from Durkheim's writings in French as "normlessness." Normlessness is often defined as a form of purposelessness experienced by a person or a group resulting from a lack of standards and values.

Robert K. Merton (1938), writing in the midst of the Great Depression, adopted Durkheim's normative concept of anomie, but he gave it a structural as well as a cultural twist by describing anomie as the result of a faulty relationship between societal goals and the legitimate means available to attain them. Merton emphasized two aspects of social and cultural structure: culturally defined goals (notably monetary success) and the acceptable means (education and employment) for their attainment. He observed that whereas in American society, success goals are widely—that is, consensually—shared, the means of attaining these goals are not. He noted that anomie results from this disparity between goals and means. The emphasis on a disparity between goals and means marks Merton's as a distinctively structural thesis.

Merton did not intend his theory simply as an explanation for why some individuals deviate. He was also interested in patterns of class relations. For example, he was interested in explaining why disadvantaged classes of individuals might deviate more than other classes of individuals. He reasoned that members of less economically advantaged classes experience most the disparity between shared success goals and the scarcity of means to attain them. Higher rates of criminal behavior among those in less advantaged class groupings are the predicted result of this structural inconsistency.

Merton's theory of anomie includes a famous typology of adaptations to relationships between goals and means. Perhaps most important for understanding crime is a category in this typology called *innovation*, which includes various forms of economically motivated crimes. However, also included are *retreatism*, consisting of escapist activities such as drug use; *rebellion*, involving revolutionary efforts to change the structural system that establishes goals and means; and *ritualism*, which describes various forms of overconforming behaviors. The most important feature of the typology is its attention to structurally induced failure, that is, failure that derives from a socially structured lack of access to achievable goals through legitimate means.

Delinquent Subculture Theories

Merton linked his theory of anomie to group-patterned behaviors by emphasizing that his explanation could account for differences in rates of crime and deviance across whole classes. Later sociologists extended this focus on class issues through the concept of subcultures. For example, Albert Cohen (1955) suggested that members of disadvantaged classes become potential members of delinquent subcultures when they experience early failures in school. He noted that when assessed using a "middle class measuring rod," working-class children often come up short. These students experience a growing sense of "status frustration" because their early experiences inside and outside the home do not prepare them to satisfy middle-class expectations. As an alternative, the delinquent subculture offers a group, often gang-based, solution. This consists of an alternative set of group-shared and group-supported criteria, or values, that working-class youth can meet.

Subcultural values may often completely repudiate middle-class standards and expectations. The delinquent subculture expresses its contempt for middle-class values and makes their opposites the criteria for status. The delinquent subculture in effect says to the onlooking middle-class society, "We're everything you say we are, and worse." The delinquent subculture inverts the values of middle-class society, taking a disreputable pleasure in being "non-utilitarian, malicious, and negativistic." It is important to emphasize that the force of this solution is that it occurs within groups that provide peer support.

Perhaps the classic application of subcultural theory is Hunter Thompson's (1967) journalistic account of a period he spent with the Hell's Angels motorcycle gang. Thompson reports that to understand the Angels it is necessary to acknowledge the stark social fact that they "are sons of poor men and drifters, losers and sons of losers" (332). "Yeah, I guess I am [a loser]," one reflective Angel commented to Thompson, "but you're looking at one loser who's going to make a hell of a scene on the way out" (334). Instead of surrendering meekly to their individual fates, then, the Angels gather in celebration of their "choppers" and each other: "They reflect and reassure one another, in strength and weakness, folly and triumph" (120). Violent mayhem is an expected part of the Angel lifestyle, but their choppers become the key symbols of the reversal of conventional values and the inverted process by which Angels collectively reclaim their status. For the Angel, "his motorcycle . . . is his only valid status symbol, his equalizer" (119).

In a variation on the subcultural theme, Walter Miller (1958; see also Banfield 1968) argues that the values of the delinquent subculture are really the "by-product of . . . the lower class system," which has a "distinctive tradition many centuries old with an integrity of its own" (19). Miller suggests that this "lower class culture" features a set of key values—trouble, toughness, smartness, excitement, fate, and autonomy—that bring affected male adolescents into conflict with the law. He concludes that simply "following . . . practices . . . of . . . lower class culture automatically violates certain legal norms" (18).

Differential Opportunity Theory

Although legitimate opportunities may be restricted in some class settings, there nonetheless may be illegitimate opportunities available that thereby become especially important in channeling individuals into specific forms of delinquency and crime. For example, a differential opportunity theory developed by Richard Cloward and Lloyd Ohlin (1960) argues that to understand the different forms that criminal and delinquent behavior can take, we need to consider the different types of illegitimate opportunities available to those who are seeking a way out of disadvantaged class settings.

Cloward and Ohlin's book, *Delinquency and Opportunity* (1960), attracted the attention of Robert F. Kennedy. When Kennedy was appointed his brother's attorney general in 1960, Lloyd Ohlin went to Washington to work in the Justice Department. Following President Kennedy's assassination and during President Johnson's administration, Ohlin continued his work and introduced some of his ideas into War on Poverty programs (Moynihan 1969). Although the eventual implementation of Cloward and Ohlin's ideas bore a tenuous connection to their original theory, this participation in a major federal government initiative likely represented the peak influence of a progressive crime theory from the age of Roosevelt in American public policy.

Cloward and Ohlin argued that different types of opportunities and settings produce different subcultural adaptations. They suggested that three types of adaptations predominate: a stable criminal subculture, a conflict subculture, and a retreatist subculture.

1. The *stable criminal subculture* is the best organized. This subculture emerges when there is coordination between legitimate and illegitimate roles and sectors in the community—for example, between politicians, the police, and the underworld. In the old-style political machines that once dominated American cities, politicians and the police provided protection for privileged forms of illegal enterprise, creating opportunities for what I earlier referred to as ethnic vice industries. Such circumstances could provide a stable base on which individuals could advance from lower to upper levels of an organized criminal underworld. A genre of films about organized crime, from *The Godfather* to *Goodfellas*, has depicted this kind of stable criminal subculture. When legitimate and illegitimate opportunity structures were linked in this way, the streets were safe *for* crime, and reliable upward mobility routes were available to criminals. Yet this is now largely seen as a romantic caricature of the American urban past that bears little resemblance to today's cities, with their more violent and disruptive crime patterns.

2. The presence of violence and conflict is disruptive of both legitimate and illegitimate enterprises. When the latter kinds of enterprise have been interconnected, violence and conflict may sometimes have been restrained. However, in the absence of effective interconnections, violence reigns uncontrolled. Cloward and Ohlin see these kinds of disarticulated communities as producing a *conflict subculture.* In these settings, street crime is common, and gangs and violent crime prevail.

3. The *retreatist subculture* consists of individuals who fail in their efforts to make it in both the legitimate and illegitimate opportunity structures. These individuals are "double failures" in Cloward and Ohlin's theory, and they are destined to the chemical crimes of drug and alcohol abuse as forms of escape from their failures.

The structural functionalist theories discussed to this point all see their subjects as impressed by the values—namely, the value attached to material success—they encounter. The valued material outcomes, usually because they are unattainable, lead to delinquent and criminal behaviors. Over the years, research in this tradition has come to focus on the issue of whether explicit disparities in the values or goals and means of individuals actually result in delinquency and crime. The question asked is whether disparities between individually held aspirations and expectations lead to delinquent and criminal outcomes. The early Mertonian emphasis of this tradition on classes and class-based solutions to disparities between goals and means has received reduced attention since the days of Robert Kennedy and the age of Roosevelt War on Poverty during the Johnson administration (Cullen 1988).

Meanwhile, another stream of the structural functionalist tradition focused on a more general absence of the goals, values, or commitment that American society valorizes. Here the emphasis was again on values and group-level processes at the neighborhood or community level. However, despite the assumption of common goals and values, it was not taken for granted that these goals and values were effectively or intensively shared.

Social Disorganization Theory

Social disorganization theory evolved out of research by Shaw and McKay (1931) beginning in the 1920s in Chicago. They observed that problems such as truancy, tuberculosis, infant mortality, mental disorder, juvenile delinquency, and adult crime clustered in neighborhoods generally near the center of the city. They observed that these problems were more characteristic of the neighborhoods than of the people in them, so that as different ethnic groups moved in and out of the neighborhoods, it was the neighborhoods and not the people who remained troubled. Since these troubles and problems were contrary to the shared values of the neighborhood inhabitants, they were indications that these neighborhoods were unable to realize the goals of their residents. In other words, they were indications of the neighborhoods' social disorganization.

Shaw and McKay also sought to determine the sources of this social disorganization by identifying characteristics these neighborhoods held in common. They concluded that poverty, high residential mobility, and ethnic heterogeneity led to a weakening of "social bonds" or controls—in other words, to social disorganization—which in turn led to high rates of delinquency. All of this referred to neighborhoods, not people.

However, as with the previous opportunity theories, researchers over time began to be concerned about what these findings meant for understanding individual behavior (Robinson 1950). One result was a shift in both theoretical and research interest to the individual level, and the development of a control theory (Hirschi 1969) that focused on the bonds of individual youths to their families, schools, and communities, as measured through survey self-reports of youthful attitudes, experiences, and delinquent behaviors.

Control Theory

Those with goals and means to their attainment bond with institutions (e.g., the family and school) that encourage conformity. Alternatively, Hirschi's (1969) control theory argues that the absence of such a social bond is all that is required to explain much crime and delinquency. He cites four sources of the social bond:

1. Attachment (e.g., to family and friends)
2. Involvement (e.g., in school and related activities)
3. Belief (e.g., in various types of values and principles)
4. Commitment (e.g., to achieving goals)

According to control theory, the less attached, involved, believing, and committed individuals are, the weaker is their bond to society; and the weaker the bond, the greater the likelihood of delinquency and crime. From this perspective, no special strain between goals and means is required to produce deviant behavior; all that is required is the reduction of the constraining social bond that holds crime and deviance in check. A prominent extension of this theory discussed in the next chapter argues that many criminals simply lack self-control (Gottfredson and Hirschi 1990). The shift in emphasis from social control to self-control reflected the changing conceptions of societal and personal responsibility that divide the theories of the age of Roosevelt from those of the age of Reagan.

Social Learning Theory

Control theory seeks to explain why, where, and when delinquency and crime are most likely to occur. Akers's (1977) social learning theory asserts that "the person whose ties with conformity have been broken may remain just a candidate for deviance; whether he becomes deviant depends on further social or other rewards" (66). According to social learning theory, deviant behavior results from a conditioning process that usually involves social groups in which rewards and punishment shape the course of the behaviors they reinforce.

This principle of social reinforcement has interesting implications that move beyond control theory, for example, in explaining how individuals shift from conforming to criminal and noncriminal forms of deviant behavior. An example involves groups with prescriptive norms that allow some drinking and in which most people drink moderately. The excessive drinking of an alcoholic usually will not challenge such a group's controls or norms until it is so far out of hand that he or she no longer is welcome in the group. However, the latter break can pave the way for a move to a group that values and rewards heavy drinking. Social learning theory emphasized this *shift*, because it illustrates how *differential reinforcement*, and not simply the absence of controls, can explain the more specific course of criminal and delinquent behavior.

An Overview of Functionalist Theories

Values or beliefs—for example, about success goals—play a key causal role in all the functionalist theories we have considered. These theories tend to argue that the presence of success goals or values without the means to attain them can produce criminal behavior, as can the absence of these goals or values in the first place. It is an emphasis on these values and on the role of the school, family, and other groups in promoting and transmitting them that ties the functionalist theories together.

There is a trend in the evolution of these theories that, counter to the intentions of many of their early exponents, has involved shifting attention from group-, neighborhood-, and class-level processes to the ways in which individuals encounter these processes. This gradual shift anticipated the transition from the age of Roosevelt to the age of Reagan. This has had the effect of deemphasizing structural and cultural issues that are at the core of this theoretical tradition to a place of secondary importance. Instead, the focus has tended to shift to issues of social psychological strain as experienced by individuals and to the loss of control over individuals. Both the group (often called the macrolevel) and individual (often called the microlevel) dimensions of analysis are important, but they were not often effectively joined in this classical period of theory development. A result is the decline of a distinctive emphasis in the early functionalist tradition on issues that rise above the individual.

The Symbolic Interactionist Theories

The symbolic interactionist theories of crime bring a subtle but important shift from an emphasis on values to the ways in which meanings and definitions are involved in explaining criminality. These meanings and definitions shape behavior and responses to it. Over time, the symbolic interactionist theories extended attention from an emphasis on how symbolic meanings and definitions derived from participation with others in delinquent and criminal behavior to the roles official agencies of social control play in imposing symbolic meanings and definitions on individuals. The extension of attention to official and symbolic meanings that began in the late years of the age of Roosevelt is the backdrop for this book's focus on the role of politics and politicians (such as Roosevelt and Reagan) in the framing of issues of street and suite crimes. To understand where the newer emphasis on the political framing of crime and criminals in part comes from, we begin with the more classical focus on co-participants in symbolic interactionist theory.

Differential Association Theory

Edwin Sutherland (1924) began to write about crime well before the Great Depression but became most influential in the early post–World War II years, as the United States was beginning to assume its superpower role in the world economy. Sutherland became probably the most revered figure in sociological criminology, largely for his concept of white-collar crime and his attention to crime in the financial suites, but also for his symbolic interactionist theory of differential association. Sutherland's concept of white-collar crime outlived Roosevelt's foreshadowing concept of "banksters." Still, Sutherland was very much of the age of Roosevelt in his awareness that accepted ideas about behaviors in the financial suites were often criminogenic. The important role of ideas and ways of thinking about criminal behavior was essential to Sutherland's differential association theory.

The concept of differential association is sometimes mistaken as referring only to associations among individuals, but it also refers to associations among ideas. Individuals only behave criminally, Sutherland argued, when they define such behavior as acceptable. To be sure, this process of association occurs through individuals, but the process also depends on the association of ideas or definitions and conceptual frameworks.

The hypothesis of differential association is that criminal behavior is learned in association with those who define such behavior favorably and in isolation from those who define it unfavorably, and that a person in an appropriate situation engages in criminal behavior if, and only if, the weight of the favorable definitions exceeds the weight of the unfavorable definitions. (Sutherland 1949:234)

Sutherland applied this hypothesis in his famous study of white-collar crime. He argued that individuals become white-collar criminals because they are immersed in a business culture that defines illegal business practices as acceptable. Common commercial clichés transmit this ideology within business groups:

"We're not in business for our health."

"Business is business."

"It isn't how you get your money, but what you do with it that counts."

"It's the law of the jungle."

Sutherland explained that such ideas become influential because of their transmission within business groups that are isolated from competing viewpoints, and because "the persons who define business practices as undesirable and illegal are customarily called 'communists' or 'socialists' and their definitions carry little weight."

Donald Cressey (1971) extended Sutherland's theory to the more specific business crime of embezzlement. After interviewing more than 100 imprisoned embezzlers, Cressey concluded that individuals committed this crime only after they had first justified their acts by redefining them with the following kinds of thoughts:

"Some of our most respectable citizens got their start in life by using other people's money temporarily."

"All people steal when they get in a tight spot."

"My interest was only to use this money temporarily, so I was 'borrowing' it, not 'stealing.'"

"I have been trying to live an honest life, but I have had nothing but trouble, so 'to hell with it.'"

Cressey (1965) believed that the definitional component of his theory had a wide application to white-collar kinds of crimes, suggesting that "The generalization I have developed here was made to fit only one crime—embezzling. But I suspect that the verbalization section of the generalization will fit other types of respectable crime as well" (15).

Neutralization Theory

An important feature of the symbolic interactionist theories is that they use the same kind of logic and conceptualization to explain crime in the upper and lower reaches of the social hierarchy. Thus, when Matza and Sykes (1961) extended some of the basic premises of Sutherland's differential association theory to explain common delinquency with their neutralization theory, they began by noting that there are "subterranean traditions" in the conventional culture that reflect ironic convergences between what are often thought of as dominant and dissident groups. Matza (1964) argues that this is so because "the spirit and substance of subterranean traditions are familiar and within limits tolerated by broad segments of the adult population" (64).

As an example of such subterranean convergence, Matza and Sykes (1961) point to Veblen's (1899) classic observation in *The Theory of the Leisure Class* that delinquents conform to the norms of conventional society's business sector rather than deviate from them when they place a desire for "big money" in their value system. They go on to note that wealth-motivated and entrepreneurial traditions in American society encourage adventure, excitement, and thrill seeking, which seemingly further promote deviance when compared with such conformity-producing values as security, routinization, and stability. The point is that the former, latent values exist side by side with the latter, more conventional values. This latter may help to explain how in the age of Reagan, extraordinary levels of risk and freedom became acceptable in a radically deregulated financial services sector that produced a series of remarkably expensive suite crimes, from the savings and loan scandal to the subprime mortgage crisis.

Matza and Sykes note that the convergences between delinquency and convention do not simply take mild or material forms. They observe that even violence is widely tolerated: "the dominant society exhibits a widespread taste for violence, since fantasies of violence in books, magazines, movies, and television are everywhere at hand. The delinquent simply translates into behavior those values that the majority are usually too timid to express" (716). The election and reelection of the actor Arnold Schwarzenegger of the *Lethal Weapon* and *Terminator* films as the "Governator" of California bears an interesting relationship to this theory. More generally, Matza and Sykes conclude that "the delinquent has picked up and emphasized one part of the dominant value system, namely, the subterranean values that coexist with other, publicly proclaimed values possessing a more respectable air" (717).

Still, Sykes and Matza also argue that common delinquents, like white-collar criminals, display guilt or shame when confronted with evidence of their acts. Like the white-collar criminal, Sykes and Matza (1957) describe the delinquent as drifting into a deviant lifestyle through a subtle process of justification or neutralization that ultimately makes him or her an "apologetic failure." "We call . . . [their] justifications of deviant behavior techniques of neutralization," write Sykes and Matza, "and we believe these techniques make up a crucial component of Sutherland's definitions favorable to the violation of the law" (667).

There are five specific neutralization techniques Sykes and Matza suggest are common among delinquents. These involve:

1. "Denials of responsibility" (e.g., blaming a bad background)
2. "Denials of the victim" (e.g., claiming that the victim had it coming)
3. "Denials of injury" (e.g., recasting vandalism as "mischief" or theft as "borrowing")
4. "Condemnations of the condemners" (e.g., calling their condemnation discriminatory)
5. "Appeals to higher loyalties" (e.g., citing loyalty to friends or family as the cause of the behavior)

We will see in the final chapter of this book how widely dispersed these kinds of techniques of neutralization can be when we consider the role of a related kind of framing process in the denial of rapes as state-led war crimes, or what I will later call "state rape." Neutralization theory anticipates the critical collective framing approach used later in this book.

Sykes and Matza suggest that techniques of neutralization cause delinquency among disadvantaged youths in the same way that verbalizations and rationalizations cause crime more generally, regardless of age, place, or class position. However, it is still the case that disadvantaged youth and young adults are more likely to get caught and punished for their misbehaviors, an issue that is of more recent theoretical concern in a variant of the symbolic interactionist tradition called labeling theory.

Labeling Theory

An early form of a labeling theory of delinquency and crime is found in the work of Franklin Tannenbaum, especially *Crime and the Community* (1938). Tannenbaum was struck by the normalcy of much delinquency. He noted that many forms of juvenile delinquency are a common part of adolescent street life, aspects of the play, adventure, and excitement that many later identify nostalgically as an important part of their youth. The problem is that at the time, others often do not view these activities in the same way but rather as a nuisance or threat, and this can result in the police being summoned.

Police intervention can begin a process of change in the way individuals and their behaviors are perceived by others, and ultimately by the individual himself or herself. Tannenbaum suggests that this begins with a gradual shift from the definition of specific acts as "evil" to a more general definition of the individual involved. The first contact with authorities is a crucial part of this process, because it can constitute a "dramatization of evil" that separates the child or adolescent from peers for specialized treatment. Tannenbaum worries that this "dramatization" can play a greater role in creating the criminal than any other experience. Individuals so signified may begin to think of themselves as the types of people who do evil things—for example, as delinquents. This turns the conventional idea of deterrence on its head by asserting that legal punishments associated with the police and courts create more problems than they solve. Tannenbaum had a solution of his own, arguing, "The way out is through a refusal to dramatize the evil" (20). He suggested that the less said and done the better.

Labeling theorists have expanded on Tannenbaum's notion of the dramatization of evil, for example, by suggesting concepts to distinguish between acts that occur before and after the societal response to deviance. Edwin Lemert (1951, 1967) does this using the terms *primary* and *secondary deviance*. Primary deviance refers to the initial acts of individuals that call out the societal response, while secondary deviance refers to the ensuing problems that arise from the societal response to the initial acts. The primary acts may occur at random or may be the product of diverse initial causal factors. The key point is that these initial acts have little impact on the individual's self-concept. That is, "primary deviation . . . has only marginal implications for the psychic structure of the individual" (1967:17).

However, secondary deviance is much more consequential. The dramatization of evil that can signal the onset of secondary deviance can also lead to a traumatization of self-concept, "altering the psychic structure, producing a specialized organization of social roles and self-regarding attitudes" (Lemert 1967: 40–41). Even more significantly, however, Lemert suggests that secondary deviance can bring with it a stabilization of the deviant behavior pattern involved: "Objective evidences of this change will be found in the symbolic appurtenances of the new role, in clothes, speech, posture and mannerisms, which in some cases heighten social visibility, and which in some cases serve as symbolic cues to professionalization" (1951:76). Again, as in Tannenbaum's analysis, the implication is that simply "leaving things be" might often be the better course of action.

The effect of not letting things be is to create *outsiders*, as expressed in the title of two classic books, one a scholarly analysis by Becker (1963) and the other a fictional treatment of adolescence and delinquency by S. E. Hinton (1967). Becker emphasizes that there is a political dimension to the creation of such groups and that "the rule-breaker may feel his judges are outsiders" (2). This political process is social in that "groups create deviance, by making the rules whose infraction constitutes deviance, and by applying those rules to particular people and labeling them as outsiders" (9). There is a crucial distinction drawn in this framing of the problem between rule-breaking *behavior*, on the one hand, and the disreputable *status* of being called a deviant on the other.

This distinction parallels a more common division often drawn in sociology between *achieved* and *ascribed* characteristics. People earn their achieved characteristics, as contrasted with the ascription of their inherited or imposed characteristics. As used here, achieved behaviors contrast with ascribed statuses. To clarify this distinction in the study of crime and disrepute, Becker suggests that "it might be worthwhile to refer to such behavior as *rule-breaking behavior* and reserve the term *deviant* for those labeled as deviant by some segment of society" (14). However, the bigger question in some ways is, who makes the rules? Becker's early answer to this question—"those groups whose social position gives them weapons and power" (18)—anticipated the conflict theories we consider next and the critical collective framing theory that I introduce later in this book. However, Becker's most pressing concern is with the consequences for the careers of individuals after the imposition of criminal and disreputable labels.

Becker draws from the sociological study of occupations to suggest that while the concept of "career" usually distinguishes success in conventional work, it can also refer to "several varieties of career outcomes, ignoring the question of 'success'" (1963:24). The analogy with more typical occupational careers involves the sequencing of movements from one position to another. "Career contingencies" are the crucial determinants of when and how these movements take place, with a key contingency in deviant careers being the imposition of a disreputable label.

Becker writes that "one of the most crucial steps in the process of building a stable pattern of deviant behavior is likely to be the experience of being caught and publicly labeled as deviant" (31). Labeling theorists more generally assert that the imposition of a disreputable label sets in motion a process in which the individual's self-concept is stigmatized (Goffman 1961, 1963) or degraded (Garfinkel 1956), and she or he becomes what others expect. Becker concludes that the labeling process is a self-fulfilling prophecy that"sets in motion several mechanisms which conspire to shape the person in the image that people have of him" (1963:34).

Overview of the Interactionist Theories

The symbolic interactionist theories broaden the study of crime and disrepute from the functionalist concern with values to include consideration of the ways social meanings and definitions, which we will later call framings, help to produce criminal and deviant behavior in a wide variety of settings. Over time, the attention of this set of theories more generally shifted from how meanings and definitions are cultivated by individuals and within groups to the ways in which meanings and definitions are imposed by members and agents of other groups, including political groups, on individuals within groups who become official outsiders.

Although the attention of interactionist theories to issues of meaning and definition is central to the sociological study of crime and disrepute, work in this tradition did not develop a longitudinal understanding that fully exploits the potential of the career analogy. We will see in the next chapter that this longitudinal analysis of criminal careers became a central focus in the age of Reagan. Nonetheless, the attention to meaning, the alertness to convergence across classes, the sensitivity to labeling processes, and the career analogy are all classic contributions to American criminology.

Conflict Theories of Crime and Disrepute

The conflict theories pick up where the labeling theories leave off, often giving emphasis to the role of dominant societal groups in imposing legal labels on members of subordinate societal groups. Conflict theories explain how and why this happens by considering differences in power and wealth in society. In doing so, attention is placed more on the groups imposing criminal labels than on the individuals who receive them.

Although we will trace the American origins of the conflict theories to the late 1950s, the rise of these theories was very much a product of the late 1960s and early 1970s. The development of conflict theories paralleled political developments in the last stages of the age of Roosevelt. The seminal events of this period, the Vietnam War and the resistance to the military draft, contributed to a new context in which American criminologists sought to locate and understand crime (Hagan and Bernstein 1979).

Conflict theorists saw the Vietnam War itself as a crime of and by the state. Neil Young's call to arms with "Four Dead in Ohio" captured the youthful mood of government distrust. This led conflict theorists to ask whether and how crimes beyond those of war connected to the state. This kind of thinking led criminologists to focus their attention on wealthy and powerful interests. They asked how crime connected to the newly scrutinized military-industrial nexus and other centers of power in society.

Conflict theories of crime peaked in prominence during the tumultuous period that marked the electoral transitions from the age of Roosevelt to the age of Reagan. (Recall here that Ronald Reagan became governor of California in 1966.) The presidential crimes of Richard Nixon's Watergate scandal underlined the connections between crime and politics and whipsawed the country between the nearly diametrically opposed policy positions and politics of the Nixon and Carter administrations. As these winds of change swirled around them, criminological conflict theorists were thinking seriously about the place of power and politics in their theories.

Group Conflict Theory

There is a link between conflict theory and subcultural as well as labeling theory. The link is that subcultural groups typically are also subordinate groups, and this makes their activities liable to the legal interventions of dominant groups who oppose them and the values they represent. George Vold (1958) recognized this point and focused his early group conflict theory of crime on the role of dominant groups in imposing their value judgments by defining the behaviors of others as criminal. Where the functionalist theories assumed a basic value consensus in society, the conflict theories focus on value conflict between opposing groups.

Vold set the perspective of his theory by referring to crime and delinquency as "minority group" behaviors. He applied this argument first to delinquency, asserting that "the juvenile gang . . . is nearly always a 'minority group' out of sympathy with and in more or less direct opposition to the rules and regulations of the dominant majority, that is, the established world of adult values and powers" (211). This theme is a cross-class staple of the American cinema, from *West Side Story* and *Rebel Without a Cause* to *Ferris Bueller's Day Off* and *Youth in Revolt*. The police and teachers protect adult values in struggles against adolescents who seek symbolic and material advantages not permitted to them under the adult code. Vold argues that this is an intergenerational conflict of values where adults prevail through their control over the legal process.

Vold analyzes four other types of crime from this group conflict perspective:

1. The first involves the kinds of political movements witnessed during the break with the Soviet Union in Budapest, Prague, and Berlin. Vold notes that the irony of such events is that "a successful revolution makes criminals out of the government officials previously in power, and an unsuccessful revolution makes its leaders into traitors" (214). Examples of this point include the contrasting fates in post–World War II Czechoslovakia of Alexander Dubcek, who was exiled to a low-level bureaucratic job in a remote setting for his earlier failed attempts to resist Russian domination through democratization, and Vaclav Havel, who was later elected president after being released from prison.

2. Clashes between business and labor interests during strikes and lockouts constitute a second type of crime considered by Vold. Here he notes that "the participants on either side of a labor dispute condone whatever criminal behavior is deemed 'necessary' for the maintenance of their side of the struggle" (216). The experiences of the late labor leader Cesar Chávez on behalf of migrant farmworkers in California and beyond illustrate this point. Chávez experienced periods of both criminal condemnation and cultural celebration for his efforts to improve the lives of migrant laborers through unionization and strikes.

3. Conflicts within and between competing unions are a third type of crime included in Vold's theory. Vold writes that "such disputes often involve intimidation and personal violence, and sometimes they become entangled with the 'rackets' and gang wars of the criminal underworld" (217). Robert Kennedy exposed illegal activities of the Teamsters Union. Marlon Brando's portrayal in the film *On the Waterfront* of a boxer broken by this corruption dramatized the criminal forms these union politics could take.

4. The last type of crime considered by Vold involves racial and ethnic conflict. Vold observes that "numerous kinds of crimes result from the clashes incidental to attempts to change, or to upset the caste system of racial segregation in various parts of the world" (217). These crimes can be violent as well as political, as in the bloodshed coincident with the rise and fall of South Africa's racial apartheid, symbolized in the life of Nelson Mandela, and in many episodes of the ongoing fight for civil rights by African Americans. Spike Lee's film biography of Malcolm X portrays a remarkable life experience of crime that moved from the personal to the political and back again, culminating for many in Malcolm's proclamation in rebellion against the U.S. mistreatment of African Americans that "violence is intelligence."

Vold did not intend that his theory should explain all crimes, advising instead that "the group-conflict hypothesis should not be stretched too far" (219). He speculated, however, that his theory was relevant to a "considerable amount of crime," and subsequent work advanced this speculation.

Theories of Crime, Law, and Order

Austin Turk presents a propositional statement of conflict theory in his book, *Crime and the Legal Order* (1969). Turk treats
criminality as a status that is conferred by others, so that
"criminality is not a biological, psychological, or even behavioral phenomenon, but a social status defined by the way in
which an individual is perceived, evaluated, and treated by
legal authorities" (25). It is critical to know, then, who does
the defining. Two groups are involved: "There are those . . .
who constitute the dominant, decision-making category—the
authorities—and those who make up the subordinate category
who are affected by but scarcely affect law—the subjects"
(33). Criminals are regarded as the subjects of lawmaking by
authorities.

An innovative aspect of Turk's theory involves a learning
process through which authorities impose their power. He
writes that "both eventual authorities and eventual subjects
learn and continually relearn to interact with one another as,
respectively, occupants of superior and inferior statuses and
performers of dominating and submitting roles" (41–42). The
result is that authorities learn "social roles of domination,"
while subjects learn "social norms of deference." However,
there is never complete agreement on the lessons, and subsequent disagreements become conflicts interpreted as challenges to authority. From this perspective, "lawbreaking is . . .
an indicator of the failure or lack of authority: it is a measure
of the extent to which rulers and ruled . . . are not bound together in a perfectly stable authority relationship" (48).

Turk's theory is systematic and propositional in making explicit the conditions in which this conflict becomes most intense, thus specifying the situations in which the highest crime
rates occur. The relative power of the persons involved is a
central consideration. Turk reasons that those who are poor
and nonwhite have the least power and therefore have the
highest rates of criminalization.

Chambliss and Seidman (1971) take the conflict theory of crime to a societal level of analysis. They suggest that societies low in specialization and stratification tend to resolve disputes through compromise and reconciliation that involves relative consensus. However, as societies become more complex and intensively stratified, a "winner-take-all" rule-enforcement approach comes to replace reconciliation as a means of dispute resolution. The selection of which rules are to be enforced and against whom becomes crucial. Chambliss and Seidman point out that bureaucratic agencies are the source of these decisions in advanced stratified societies. In these settings, they write, "rule creation and rule enforcement will take place when such creation or enforcement increases the rewards for the agencies and their officials, and they will not take place when they are conducive to organizational strain" (474). The implication is that the guiding principle of legal bureaucracy is to maximize organizational gains while minimizing organizational strains.

This principle leads to what Chambliss and Seidman paradoxically call a rule of law: "the rule is that discretion at every level . . . will be so exercised as to bring mainly those who are politically powerless (that is, the poor) into the purview of the law" (268). Chambliss and Seidman reason that this is because the poor are least likely to have the resources to create organizational strains that provide protection against prosecution. This makes it probable that "those laws which prohibit certain types of behavior popular among lower-class persons are more likely to be enforced" (475). The implication is that the poor and minorities form a large component of our official crime statistics more because of class bias in our society and the dynamics of our legal bureaucracy than because of differences in behavior.

A Social Realist Theory of Crime

Richard Quinney's (1970) social realist theory integrates the formulation and application of criminal definitions with the occurrence of criminal behavior. Several sources of criminal

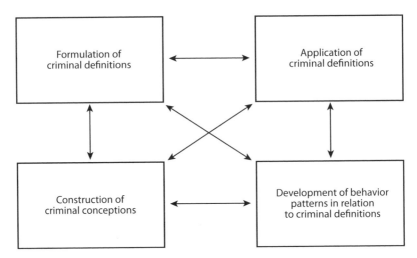

Figure 3.1 Model of the social reality of crime. Source: Quinney (1970:24).

behavior are identified, including (1) structured opportunities, (2) learning experiences, (3) interpersonal associations and identifications, and (4) self-conceptions. The key assumption that links behaviors with definitions in this theory is that "persons in the segments of society whose behavior patterns are not represented in formulating and applying criminal definitions are more likely to act in ways that will be defined as criminal than those in the segments that formulate and apply criminal definitions" (21). This involves the first two elements of the theory, opportunities and learning, in a process through which the better-off in society are involved in criminalizing behavior patterns that are learned, often in response to differential opportunities, by those who are less well off.

For Quinney, the key to this process involves *conceptions* of crime, which I later call framings of crime, held by powerful segments of society. These conceptions appear in personal and mass communications that articulate powerful elite definitions of the "crime problem," which in turn become real in their consequences. This is "the social reality of crime," and it takes effect in the following way:

In general . . . the more the power segments are concerned about crime, the greater the probability that criminal definitions will be created and that behavior patterns will develop in opposition to criminal definitions. The formulation and application of criminal definitions and the development of behavior patterns related to criminal definitions are thus joined in full circle by the construction of criminal conceptions. (23)

This is a broadly integrative theory that brings together the key ideas of labeling and conflict theory with those of opportunity, differential association and learning theories of crime. Figure 3.1 presents an overview of this theory.

Critical Conflict Theories

A final group of conflict theories explicitly incorporate ideas about economic conflict, which have captured the attention of sociological criminologists at several junctures, first in Europe and then in America (Bonger 1916; Greenberg 1981; Rusche and Kirchheimer 1939). A group of English criminologists, Taylor, Walton, and Young (1973), joined this tradition by calling for a "new criminology." This school of thought sees the criminal law as the product of an alliance between business interests and the state.

The new criminologists argue that this alliance imposes "an ethic of individualism" that holds *individuals* responsible for their acts, while at the same time diverting attention from the *environmental* structures from which these acts emerge. They argue that this ethic restrains only the disadvantaged classes because the "labour forces of the industrial society" are bound by this ethic through the criminal law and its sanctions. In contrast, "the state and the owners of labour will be bound only by a civil law which regulates their competition between each other" (Taylor, Walton, and Young 1973:264). The effective result is a double standard of citizenship and responsibility in which the more advantaged are "beyond incrimination," and therefore beyond criminal sanction as well (see Swigert and Farrell 1980). This double standard is a source of the distinction between crimes of the streets and crimes in the suites highlighted throughout this book.

Spitzer (1975) provides a further application of critical conflict ideas in the study of crime and disrepute. He reasons that "we must not only ask why specific members of the underclass are selected for official processing, but also why they behave as they do" (see also Colvin and Pauly 1983). Spitzer argues that "problem populations" emerge when, because of their behaviors, personal qualities, and positions, groups of individuals generate costs or threats for powerful groups in society.

Two broadly defined problem populations result. The first is *social junk*, which from the perspective of the dominant class is a costly but nonetheless relatively harmless burden to society. Examples of this category include the dispossessed and the homeless, who may also be aged, disabled, and physically or mentally challenged, as well as sometimes involved with alcohol and drugs. In contrast is Spitzer's second category, characterized as *social dynamite*. The uniquely more dangerous feature of this grouping is "its potential actively to call into question established relationships, especially relations of production and domination" (645). This second group tends, according to Spitzer, to be more youthful, alienated, and politically volatile than social junk. However, social junk transforms in some political circumstances into social dynamite. The U.S. ghetto riots, especially in the 1960s, may have been such a moment of incipient rebellion.

A Conflict Theory of Ghetto Revolts and the Courts

Spitzer's (1975) concept of social dynamite is exemplified in the 1992 riots that followed the acquittal of Los Angeles police officers accused of beating Rodney King and in the earlier ghetto riots of the 1960s, including the 1965 Watts revolt, the 1967 Detroit rebellion, and the 1968 Chicago riot. These riots posed major challenges to law enforcement authorities, as analyzed from a conflict perspective by Isaac Balbus (1973). Balbus found court authorities in each of the cities conscious of their role in assisting political elites in stopping the "fires in the streets" that had engulfed their cities. Their first concern was to reestablish *order.*

Yet this concern to impose order did not operate alone or without check. Legal procedures were also under scrutiny during this period, so that a semblance of *formal rationality* also had to be preserved. Considerations of *organizational maintenance* also operated, in that the riots placed heavy pressures of sheer volume on the courts of each city. Balbus argues that these shared concerns about order, formal rationality, and organizational maintenance affected the courts of the three cities in parallel ways, resulting in a similar sequence in the patterned responses of authorities across the cities. This sequence conditioned the fairness of the treatment offenders received.

The beginning phase in each city involved an urgent concern with order that outweighed attention to formal rationality and organizational maintenance. Serious and widespread abrogation of standard procedures characterized the processes of arrest, charging, and bail-setting. For example, judges indiscriminately implemented preventive detention policies by imposing excessively high bail requirements. The intent was to "clear the streets" and keep them clear for the duration of the revolts. However, even here standards of justice were not completely abandoned, and some formal rationality prevailed during this period. Balbus describes the legal response this way: "Although the police and military response was often brutal and led to considerable destruction of life, there was no wholesale slaughter of riot participants. Martial law was *not* declared, and *some* concern for the legality of arrests was exhibited" (234). Balbus explains that a level of legality was preserved, if only out of the desire to formally treat the ghetto rebellion as involving "ordinary crimes" rather than as distinctively different acts of political protest and rebellion.

Meanwhile, although the priority during the revolt was to prosecute virtually all those arrested on serious charges, in the weeks and months that followed concerns about formal rationality and organizational maintenance produced convictions on less serious charges and lenient sentences. Balbus notes that this pattern reverses the more typical tendency for dismissal and leniency to decrease with movement through the criminal justice system. He observes that

> we found . . . a striking reversal of the standard model of the criminal process which posits a series of screens whose holes progressively diminish in size and from which the defendants thus find it increasingly difficult to escape; following the Los Angeles and Detroit major revolts, in contrast, the "holes" became progressively larger, and it was much easier to "escape" at the preliminary hearing and trial stages than it was at the earlier prosecution stage.

Balbus argues that it could not have been otherwise.

The justice system needed to help authorities put down the riots by providing swift and harsh treatment at the outset of the disturbances. However, as time passed, the requirements of formal rationality made it difficult to sustain this severe treatment in open court settings or in the face of an overcrowded justice system whose simple maintenance required a reduction in case volume. This application of conflict theory accords a measured "autonomy" to the state in resisting an inclination toward a more pervasive expression of class bias.

Overview of the Conflict Theories

Conflict theories are important in explaining why some forms of social deviance are criminal. A fundamental insight from conflict theory is that activities common among the socially and economically disadvantaged are more likely to be designated criminal than are activities more common among the powerful. The treatment of crack versus powder cocaine is a striking example considered in this book.

Nonetheless, Vold's advice that the conflict hypothesis "not be taken too far" anticipates much of the modern criticism of this group of theories. Vold's advice reiterates the distinction drawn in chapter 2 between consensus and conflict crimes. This distinction acknowledges that most people most of the time, across several centuries and in most nations, rather consistently have called *some* behaviors criminal. Conflict theories have sometimes dismissed this social fact and correspondingly discounted the importance of explaining these behaviors.

It is in part for this reason that Austin Turk (1976) explicitly asserted that "conflict-coercion theory does not imply that most accused persons are innocent, nor that more and less powerful people engage in conventional deviations to the same extent. It does not even imply that legal officials . . . discriminate against less powerful and on behalf of more powerful people" (292). Rather, Turk expressed the view of an increasing number of conflict theorists that there *are* class-linked differences in criminal behavior patterns and that authorities *vary* in their treatment of minority and class groupings across different kinds of social circumstances. The attention these theories give to structured inequalities of wealth and power and to the role of the state in explaining these patterns makes their contributions very important (see Zatz and Chambliss 1993).

The Classical Theories

The three classical traditions—structural functionalism, symbolic interactionism, and conflict theory—persist in contemporary criminology. Each tradition makes a distinctive contribution. Structural functionalism emphasizes that the presence of success goals and values without the means to attain them can produce delinquent and criminal behavior, as can also the absence of these goals and values in the first place. Symbolic interactionism alerts us to the role of group-enhanced and group-imposed meanings and definitions in the production of delinquency and crime. The conflict theories further address the role of dominant societal groups in imposing legal labels on members of subordinate societal groups rather than on members of their own groups. Over time, this emphasis led to more attention being paid to white-collar and political crimes.

Yet despite these notable contributions, the influence of all three of these theoretical traditions from the age of Roosevelt declined considerably during the age of Reagan. The riots of the late 1960s may have sown the seeds of the decline, as foreshadowed in Edwin Meese's story, recounted in the prologue, about Ronald Reagan during the Washington riots following the shooting of Martin Luther King. These riots set off a shock wave of fear across the political landscape of America. Criminologists responded with a new set of theoretical ideas that resonated with the fears of street crime associated with these riots. The politics of the age of Reagan articulated and responded to these fears.

Each of the classical traditions from the age of Roosevelt has its points of weakness. The structural functionalist theories too often abandoned their distinctive early attention to macro- or group-level processes that generate crime; the potential of the career analogy that is central to the symbolic interactionist tradition is not yet fully developed; and the conflict theories tended to deflect attention from the explanation of criminal behavior in and of itself. Nonetheless, American criminology is the beneficiary of a rich classical tradition of theoretical diversity that has stimulated much research. It is obviously necessary to acknowledge shifts in the national and world economy and to confront the fast-changing reality of America's problems of poverty and crime. The classical theories can advance our understanding of these new realities, but to do so, these theories of the age of Roosevelt must be adapted, elaborated, and often superseded. We urgently need, in short, to move on. Unfortunately, the politics of the age of Reagan often did not help criminologists to do this.

Chapter 4
Explaining Crime in the Age of Reagan
||||||||||

Ronald Reagan and the Radical Criminologists

The University of California at Berkeley established the first nonsociological doctoral degree program in criminology in 1966, the year California elected Ronald Reagan its governor. At Berkeley and elsewhere, the U.S. Department of Justice's Law Enforcement Assistance Agency (LEAA) had launched new state and local crime control programs and spurred much of the early growth of the new field of criminology with government funding (Savelsberg 1994). Yet the trajectory was hardly smooth or uncontroversial. Despite an early emphasis on policing supported by LEAA funding, by the late 1960s the Berkeley School of Criminology had emerged as a battleground in the politics of crime and social justice, and Ronald Reagan and Edwin Meese made the school a subject of their attention.

A leading figure in the conflict was Tony Platt, who about this time published an influential book, *The Child Savers: The Invention of Delinquency* (1969). This book questioned at a crucial moment the role of the state in defining and punishing youthful deviance. Platt's critique of "child-saving reformers" from an increasingly politicized left side of the field anticipated later criticism from the political Right of the "rehabilitative ideal" in sentencing and treatment programs in America. The radical criminologists were deeply suspicious of both the reformist "helpers" and the repressive "controllers," thinking they were in many respects much the same.

Platt and his more senior colleague Paul Takagi forcefully advocated for a radicalization of criminology at Berkeley that would break away from the crime control focus of the LEAA. The following recollection from a seminar held years later to honor Takagi captures a sense of the period:

> At the award ceremony, Professor Takagi's former students and colleagues discussed the turbulent, exciting years at Berkeley's School of Criminology, with its deep involvement in struggles for prison reform, community control of the police, decriminalization of drug offenses, and rape crisis intervention, as well as close links with the Black Panther Party, the United Farm Workers Union, and the antiwar (Southeast Asia), feminist, and antiracist movements. Despite the School's unique educational role and unbridled popularity—some 700 students attended the introductory criminology course co-taught by Paul Takagi, Barry Krisberg, and Tony Platt—it was closed due to pressure emanating from law enforcement officials and Governor Ronald Reagan's office. (Shank 2008)

The classrooms of the radical criminologists at Berkeley strongly resonated with the movement politics that were thundering across American campuses in the late 1960s.

Governor Reagan appointed Edwin Meese to the school's advisory council in the early 1970s, and the University of California at Berkeley formally closed the doors of the School of Criminology in 1976. Elliott Curie offered an ironic and cogent denial that what radical criminologists had attempted during the previous decade was actually very radical:

> Some examples: it wasn't "radical" to point out that frightening and potentially abusive techniques of "be-

havior control" were being used in some prisons (which we said), or that prisons were increasingly being used to contain the consequences of larger economic and racial inequalities (which we said), or that some American actions in Vietnam came under the definition of crimes by any intelligible standard, or that the police in many cities were increasingly getting involved, since the riots of the sixties, in scary and professionally troubling forms of paramilitary surveillance and penetration of the ghettoes. Nor was it particularly "radical" to point out that contemporary capitalism contained powerful pressures toward crime and violence. All of this was just true, and the fact that all too many "mainstream" criminologists were mostly silent about these things was more a reflection of their timidity and retreat from social engagement than of our radicalism. (1999:16)

Platt and the other editors (1976) of the movement's journal, *Crime and Social Justice*, took some of the responsibility for "a naive political analysis" that failed to stave off the closure of the Berkeley school, but the fingerprints of the age of Reagan were all over the demise of the Berkeley program, and its termination was emblematic of changes to come.

The close of the Berkeley school in fact marked more of a new beginning than an end, coinciding with the transition from the age of Roosevelt to the age of Reagan in American criminology. Criminology made its first serious claims to being a separate field in the mid-1970s and the beginning of the age of Reagan. By the early 1990s, more than 1,000 universities and colleges offered separate undergraduate degrees in law enforcement, criminology, or criminal justice, while ninety-five graduate programs offered advanced degrees in criminology or criminal justice and eight major programs offered doctoral degrees (see Akers 1995). The carryover from the early government LEAA funding was a professional and pragmatic emphasis on crime control.

Crime and the Age of Reagan

There is no sharp divide between the age of Roosevelt and the age of Reagan. Neither political nor criminal history is that simple. As the Princeton historian Sean Wilentz (2008) writes in his *Age of Reagan*, "Like all major periods in our political history, the Reagan era had a long prelude, in which an existing political order crumbled and the Republican right rose to power, as well as a long postlude, in which Reagan's presidency continued to set the tone for American politics" (3–4). Wilentz thus locates a prelude to the Reagan era in the 1970s, during the latter part of the Nixon administration and the successor post-Watergate administration of Gerald Ford. Holdover Nixon-Ford figures such as George H. W. Bush, Donald Rumsfeld, and Dick Cheney were architects of a "powerful surge of conservative politics" that covered much of the following forty years. The conservative politics of this age of Reagan influenced all aspects of American society, with both direct and indirect influences on criminology.

This is, of course, because the politics of an era influence criminologists along with their fellow citizens (Savelsberg, Cleveland, and King 2004; Savelsberg and Flood 2004; Savelsberg, King, and Cleveland 2002). The age of Reagan was marked by distinctive changes in the economy and surrounding society. The preceding period of remarkable post-Depression and postwar economic growth had broadened the middle class and set an apparent foundation for lifelong jobs and long-term economic security with programs like Social Security and Medicare. This postwar period lasted in broad terms from the 1950s through the 1960s and into the 1970s. In contrast, the later 1970s were firmly part of the age of Reagan, with major changes in economic and social relations.

The 1970s marked the emergence of a fast-changing and turbulent economy that was increasingly polarized. This new dual economy included a bottom tier that required less educated and skilled workers to now rapidly change jobs and even jump sectors within the economy—often requiring relocations of work and residence and retraining in new skills and work arrangements, with fewer benefits and less control over work conditions. In the top tier, highly educated Americans as well became more mobile in terms of where they lived and worked, but they also gained in earnings and retained access to benefit programs. The top tier of the class structure raced ahead in the age of Reagan.

The result was increasing labor force inequality characterized by growing gaps between top and bottom ranks of an increasingly stratified economy. The postwar emphasis on growing the middle class gave way to a bipolar class system with radically differentiated lifestyles and prospects. Minority and less educated males who gained most during the postwar period from their migration to urban factory jobs in the North later lost the most, as the availability of unskilled manufacturing work declined.

There are many ways to illustrate the growth of income inequality. The Congressional Budget Office reports that in 2005, the average after-tax income of the bottom fifth of the income distribution was just over $15,000, compared to more than $1 million for the top 1 percent of this distribution. That is, after taxes, the top 1 percent made about seventy times the bottom 20 percent. The earnings ratio of top to bottom earners was 23 in 1979—before tripling in magnitude in the quarter century that followed (Bernstein 2007).

In addition to the jump in income inequality, no less striking changes were taking place in household size, composition, and location. Access to birth control, education, work, and cars radically altered the options available to women as well as men who could access those options. One-car families became multiple-car families, while advantaged women as well as men gained better access to higher education and careers outside the home. By 1980, more than half of married women in the United States had joined the labor force. Marriage itself was changing, as was parenthood. Divorce increased, and family size declined.

Even earlier, in 1965, Daniel Patrick Moynihan had sounded an ominous warning about worrisome trends among minority households in a controversial report anachronistically titled *The Negro Family* (1965). In describing a "tangle of pathology" in this troubling work, Moynihan predicted that rising numbers of female-based households would result in higher rates of delinquency and crime. Moynihan was widely criticized for his motives and message.

By the 1990s, about 70 percent of African American children were born to and raised by single mothers, a figure that proved stubbornly resistant to change over the following decades. Americans grew increasingly fearful about the changing face of the urban landscape. Suburban housing tracts and shopping malls drew white Americans away from the cities in mounting numbers, taking jobs with them. A combination of white flight and the northern migration of African Americans created increasingly segregated urban ghettos with fewer jobs, weakening tax bases, declining schools, and imperiled families. At the same time, a growing mass media culture built around television and movies fed an appetite for consumer goods that were ever more visible and desirable to Americans, from top to bottom in the new dual economy.

Those who had more of the mass-marketed consumables were increasingly fearful of those who did not. Moynihan had struck a raw nerve when he wrote about the changes that were emerging in this polarized political economy with its segregated and highly stratified spread across the landscape of America's suburbs and cities. Moynihan added to the discord he had earlier helped to provoke in a 1970 Nixon administration memo suggesting that "benign neglect" might be the best response to the associated policy problems. "The issue of race," Moynihan suggested, "could benefit from a period of benign neglect" (*New York Times* 1970). This fearfully turbulent and polarized political context produced the culture wars, to which criminology adapted in ways that would alter the evolution of this field for years to come.

Developmental Criminology: The Chronic Criminal

The first signs of a changing criminology in the age of Reagan came in the form of a finding associated with a new emphasis on longitudinally designed research. This research, which mirrored state-of-the-art methods used in medical studies, tracked the development of individuals and their involvement in crime over the life span. An early study that attracted widespread attention, *Delinquency in a Birth Cohort*, was first published in 1972, based on research led by the University of Pennsylvania criminologist Marvin Wolfgang. This study astonished many readers in reporting that a very small proportion of criminals accounted for a very large amount of crime. This study marked not only a new interest in the collection of longitudinal data but a return to a concern with common law types of street crime and delinquency. The renewed attention to crimes of the streets and gathering blindness to crimes of the suites endured as a longlasting influence of the age of Reagan.

Wolfgang's research team studied the records of about 10,000 males in Philadelphia from birth to age eighteen. They found that these youths committed more than 10,000 offenses, or an average about one offense each. Yet this average of one offense per youth was misleading. On closer examination of the records it became apparent that more than half the offenses were committed by only one-sixth of the delinquents. These delinquents, whom Wolfgang called "chronic offenders," formed just 6 percent of the entire population.

A London study by West and Farrington (1977:109) similarly found that about 5 percent of the families they sampled accounted for almost half of all convictions in their research. When the Rand Commission later surveyed adult prison and jail inmates, they found that half of all burglars committed about six crimes a year, while the top 10 percent committed an average of more than 200 offenses in a year (Visher 1986). A relatively few chronic criminals, it seemed, accounted for an inordinate amount of crime.

Ronald Reagan was one of many who embraced this research about "chronic offenders" and saw it as an important foundation for crime policy. If there was a single finding about crime that captured Reagan's imagination and set the agenda for much of the crime research in the age of Reagan, the documented high rates of offending by chronic criminals was it. Reagan cited a batch of studies about chronic criminals in a celebrated speech he delivered before an assembly of police chiefs in New Orleans in 1981. He said,

> Study after study has shown that a small number of criminals are responsible for an enormous amount of the crime in American society. One study of 250 criminals indicated that over an 11-year period, they were responsible for nearly half a million crimes. Another study showed that 49 criminals claimed credit for a total of 10,500 crimes.

Reagan leaned on this research and on the image of the chronic offender in advancing his ideas about crime and punishment. He insisted:

> It's time for honest talk, for plain talk. There has been a breakdown in the criminal justice system in America. It just plain isn't working. All too often, repeat offenders, habitual law-breakers, career criminals, call them what you will, are robbing, raping, and beating with impunity and, as I said, quite literally getting away with murder. The people are sickened and outraged. They demand we put a stop to it.

The American president was now using the very language of crime research to support his policy agenda. Criminologists followed suit by deepening their involvement in research on the development of chronic criminals and their criminal careers.

Contesting the Criminal Career Paradigm

A major development in the emergence of the field of American criminology during the age of Reagan was the increasing focus on the study of career criminals and criminal careers. David Garland (2001) in retrospect suggests this was a period and a paradigm characterized by a "culture of control," echoing the earlier attention of Platt and others to the heavy hand of the state. Garland urges the importance of studying the actual persons, as well as the social and political forces that created and contested this culture. "Instead of talking in the abstract about 'structural alignment,' or assuming that 'underlying forces' are capable of automatically working their effects across different social fields," Garland (104) writes, "we should instead attend to specific actors and agencies" (104). He adds, "We must also inspect the motivations and thought-processes of the authorities who select and implement them, and the cultural and political contexts in which their choices are validated" (105).

Garland is telling us that criminologists and politicians use ideas like "career criminals" and "criminal careers" to compete for approval and advancement in their respective worlds, and that we need to analyze the competition among such concepts and between specific academics to understand the development of the fields of criminology and crime policy (see also Bourdieu 1989). He insightfully insists that "If this field is to have any self-consciousness, and any possibility of self-criticism and self-correction, then our textbooks need to be rewritten and our sense of how things work needs to be thoroughly revised" (5). As president of the American Society of Criminology, John Laub (2003) similarly observed that we need a narrative that reflects the history of the field of criminology.

A major focal point around which crime policies and academic criminology revolved in the age of Reagan was the criminal career paradigm. The novelist and social philosopher Saul Bellow, who was widely read by academics during this era, observed that "without concepts it is impossible to advance or publicize your interests," and that "the universities have become a major source of the indispensable jargons that flow into public life" (1987:16). Like Garland, Bellow was interested in how academics advanced their ideas in public discourse and policy circles. Travis Hirschi demonstrated how contentious this discourse could become with an incisive speech in 1986 to the membership of the American Society of Criminology about the criminal career paradigm. Hirschi drew on work later published with Michael Gottfredson (1986) in the society's flagship journal, *Criminology*, under the provocative title "The True Value of Lambda Would Appear to Be Zero." Lambda was the mathematical symbol that Hirschi and Gottfredson's academic rival, Alfred Blumstein, used to represent the extent to which criminals might persist in offending at a near constant rate regardless of age. In other words, the constant rate of offending might be an academic myth.

In contrast to Gottfredson and Hirschi's ironic assertion that the value of lambda might be zero, Blumstein, Cohen, and Farrington (1988:21–22; see also Blumstein and Cohen 1987) speculated that the potentially constant non-zero value of lambda—or the tendency of offenders to keep offending at a constant rate—might be profound. They suggested comparisons with such invariants in science as the speed of light, Boyle's law, and other homeostatic processes, including the stability of body temperature under radically variable external conditions. This constancy of lambda or criminal offending was tantalizing to criminologists and crime policymakers in the age of Reagan because it represented the prospect of accurately identifying the relatively few offenders, like those highlighted in Marvin Wolfgang's cohort study, whom Ronald Reagan and his constituents so desperately hoped they could lock away and incapacitate from future offending.

Hirschi and Gottfredson were concerned that an alliance of academic criminologists and policymakers during the Reagan administration was building a field of study monopolized by the notion of chronic offenders and career criminals. The distinction between the "career criminals" and "criminal careers" was slippery. The concept of career criminals evoked the image of the unremorseful and unyielding lifelong "superpredator" that preoccupied the politics of punitiveness in the age of Reagan (Bennett, DiIulio, and Walters 1996). In contrast, the concept of criminal careers treated the persistence of such criminal behavior as a key variable for explanation and looked for possible sources of change in these careers.

Gottfredson and Hirschi noted that the terms were frequently used interchangeably, and questioned the motives of government agencies and criminologists who mixed the concepts. "Academics supply the terms," Goffredson and Hirschi charged, "that justify the funds provided them" (1986:214). They implied that criminological researchers were using their concepts ambiguously to satisfy a punitive political bias and thereby improve funding for their research.

Pronouncements by the heads of major government funding agencies provided evidence for Hirschi and Gottfredson's concern. For example, during the Reagan administration the director of the National Institute of Justice observed that "Few issues facing criminal justice are more urgent than safeguarding the public from those who make a career of crime." Similarly, the administrator of the Office of Juvenile Justice and Delinquency Prevention remarked that "The main objective of our intervention strategies should be to incapacitate the small proportion of chronic, violent offenders" (Tracy, Wolfgang, and Figlio 1985). Blumstein and his associates (Blumstein, Cohen, and Farrington 1988:23) did not deny the political dimension of government support for the criminal career paradigm but suggested that "When resources are limited . . . finding issues in which both researchers and potential users are interested may be one of the few ways of stimulating greater interest in research by potential funding sources."

For criminologists, the issue increasingly became what concepts and questions this criminal career paradigm would explore, and what answers the resulting research would bring. The concepts and questions were outlined in a pair of influential National Academy of Sciences panels led by Alfred Blumstein and these panels' reports, *Deterrence and Incapacitation: Estimating the Effects of Criminal Sanctions on Crime Rates* (Blumstein, Cohen, and Nagin 1978) and *Criminal Careers and "Career Criminals"* (Blumstein et al. 1986). The placement of the career concept in quotation marks was a way of acknowledging its contentiousness. Three central concepts drove the resulting paradigm: incidence, prevalence, and lambda.

The authors argued that a distinction had to be made between prevalence (i.e., participation) and incidence (i.e., frequency) of crime, whereas the paradigm tended to focus more on the incidence or the chronic aspect of offending. The emphasis on incidence or frequency was in part to better establish subtypes of criminality, but also in the hopes of reducing high-frequency criminality. Particular attention was given to the possibility that some offenders were sufficiently persistent in their criminality as to offend at a near constant rate, and this recurrence was operationally measured by the age-specific ratio called lambda. To those who might complain that this reference to lambda was obscure or pretentious, its advocates explained that it was more efficient than awkwardly repeating the phrase "the frequency of offending by active offenders."

The career criminal paradigm also gave attention to the onset, duration, and desistence from criminal activity. However, the policy-driven concerns about chronic offending shifted the emphasis in criminology from the causes of someone ever committing a crime—a prominent concern in the age of Roosevelt—to the causes of someone chronically continuing to commit crimes, which became *the* prominent concern in the age of Reagan.

Blumstein and his associates (Blumstein, Cohen, and Farrington 1988:6–7) formally maintained an agnostic position on the value of studying participation or frequency—with the latter's emphasis on lambda—even if their disproportionate attention to lambda suggested otherwise. They were clear in noting the alternative policy implications of the two approaches, pointing out that a focus on participation encouraged prevention strategies in the general population, while a focus on frequency and lambda encouraged a more restrictive attention to chronic offenders. They reasoned that "so far, the evidence on both approaches is sufficiently inconclusive that neither is clearly preferable, and pursuit of either should not preclude interest in the other" (7). But they also conceded their own greater interest in frequency and lambda, and this was consistent with Blumstein's earlier leadership on the National Academy of Sciences panel that produced the report on deterrence and incapacitation (Blumstein, Cohen, and Nagin 1978).

The seductive power of the career criminal concept is not difficult to explain: it is the promise of selective incapacitation (Sampson and Laub 2005). As Gottfredson and Hirschi (1986) observed, "To the policy-oriented, the idea of a career criminal suggests the possibility of doing something to or for a small segment of the population with notable reductions in crime rates."

One other academic figure, James Q. Wilson, is essential to complete our discussion of early developmental criminology and the criminal career paradigm during the age of Reagan. Early in his presidency, Reagan converted his summary of tentative empirical findings about chronic criminals into a characteristically concise political message: "We can begin by acknowledging some absolute truths. . . . Two of those truths are: men are basically good but prone to evil; some men are very prone to evil—and society has a right to be protected against them." To this, Reagan added a still more frightening vision of the "stark, staring face—a face that belongs to a frightening reality of our time: the face of the human predator. . . . Nothing in nature is more cruel or more dangerous" (cited in Beckett 1997:47).

James Q. Wilson simultaneously provided Harvard-based academic reinforcement for Reagan's images with his books, *Thinking About Crime* (1975) and, with Richard Herrenstein, *Crime and Human Nature* (1986). Wilson (1993:492) echoed President Reagan's hyperbolic and dehumanizing rhetoric with his own depiction of "the blank, unremorseful face of a feral, pre-social being."

Wilson attached an unabashed argument for incapacitation to Wolfgang's account of chronic offenders. Wilson and Herrenstein (1986:144) reported that chronic offenders accounted for "as many as 75 percent of offenses" and also for "a disproportionately serious brand of crime." Wilson emphasized what Reagan's presidency made obvious, that policymakers wanted instruction for action, and he warned that criminologists would be ignored if they did not provide such instruction. With this in mind, Wilson was willing to lend his academic authority to a rejection of the "rehabilitative ideal" of mainstream criminology from the age of Roosevelt (see also Bennett, DiIulio, and Walter 1996).

In place of the Roosevelt era's attention to rehabilitation, Wilson offered justifications for the crime policies of the age of Reagan, optimistically opining that "the gains from merely incapacitating convicted criminals might be very large" (1975:22). Of course, like Blumstein in his leadership of the panels that wrote the influential National Science Foundation reports on crime, Wilson was not certain of this. Still, he was certain enough to encourage the criminal career paradigm of research and advocate for increased punishment of chronic offenders. Later Wilson (1994:38) would suggest a change of heart with a lament that "very large increases in the prison population can produce only modest reductions in crime rates." However, this is getting ahead of our story.

A General Theory of Self-Control

Probably the most cited work from the age of Reagan is Gottfredson and Hirschi's *A General Theory of Crime* (1990). Gottfredson and Hirschi (1988, 1990, 1995) reject the idea that their general theory of self-control is a developmental theory of crime, and they would probably be even more likely to deny that this theory of self-control is tied to the age of Reagan. Yet there are sound reasons to argue otherwise.

The key to understanding Gottfredson and Hirschi's self-control theory as developmental is its endorsement of the "early establishment" in childhood of self-control, which becomes an enduring trait, with only its specific consequences changing forms across the life span: "The evidence suggests to us that variation in self-control is established early in life, and that differences between individuals remain reasonably constant over the life course" (Hirschi and Gottfredson 2002:204). This focus on self-regulation from early in life is a hallmark of age of Reagan thinking about development.

However, Gottfredson and Hirschi distinguished themselves from Reagan administration policies by consistently insisting on the limits of state regulation, especially lengthy imprisonment for the purposes of incapacitation. Their concern was that "such policies inevitably incarcerate people after they have moved beyond the teen years, the age of maximum participation in crime" (1995). Yet a capacity for "evil" they assumed as part of human nature made their theory highly compatible with the age of Reagan. Gottfredson and Hirschi (1990:117) made clear that their theory also assumed "that people naturally pursue their own interests and unless otherwise socialized will use whatever means are available to them for such purposes."

Thus, Gottfredson and Hirschi regard low self-control as a "latent trait" that is established early in life and expressed in various ways throughout life, although most prominently in the middle to late teenage years. They are especially impressed with continuity over time, reasoning that the correlation between children who offend by whining and pushing and shoving are actually behaving in ways that in theoretical terms are equivalent to robbing and raping in adulthood. "If deviant acts at different phases of the life course are engaged in differently by the same individuals," Gottfredson and Hirschi reasoned (2002:204), "the underlying trait must be extremely stable over time."

Gottfredson and Hirschi (1987) even hold the trait of low self-control responsible for white-collar crime, which they explain may simply develop later in the life course because it takes time for individuals to move into the occupational positions where it can manifest. Gottfredson and Hirschi's attention to white-collar crime was a welcome variation from the emphasis on street crime and common forms of delinquency in the age of Reagan, yet their approach to the topic essentially reinforced that concern with white-collar crime was a distraction, since its causes were the same as other infractions.

Even though they referred to the life course concept, Gottfredson and Hirschi (1995) did not actually endorse it, arguing instead that continuity across time and place in the trait of self-control was more essential to explaining crime. In contrast to the general theory of self-control, I argue in the remainder of this chapter that understanding the sources of variability in crime rather than its continuity is key to reducing crime and its consequences. I discuss first variability across time and then variability across communities.

Life Course Criminology: The Life Course from Roosevelt to Reagan

Developmental criminology, the criminal career paradigm, and the concept of self-control that were so central to explaining crime in the age of Reagan had relatively little power in explaining the dramatic social changes that characterized this period. The life course theories that became prominent toward the end of the Reagan administration shared the developmental theme of this era, but they exposed a notable deficiency in the developmental approach by acknowledging influences of time and place in the explanation of crime. While still centered on individuals, the life course theories increasingly examined the settings in which individuals conduct their lives. This sensitivity to societal setting reflected a discomfort among many criminologists with the premises and themes of the Reagan era, even though life course criminology also incorporated a developmental orientation.

A life course approach recognizes that involvement in delinquency and crime can be a transitional period that in turn flows into a longer life trajectory (Hagan and Palloni 1988, 1990; Sampson and Laub 1990, 1992, 1993). As Elder (1985) notes, "transitions are always embedded in trajectories that give them distinctive form and meaning" (31), and "the same event or transition followed by different adaptations can lead to very different trajectories" (35). These adaptations can distinguish those whom Moffitt (1993) describes as the more common "adolescent limited" in contrasted to the less common "life course persistent" offenders against social and legal norms. To capture the full range of such trajectories, Elder (1985; see also Sampson 1993) urges that historical and intergenerational dimensions be included in research designs.

Although life course criminology has not typically exploited the opportunities to include the historical dimension in its theory or research, there are notable and informative instances of doing so. For example, Joan McCord (1995) used a life course perspective on the relationship between age and crime to highlight what she calls "crime in the shadow of history." She did so by analyzing three male birth cohorts from high-crime-rate neighborhoods of Cambridge and Somerville, Massachusetts, two satellite communities of Boston. Birth cohorts are defined by the period in which sampled groups are born, and in this case two of the cohorts were fathers of the third. The first cohort of fathers was born between 1872 and 1896, the second between 1897 and 1913, and third cohort, consisting only of sons, between 1926 and

1934. This meant that the last cohort of sons from the first two cohorts of fathers reached adult-hood during the later post–World War II phase of the age of Roosevelt.

The most intriguing of McCord's findings is that the age for committing crimes seems to have declined between the first two cohorts of fathers and their sons, that is, from the time before to the period during the age of Roosevelt. McCord found that the age at onset of crime convictions came earlier in the later cohort. In other words, criminal convictions began at younger ages in the cohort that was born later. The likely explanation involves the emergence of adolescence as an early (and turbulent) transitional stage in the life course in the postwar period.

Researchers identified adolescence as a new developmental life stage that took on increased meaning after World War II. The end of the war and the postwar boom in the later phase of the age of Roosevelt brought new opportunities for independence in the teenage years. This new independence allowed earlier onset of and experimentation with delinquency, which in Moffit's terms was usually adolescent limited, leading to early desistence from delinquency as well. McCord used her findings to warn that studies limited to a single time period risked confusing historically contingent features of crime with conditions identified as consistently related to crime throughout time.

Laub and Sampson (1995) used a different longitudinal study of Boston males developed by Sheldon and Eleanor Glueck (1950, 1968) that corresponds temporally to McCord's third cohort. Like McCord's third cohort, this sample also came into adulthood during the period of strong post–World War II economic growth and the emergence of adolescence as a distinct life phase with greater opportunities than previously for behavioral expression. There was an opportunity in the Boston data to further exploit in a more penetrating way the birth dates of the subjects. Laub and Sampson separated their sample into three birth cohorts and then compared the first cohort, born in 1924 and 1925, with the last cohort, born between 1929 and 1935. The latter group reached adolescence and young adulthood during the rapid expansion of economic opportunities following World War II.

Although Laub and Sampson observed notable similarities between the entries of their first and last cohorts into adulthood, they also found a notable difference: the younger cohort experienced a first arrest somewhat earlier. This finding is striking when placed alongside the previously noted declining age at onset of delinquency and crime in McCord's Cambridge-Somerville research. Together, these studies suggest that the evolution of adolescence as an early and distinct stage in the life course led to an advance in the age at onset of criminal activity and an earlier peak age of youth crime. These analyses of individual-level longitudinal data provide important empirical support to an overview by Steffensmeier and colleagues (1989) of aggregate-level official data indicating an earlier peak in the age-crime curve during the twentieth century in the United States, a decline that again seems to have become apparent during the age of Roosevelt.

Of course, the circumstances of the age of Reagan were quite different. Economic times were more precarious, with rising inequality. The concern in the Reagan era was with criminal careers marked by high-frequency offending (lambda) into and through adulthood. In Moffit's terms, the concern was with life course–persistent as opposed to life course–limited involvement in delinquency and then crime. In the age of Reagan, it was feared that many adolescents were becoming more firmly embedded in problems of crime and unemployment (Hagan 1993), especially in distressed minority communities (e.g., Sullivan 1989), and that these youths were experiencing increasing difficulty breaking away from what might otherwise have been transient adolescent limited involvements in delinquency (Moore 1991).

We have already noted the influence of Marvin Wolfgang's (1972) finding of chronic offending by relatively few offenders as an academic starting point for rising fears about crime in the age of Reagan. Wolfgang (1995) also brought his Philadelphia research to bear on the issue of life course persistence in crime by adding a further analysis of two cohorts born in that city in 1945 and 1958. These two cohorts came of age in Philadelphia toward the end of the age of Roosevelt (the mid- to late 1960s) and the beginning of the age of Reagan (the mid- to late 1970s). Thus, the first cohort transitioned from adolescence to adulthood during the latter stages of the age of Roosevelt post–World War II economic boom, while the second cohort entered adulthood during the rising economic inequality that ushered in the age of Reagan and characterized much of that era.

Wolfgang's analysis revealed that in the first age cohort, about 30 percent of white offenders and 52 percent of nonwhite offenders were life course–persistent criminals, while in the second cohort these proportions increased to nearly 50 percent and 64 percent, respectively. The implication was that rising economic inequality negatively affected both white and nonwhite offenders. This variability across groups and temporal periods complicated assumptions about constancy in a developmental criminology. These trends become increasingly important when we turn to an elaborated life course theory of punishment and inequality below.

An Age-Graded Theory of Social Control

Sampson and Laub's (1993) rediscovery of the Gluecks' Boston data in the basement of Harvard Law Library allowed them to undertake a landmark reanalysis of longitudinal data charting human lives, with copious measurements of criminality across eight decades of the twentieth century, from early childhood to the onset of old age (Laub and Sampson 2003). Many members of this sample were World War II veterans and experienced the postwar expansion; few used narcotic drugs or handguns, whereas alcohol use was pervasive. The 500 officially defined delinquents and nondelinquents in the sample were matched for age, race or ethnicity (most were white), neighborhoods, and measured intelligence. There was widespread poverty in these Boston neighborhoods, but they "were considerably more cohesive and socially integrated than modern poverty neighborhoods" (Laub and Sampson 1995:127).

The first part of Sampson and Laub's work established the influence of social capital and social bonds in controlling delinquency. Social capital is an emergent productive capability that is created through socially structured relations between individuals in groups, including, during childhood, through families, schools, and peers. However, the social relationships that produce social capital change over the life course and in early adulthood also include marriage and employment. Sampson and Laub demonstrated how this process of informal social control evolved over the full cycle of the life course.

Sampson and Laub's (1993) work is extremely important because it clearly established two contrasting themes that stretched beyond the authors' reconfirmation of the importance of early life course effects of family, peer, and school experiences. The first theme was that youth who are seriously delinquent and officially labeled as such through arrest and punishment accumulate disadvantages as they age. Laub and Sampson showed that these "cumulative disadvantages" pile up, or "snowball," over time, with the result that it becomes increasingly difficult for young people labeled as delinquent to escape a life of crime and deviance. The second theme was that, nonetheless, youth who married a supportive spouse or found a good job often turned their lives around. Military service was also a "turning point" in the life course for members of this sample.

These life changes shared some common elements: a sharp shift or "knifing off" from past patterns, new sources of supervision and monitoring as well as opportunities for support and growth, and finally prospects for shaping new identities—for example, turning from being "a hell-raiser to a family man." Sampson and Laub found that even some very committed offenders moved away from crime over their lives, and some of these changes occurred surprisingly late in life.

Yet as their research on the Boston sample continued, Laub and Sampson also found that involvement in crime was often intermittent, with a zig-zag quality that added complexity and made problematic simple groupings of offenders as persisting or desisting from crime, despite the evidence of desistence in their own earlier work (Laub, Nagin, and Sampson 1998). It was not that the earlier research on chronic offending was necessarily wrong in its goals or methods but rather that efforts to predict the onset of chronic offending and to produce desistence were not very successful and were often counterproductive for those mistakenly caught up in the massive dragnet involved in the growing resort to incarceration during the age of Reagan. Laub and Sampson provided an empirical foundation for the warning flags earlier raised by Malcolm Feeley and Jonathan Simon (1992) about a "new penology" of criminal justice administration in America.

The later work of Laub and Sampson is therefore especially noteworthy for its increased skepticism about efforts promoted by James Q. Wilson and others during the age of Regan to predict, identify, and incapacitate chronic offenders or career criminals. Sampson and Laub emphatically reject claims that there is a basis in research for expecting much success with such policies. In a comment that likely marked an important academic turning point, they observed that "why criminologists continue to search for a small number of groups and remain seduced by the idea of ever-more perfect prediction from the distant past is something we leave for future historians of the field" (Sampson and Laub 2005:907–8). The field of criminology was coming to terms with how profoundly consequential for disadvantaged groups the wholesale pursuit of incapacitation through mass imprisonment had become during the age of Reagan.

A Life Course Theory of Punishment and Inequality

Chapter 2 noted the increase in African American rates of incarceration from the age of Roosevelt to the age of Reagan. Late in the age of Reagan this major change in American society became a growing theme in important work in American criminology that challenged earlier treatments of topics such as chronic offending and incapacitation. Bruce Western (2006) and his collaborators led much of this new documentation and analysis effort with an approach that paid attention to the life course implications for convicted offenders of the massive growth in imprisonment in the last quarter of the twentieth century.

Western's work emphasizes that for less educated young black men, the prison system emerged as a major competitor with the military and the educational system. From the age of Roosevelt to the age of Reagan, the chances of young black high school dropouts going to prison more than tripled, from less than 20 percent for the 1945–49 birth cohort to nearly 60 percent for the 1965–69 cohort (Western 2006:27). By the turn of the twenty-first century, non-college-educated black men were more than twice as likely to have been imprisoned as to have served in the military. Western concludes that in the language of life course theory, prison had become a modal event or "normal stopping point" on the path to midlife.

The picture that emerges from the research of Western and his colleagues on the growing role of prison in the life course of young black men and their families in the age of Reagan is pervasively grim. Western and Pettit (2005) report that American black males in their thirties are more likely to go to prison than to college, and that 60 percent of black male high school dropouts in their thirties have served time in prison (Pettit and Western 2004; Western 2006; Western, Pettit, and Guetzkow 2002). These statistics have devastating implications not only for black men but also for their families (Hagan and Dinovitzer 1999; see also Lynch and Sabol 2004; Rose and Clear 1998). Wives and mothers are greatly affected by the imprisonment of men (Comfort 2008), and the majority of prison inmates are parents (Mumola 2000).

Western (2006:138) observes that as imprisonment has become a "normal life event" for disadvantaged young black men, paternal imprisonment has also become "common place" for their children. There was a historic sixfold increase in children of incarcerated black fathers in the United States between 1980 and 2000, resulting in more than one in five black children having had a father in prison or jail (Wildeman 2009; see also Foster and Hagan 2009). There is growing evidence of the negative impact of imprisoning fathers on the educational outcomes of their children (Foster and Hagan 2007). This consequence gives credence to the observation that mass imprisonment is a form of "marking" (Pager 2003, 2007) and "race-making" (Wacquant 2000:103–4): a process of "attaching the marker of moral failure to the collective experience of an entire social group" (Western 2006:57).

Western's elaboration of the racial implications of life course theory in the age of Reagan reveals how devastatingly interconnected is the imprisonment of young black men and the outcomes for their families and the communities in which they live. By the midpoint of the age of Reagan, the lessons of developmental and life course criminology were overlapping in a renewed look at communities.

Everyday Criminology and Communities: Routine Activity and Lifestyle Theories

A classic insight at least since the age of Roosevelt and Cloward and Ohlin's (1960) opportunity theory considered in chapter 3 is that crime is not just a product of the acts of motivated individual criminals but also of the opportunities available to them in the community settings where their crimes occur. This insight turns the spotlight from the criminal to his or her victims and the communities in which they are found. This brings further attention to changes in the routines and lifestyles across the range of times and places where criminal victimization can occur. These lifestyles and routines markedly changed from the age of Roosevelt to the age of Reagan, and they continue to change across the unfolding time and space of the American landscape.

Hindelang, Gottfredson, and Garoffalo's book, *Victims of Personal Crime* (1978), first formally introduced the concept of lifestyle exposure to crime. The key idea of their lifestyle theory was that where and how people from youthful teenagers to elderly adults carry out their daily lives influences their risks of criminal victimization. Thus, elderly women who seldom leave home are at very low risk of criminal victimization, while young black males who hang out in open air drug markets are at much higher risk of personal crime victimization, both by their peers and by the police, and this helps to explain how crime itself becomes a lifestyle. The reality of such differences associated with lifestyles gave new importance to understanding where, how, and when crime occurs.

Cohen and Felson (1979) elaborate these ideas in their routine activities theory of crime. They conceptualize crime as involving motivated offenders, available targets (e.g., homes and businesses) for their crimes, and an absence of guardians (e.g., protectors) to restrict access to targets. We noted at the outset of this chapter how the persons Cohen and Felson see as targets and guardians were changing in their roles from the post–World War II era on. These changes included not only growing income inequality but also changes in household size, composition, and location.

Women's access to birth control, higher education, and new careers caused radical changes not only in their lives but in the lives of men as well. By 1980, more than half of American married women were working outside the home, and the institutions of marriage and parenthood themselves were being transformed as divorce rates increased and family sizes shrank. In addition, as households with multiple cars became more common, both women and men were able to travel longer distances to find jobs.

Routine activities theory argues that the emergence of suburbia and exurbia in the late Roosevelt postwar period initially presented fewer opportunities for crime. Youth had less access to cars and therefore could not range as widely. There was more space between stores and residential areas, and mothers still worked at home and could protect their possessions. However, Felson (1994) emphasizes the changes that soon would spread rapidly across America during the shift from the age of Roosevelt to the age of Reagan.

As individuals and families became more mobile, the property and possessions in their homes became more vulnerable. More persons possessing more movable things spent more time away from home, leaving their possessions increasingly available for theft. The combination of more targets and less guardianship was a recipe for more property crime.

Felson explains that urban areas evolved in the postwar period toward the concentration of "convergent [inner] cities" and the dispersion of "divergent [outer] metropolises." We are accustomed to thinking of inner and central cities as having lower social control, but Felson argues that divergent exurban metropolises were also low in social control. This resulted from the dispersal of "people over more households, households and construction over more metropolitan space, travelers over more vehicles, and activities away from household and family settings" (70). Again, his point is that these processes increased the available targets while decreasing guardian social control.

Felson concludes that "The vast increment in purely public space within the divergent metropolis plays a major role in undermining the capacity of local people to control their environment and prevent crime. This helps us to explain why crime rates are so high in the United States" (70). A major contribution of the theories of everyday criminology is thus to increase our attention to variation in the social organization of communities across time and place.

A Community-Level Theory of Criminal Capital and Embeddedness

We earlier saw in Sampson and Laub's research how social capital and social bonds evolved in a sample of Boston males born in the first half of the twentieth century. A related theory of criminal capital explains patterns of street crime and its variation across highly urbanized community settings (Hagan and McCarthy 1997). This theory is distinctive in its emphasis on macrosocial and economic processes such as "capital disinvestment" and "criminal capitalization." Capital disinvestment from minority communities intensified during the age of Reagan and contributed to growing economic inequality, residential segregation, and a growing racial and ethnic concentration of poverty (Sampson and Wilson 1994).

This capital disinvestment process meant that core manufacturing jobs in auto plants and steel mills began to disappear from U.S. cities in the Northeast and Midwest. These jobs, which had provided earlier advancement for immigrants and minorities, were replaced with less well-paying and insecure service sector jobs. New jobs also emerged in the information and financial sectors, but these positions were rarely available to immigrants and minorities. The new economy's better jobs were educationally and residentially out of reach. Minority men and women were trapped in inner cities with few legitimate opportunities. As a result, feelings of injustice intensified (Hagan and Albonetti 1982; Hagan, Shed, and Payne 2005; LaFree 1998).

Capital disinvestment limits and destroys conventional processes of social capitalization while encouraging alternative recourse to the acquisition and accumulation of criminal capital. Individuals and groups in communities organize and embed themselves in the resources that are available to them, including illegal services and commodities, such as prostitution and drugs. The resulting sites are sometimes called "deviance service centers" and are comprised of the street corners and open air markets where illicit services and commodities are provided for a price. These sites and centers are not new; we noted in chapter 2 that ethnic vice industries have a long history in America and other countries. The embeddedness of young people in these crime networks increases their risk of becoming isolated from pro-social networks and the accumulation of the social capital in more legitimate settings (Hagan 1993).

Hagan and McCarthy (1997) applied this theory of capital disinvestment and criminal capitalization and embeddedness in a study of two Canadian cities, Toronto and Vancouver. For most of the past century, Toronto and Vancouver have differed in their experiences with street crime. Although Toronto's population has consistently been larger than Vancouver's, its crime rate typically has been lower. Hagan and McCarthy looked at how these cities approached their respective problems of homeless youth and street crime.

Toronto's orientation to street youth had many features of a social welfare model. Youth over sixteen living on the street were treated as adults and could receive welfare support and shelter in a system of youth hostels. The hostels had their problems, but they were valued by most youth otherwise living on the street. The Toronto policies represented a modest attempt to remedy the lack of access to normal social capital among homeless youth. Vancouver was much different. Youth could not live legally apart from their families until age nineteen and so could not receive welfare support. There was no system of hostels available. Vancouver, which has much in common with West Coast U.S. cities, followed a more American crime control model, in contrast to the more northern European social welfare model adopted in Toronto.

The result was that youth in Vancouver were more often on the street than youth in Toronto, leaving them more liable to police charges. Hagan and McCarthy tracked the youth in Toronto and Vancouver in a summerlong longitudinal panel study. Over the summer, the Vancouver youth were significantly more involved in theft, drugs, and prostitution. As Hagan and McCarthy had hypothesized in selecting the two cities for their comparative study, Toronto's social welfare or investment model, which provided access to overnight shelters and social services, diminished involvement in such street crimes, whereas Vancouver's crime control model and absence of assistance made street crimes more common. Vancouver youth's exposure to the streets and its criminal opportunities intensified a process of criminal capitalization and embeddedness. Vancouver youth also were more likely to be charged by the police for involvement in nonviolent street crimes. The effect was to embed the Vancouver youth further into the street culture, which encouraged their reliance on the street for the limited prospects of criminal capitalization it provided.

The variation Hagan and McCarthy observed in the treatment of homeless street youth in Vancouver and Toronto has no certain generalization to other urban settings. However, a key difference between the city settings was the amount of exposure to criminal opportunities, that is, to possibilities for criminal capitalization and criminal embeddedness. Vancouver's crime control model seemed to produce counterproductive results, and Toronto's modest efforts at social investment seemed to moderate the harmful effects of the street. This research renewed and encouraged attention to the likely importance of variation in the causes and consequences of crime across community settings.

A Multi-Community Developmental Study and the Theory of Collective Efficacy

One of the most important events for the field of criminology during the age of Reagan was the establishment in 1990 of the Project on Human Development in Chicago Neighborhoods. The developmental theme of this project was an outgrowth of the earlier National Academy of Sciences panels led by Alfred Blumstein and a new National Academy report, *Understanding and Preventing Violence*, reflecting work that was begun in 1989 and led by Yale sociologist Albert Reiss. The distinctive feature of this report was its added attention to the community settings in which human development and violent behavior occurs. Three very senior and distinguished criminologists— Marvin Wolfgang, Alfred Blumstein, and Albert Reiss—now were participants in the planning of a major research agenda for the study of crime in America. The panel's report explicitly recommended a multi-community longitudinal approach and announced that the National Institute of Justice and the Mac-Arthur Foundation had begun this work through their Program on Human Development and Criminal Behavior.

The panel expected the program would lay a necessary scientific groundwork for the next generation of "preventive interventions" aimed at "aggressive, violent, and antisocial behaviors." It was widely thought that Wolfgang, Blumstein, and Reiss would all want to lead the project. Reiss was the most prominently located, at Yale; he was the leader of the most recent panel report; and he had placed his own stamp on the recommended project design by advocating a multi-community approach. Ultimately, this multi-community emphasis became a multi-neighborhood design situated in the city of Chicago. Reiss played a guiding role, but as the project evolved, the Harvard psychiatrist Felton Earls also assumed a leadership role.

Wolfgang, Blumstein, Reiss, and Earls all began their professional careers as part of a post–World War II cohort of scholars recruited into America's fast-growing universities in the 1950s. Savelsberg and Flood (2004) urge that we think not just of criminals but also criminologists as members of cohorts and as doing their research in distinct periods, in this case during the age of Reagan.

Enter Robert Sampson, who joined the field decades after his senior counterparts and whose life course developmental research with John Laub was now attracting widespread attention. Sampson was also well located at the University of Chicago to help guide the new project. Sampson emerged as the locally powerful figure in the Chicago project and represented a generational change in leadership with a strong inclination to make neighborhoods rather than individuals' development the focus of investigation. In particular, Sampson was skeptical of the single-minded concentration on prediction and incapacitation of the chronic offender and career criminal paradigm.

The scale and prominence of the Project on Human Development in Chicago Neighborhoods destined it to play an important role in the subsequent evolution of American criminology. The project described itself as a large-scale, interdisciplinary study of how families, schools, and neighborhoods affect child and adolescent development. Its Internet home page description still reads, "It was designed to advance the understanding of the developmental pathways of both positive and negative human social behaviors. In particular, the project examined the causes and pathways of juvenile delinquency, adult crime, substance abuse, and violence." However, this description then goes on to note that "At the same time, the project also provided a detailed look at the environments in which these social behaviors take place by collecting substantial amounts of data about urban Chicago, including its people, institutions, and resources."

An indication of the change from a developmental to a neighborhood emphasis in the project was that when attention turned to describing its two components, the neighborhood component came first. The project was thus first described as "an intensive study of Chicago's neighborhoods, particularly the social, economic, organizational, political, and cultural structures and the dynamic changes that take place in the structures over time." Only following this introduction did the project description turn to its "accelerated cohort design" involving a series of youth of different ages with which its longitudinal design began. Thus, "The second component was a series of coordinated longitudinal studies that followed more than 6,000 randomly selected children, adolescents, and young adults over time to examine the changing circumstances of their lives, as well as the personal characteristics that might lead them toward or away from a variety of antisocial behaviors."

It should perhaps therefore not be surprising that the most widely cited conceptual innovation and empirical finding of the study emerged at the community and contextual level rather than at the individual and developmental level. This contribution was Robert Sampson's concept of collective efficacy. The concept of collective efficacy builds on the foundation of the psychologist Albert Bandura's conception of self-efficacy, but it differs by emphasizing that individuals can organize themselves collectively in neighborhoods that have their own distinctive qualities. This is a sociological kind of focus on group level processes linked to the classical anomie, opportunity, and social disorganization traditions of criminological theory rooted in the age of Roosevelt explanations discussed in chapter 3.

Sampson made the move between individual level to group level explicit. He observed that "Just as individuals vary in their capacity for efficacious action, so too do neighborhoods vary in their capacity to achieve common goals" (Sampson, Raudenbush, and Earls 1997:918). The community and surrounding society value this communal capacity, even if or because subgroups might rebel against them. The point is that the community shares in these evaluations.

For example, shared goals can promote a "neighborhood efficacy" based on the communal supervision of children and the collective maintenance of social order. Sampson emphasizes that efficacy occurs not just as a response to the action of individuals within families but also because of processes at the level of neighborhoods. His research with colleagues (Sampson, Morenoff, and Earls 1999; Sampson, Raudenbush, and Earls 1997) and using the Chicago Project on Human Development data demonstrates that even with individual-level factors statistically held constant, some neighborhoods exhibit an enhanced capacity to perform monitoring and order-maintaining tasks in ways that prevent and reduce crime. Sampson's work on collective neighborhood efficacy supports the African aphorism that "it takes a village."

As noted in chapter 2, this conceptual attention to processes of collective efficacy and the related concept of social capital has proven useful in explaining how otherwise disadvantaged immigrant communities, including Latino communities in the United States, have been able to maintain low levels of criminal behavior. Recently, Sampson and Wikstrom (2009) have added a broader global dimension by comparing findings from the Chicago project with data gathered in Stockholm, Sweden.

Of course, Stockholm is far different from Chicago. In comparison to the stark differences in resources across Chicago neighborhoods, Stockholm's neighborhoods tend to be more peaceful and equal in resources, while Chicago is distinctive in its violence and economic inequality. Sampson and Wikstrom nonetheless find some striking similarities: in Stockholm as well as in Chicago, differences within and between neighborhoods in resources, including both concentrated disadvantage and collective efficacy, account for notable variation in levels of violent crime. The attention to concentrated disadvantages in economic resources is an important recurring theme in Sampson's work that echoes the age of Roosevelt, while the focus on collective efficacy is a newer and novel contribution from his more recent research in Chicago neighborhoods.

With other factors held constant, Sampson and Wikstrom (2009:117) find that social control, social trust, and the collective involvement of residents in social control of public spaces lead to reduced violence in both cities. This is in spite of a large residual difference in violence between the two cities that none of their measures can fully explain. Sampson and Wikstrom therefore conclude that "the 'Chicago' effect remains large, possibly owing to cultural differences. Still, it appears that there is something fundamental and generic about community social order and violence that cuts across international boundaries."

Collective Action and Social Efficacy

In extending his individual-based differential association theory of crime, introduced in chapter 3, to the level of group organization, Edwin Sutherland (1943) introduced the concept of "differential social organization" to explain how citizens mobilize to counteract organization around criminal opportunities within communities. Similarly, Ross Matsueda (2006) recently added the concept of social efficacy to refer to the capacity of particular individuals to mobilize others in realizing shared communal goals of the kind Sampson calls collective efficacy. Thus the concept of social efficacy is a linking mechanism that highlights the acts of individual initiative or agency that inspire others to join together in collectively organized communal action; for example, organizing individuals in a neighborhood for the joint supervision of children and the collective maintenance of public order. Social and collective efficacy can combine to control crime in some communities.

This discussion leads back to the earlier realization of Sutherland and other criminologists that similar but opposing processes of social and collective efficacy organize both crime and responses to it. The challenge is to understand the competition between these collective crime and control processes in contemporary society. Matsueda links the concepts of social and collective efficacy with further ideas about collective action (e.g., Gamson 1990) and frame analysis (Goffman 1974; Snow and Oliver 1995). Similarly, Sampson and Wikstrom (2009:101) draw on Portes and Sensenbrenner (1993:1323) to recharacterize the concept of social capital as "expectations for action within a collectivity."

The linkages drawn by Matsueda and Sampson between individual actors and collective behavior—through their concepts of social and collective efficacy—bring us full circle to the importance attached by David Garland (2001) and Jonathan Simon (2007) to the roles of specific academic and political actors in the formation of crime policies. Following such leads, I use what I call a critical collective framing approach to organize the remaining chapters of this book.

A Critical Collective Framing Perspective

The challenge in the rest of the book is to mobilize what we have learned from the age of Roosevelt through the age of Reagan to advance our understanding of crime and its control in the United States and internationally. The theoretical approach I propose for meeting this challenge applies a critical framing perspective to the collective behavior of crime and the failed policies for its control in the age of Reagan. Oberschall

(2000:989, drawing on Snow et al. 1986; see also Benford and Snow 2000) usefully defines a cognitive frame as "a mental structure which situates and connects events, people and groups into a meaningful narrative in which the social world that one inhabits makes sense and can be communicated and shared with others." Cognitive and collective frames— which can be as different as career criminals and collective efficacy—are the narrative conceptual devices academics, politicians, and policymakers use to advance their ideas about crime and its control.

The failed policies of the age of Reagan notably include the resort to mass incarceration in response to fears of ghetto street crime, resulting in more than two million Americans imprisoned. In the following chapter, I will also show how this failed response to street crime is in stark counterpoint and yet in important ways connected to an offsetting counter trend, the retreat from the criminal regulation of elite suite crimes, recently resulting in trillions of dollars in financial losses and economic collapse. In this chapter, I have emphasized academic actors, from Alfred Blumstein and Travis Hirschi to Robert Sampson and Ross Matsueda, who provided theoretical framings for criminological debates related to developments in the age of Reagan. In the following chapters I shift the focus to political actors—from Ted Kennedy and Joe Biden to Ronald Reagan and ultimately Barack Obama—who have provided political framings for legislative debates in the age of Reagan and potentially beyond.

I will analyze how the age of Reagan enabled collective phenomena such as mass incarceration and the economic collapse through framing processes that led to counterproductive crime-linked forms of collective behavior and its control, or, equally importantly, lack thereof. These were respectively the policies of collective *action* in response to street crime, on the one hand, and on the other, policies of collective *inaction* in response to suite crime. Frame realignment processes were instrumental to both, with the field of criminology accommodating and contributing to the former while underestimating and neglecting the latter. The former preoccupation of criminologists with chronic street criminals during the age of Reagan and this era's emphasis on mass imprisonment notably diverted energy and resources from the scrutiny of suite crimes and corporate criminals.

Oberschall (2000:989) extended his definition of framing presented above to further distinguish narrative processes that are "normally framed" from those that involve "crisis framing." What emerges as "normal" versus "crisis" can be highly influenced by power and politics, and this was conspicuously the case during the age of Reagan. This attention to power and politics adds a critical dimension to the collective framing approach. The challenge in responding to the age of Reagan is to use the preceding terms and this critical collective framing approach to understand both the resort to mass imprisonment and the retreat from regulation of financial crimes in America.

The thesis I advance in the following chapter is that while power politics during the age of Reagan enabled the crisis framing and the ensuing fear of street crime that led to mass imprisonment, a corresponding normalized framing encouraging a misguided absence of fear resulted in a retreat from the regulation of suite crimes and thereby contributed to the economic collapse.

Chapter 5
Framing the Fears of the Streets
||||||||||

THE CLASSICAL AMERICAN THEORIES of crime, from class-based structural anomie theory to state-based radical conflict theory, emerged in what I broadly have called the age of Roosevelt, from 1932 to 1968. However, the age of Reagan, from about 1968 to 2008, reconfigured the world of crime and criminal justice. A critical collective framing theory can further help to explain this criminological turn, a change that in important ways upended the study of and response to crime. The upending involved a move away from rehabilitation and toward the incapacitation of street criminals, accompanied by a move away from the prosecution of white-collar criminals and toward the deregulation of the financial industry.

A critical collective framing theory considers how political and powerful groups are involved in defining and denying—that is, framing—criminality. Goffman (1974) analyzed more broadly how this happens through what he called "frame analysis," and Snow and colleagues (1986) later referred to this as "frame alignment." A framing process in the age of Reagan realigned the meanings of street crimes and suite crimes by vilifying the feared offenders of the streets and valorizing the newly freed entrepreneurs of the suites, the respective occupants of the mean streets and the corporate suites of a changing world.

The policies of the age of Reagan may have led Americans to fear both too much and too little. On the one hand, the

Reagan administration pursued stricter drug policies and sentencing laws in response to a crack epidemic that it failed to avert or contain. It failed by allowing a surge in the flow of cocaine into the United States. The Reagan administration responded to its failed interdiction mission with a fear-driven trajectory of mass incarceration focused on the drug abuse of young minority males.

At the same time, the Reagan administration deregulated investment and financial services, freeing these institutions to indiscriminately alter lending practices, resulting in large losses that were passed on to taxpayers and compensated with government bailouts. These programs and practices disproportionately victimized the minority working poor as well as others by facilitating the unfettered expansion of an underregulated and undercapitalized financial sector. This model was further abetted by a reckless "too large to fail" policy of corporate immunity providing a nearly fail-proof freedom for many financial institutions to expand risks that led to massive losses.

A critical collective framing theory focuses on the class and state policies that increased regulation of the risk-takers on the nation's streets even as they simultaneously deregulated the risk-taking occupants of the corporate suites. This redistribution of control was the dual legacy of the age of Reagan. However, the age of Reagan has extended well beyond the years Reagan was in office, and the policies from this era have shaped the views of leaders and members of both major parties. An example of such long-lasting effects can be found in the leading roles played by Senators Ted Kennedy and Joe Biden in passing the 1980s sentencing guidelines that resulted in disproportionately long prison terms for crack cocaine crimes. Moreover, both political parties were involved in the savings and loan (S&L) scandal and the subsequent subprime mortgage crisis. The age of Reagan was an era with a surprising degree of bipartisan support for the breadth and depth of the framing processes it promulgated.

The Alignment of Collective Action Frames

Several concepts from the study of collective action frames can help us to understand the changing definitions and meanings of crimes and misdemeanors during the age of Reagan. For example, it may be useful to think of the realignment of street and suite crimes that occurred during the Reagan years as involving "boundary framing" (Hunt and Benford 1994) and "adversarial framing" (Gamson 1995). These are framing processes that seek to build consensus around new definitions and meanings with the goal of mobilizing support for action. President Reagan and others excelled in crafting phrases, speeches, anecdotes, and metaphors that offered such motivational frames for action. Reagan's image of the "stark, staring face" and James Q. Wilson's "feral face" noted in the previous chapter are apt examples of this frame building for adversarial motivational purposes. These were fearful and dehumanizing images that offered motivation and justification for action.

Benford and Snow (2000:623) suggest that "what gives the resultant collective action frame its novelty is not so much the originality or newness of its ideational elements, but the manner in which they are spliced together and articulated, such that a new angle of vision, vantage point, and/or interpretation is provided." Often this splicing took the form of connecting overlapping or logically linked issues in a way that elicited a broad cultural resonance, for example, when prohibitions of pornography and drugs are joined under the master frame of the general rubric of law and order.

However, frame alignment can also bring together disparate issues, such as the incapacitation of street criminals and the deregulation of business relations and practices. Thus, Benford and Snow (2000:629) also observe "that changing cultural resonances and collective action frames reciprocally influence one another and that framing processes typically reflect wider cultural continuities and changes." This is the kind of frame realignment that the Reagan administration persistently pursued by simultaneously advocating more severe punishment of American street crime and the deregulation of American business practices.

Thus, President Reagan argued that "the growth of government and the decay of the economy . . . can be traced to many of the same sources of the crime problem." He reasoned that "this is because the same utopian presumptions about human nature that hinder the swift administration of justice have also helped fuel the expansion of government" (Reagan 1981). The convergence emphasized in this framing was that "due process liberals" simply needed to "get out of the way." They needed to do this in the criminal area by contracting provisions such as the exclusionary rule restricting use of illegally obtained evidence, so that courts could swiftly convict and sentence street criminals. At the same time, the government simultaneously needed to free up entrepreneurs and institutions to pursue more easily their private enterprise initiatives. "Government interference in our lives," the president opined, "tends to discourage creativity and enterprise . . . [in] the private economic sector." The attorney general was the agent and the Department of Justice was the agency to implement this collective action framing of the president's plans.

The President's Legal Counselors

Although President Reagan railed against the growth of government, he was not reluctant to utilize the resources of the attorney general and the Department of Justice, which Jonathan Simon (2007:45) describes as having by the age of Reagan "swollen into a planetary giant within the executive solar system." President Reagan appointed the corporate labor lawyer William French Smith as his first attorney general, and Edwin Meese, the former Alameda Country district attorney who closed down Berkeley's School of Criminology and who was Reagan's first presidential chief of staff, as his second attorney general. Meese's appointment was nearly derailed by an Office of Government Ethics investigation, which concluded he had committed violations in securing federal jobs for associates, and he eventually resigned under the cloud of ethics scandals that threatened his impeachment.

There was little doubt that links between Ronald Reagan's Department of Justice and the business community encouraged his plans for street criminals and for economic entrepreneurs. Wilentz (2008:181) writes that Meese helped Smith "assemble and galvanize a cohort of well-schooled, activist ideologues, including religious conservatives and adherents of the pro-free-market, so called law and economics movement." As Reagan's closest legal advisers, Meese and Smith developed a set of policies that linked the racial divisions involved in street crimes with a tolerant attitude toward the corporate suites. Wilentz concludes that through the successive tenures of Smith and Meese, "the Reagan administration, and in particular the Justice Department, was quietly waging its own pragmatic version of the culture wars with a long-term strategy that was as comprehensive as it was deliberate" (187).

The street crime side of the Justice Department agenda initially involved a selective neglect and then a punitive prosecution of crack cocaine use and distribution in a national symbolic crusade. This crusade first tried ineffectual drug interdiction policies in Latin America, which failed to contain the threat posed by crack cocaine. It then turned to the passage of determinate sentencing laws and sentencing guidelines that imposed draconian punishments on crack cocaine offenders. The simultaneous suite crime component of the Justice Department agenda entailed deemphasizing white-collar crime prosecutions and deregulating the financial sector in ways that set the foundation for the S&L scandal as a forerunner to the subprime mortgage collapse and the recent credit crisis.

The long-term, joined effects of these age of Reagan policies led to social and economic crises in black and white America. These crises included (1) the mass imprisonment of more than a million African Americans, (2) mergers and acquisitions that enabled vertically integrated mortgage schemes, leading to foreclosures on millions of homes, and (3) trillions of dollars in government-led bailouts and debt to refinance these failed financial ventures. The racial divisions underlying these policies were visible from their outset, as were their outcomes.

From the outset, William French Smith (1991) took a strong interest in deregulation—for example, by relaxing antitrust policy. He opposed prosecution of antitrust cases and maintained that "bigness" in business—businesses that eventually became "too big to fail"—was not necessarily bad, and that the government should be concerned only with grossly anticompetitive behavior. He developed a favorable legal climate for mergers that reflected the white shoe culture of the corporate law firm culture he came from and led to the wave of mergers in the banking and housing finance sectors that characterized the 1980s and beyond. The financial deregulation had indirect race-linked consequences for home mortgages and foreclosures, while the racial origins and impact of the drug and sentencing policies were more immediately and directly apparent.

Edwin Meese established an early race-linked law and order agenda that had attracted Ronald Reagan's attention in response to community and student activism in Oakland and Berkeley, California, and he carried this agenda to his role in Reagan's governorship from 1966 to 1975. Meese (1992:30) summed up his early years in Sacramento with the recollection that "I saw a lot of flower children, and some vicious attacks on police officers." But Meese's role was far more significant than his off-hand characterization might suggest.

Powerful politicians often have "fixers," "bag men," and "hatchet men," if not "henchmen," who resolve their most difficult dilemmas. A story told by Meese suggests how significantly he fulfilled such functions for Ronald Reagan from an early point in his career. In Meese's own words:

Many developments in Sacramento presaged what was to occur later in Washington. One of the earliest decisions

> the governor had to make was a capital punishment case involving a convicted murderer, Aaron Mitchell, who had killed two police officers. Reagan's predecessor, Pat Brown, had opposed capital punishment, and strong efforts were being made to abolish it before both the California and the U.S Supreme Courts. On my recommendation, and despite loud public outcry by opponents, the governor allowed Mitchell's execution to proceed. That sent a message, early on, that Reagan was prepared to make some tough, and controversial, decisions. (Meese 1992:31)

This was false modesty: Meese assumed a very visible public responsibility for the decision to execute Mitchell.

Meese's account also fails to mention that Aaron Mitchell was African American and that he was the only person put to death in California in the five years preceding and the twenty-five years following this 1967 execution. Michael Radlet (1989:26) wrote of the day of the execution that "It was Mitchell's color that had drawn [the American Nazi Party's Norman Lincoln] Rockwell to San Quentin that morning. His placard read, 'GAS—THE ONLY CURE FOR BLACK CRIME.'"

Meese selectively invoked social science findings to build arguments for Reagan administration practices. He frequently cited Marvin Wolfgang's signature finding about chronic offenders, cogently observing that "It is a little-known fact that huge numbers of crimes are committed by a relatively small group of people who engage in criminal acts repeatedly" (1982:306). Meese also has written about his use of government task forces and commissions to overcome the "rehabilitation frame," first in California and then in Washington:

> In still another initiative of the early 1970s, Governor Reagan appointed a task force to look into the criminal justice system. One of its principal findings was that serious felons, when caught and convicted, seldom went to prison. In their zeal to rehabilitate, rather than incarcerate, convicted

criminals, courts and other authorities had been sending
them just about anywhere but to jail. Fewer than one in ten
of the felons were actually serving prison time. The task
force, unsurprisingly, recommended much tougher sentencing. (Meese 1992:37)

Toughening the federal sentencing laws was the most consequential criminal justice innovation overseen by Meese during
the Reagan administration.

When Reagan ran for president in 1980, he leveraged the
law and order reputation he had developed in California with
Meese into a national campaign that began with a version of a
southern law and order strategy earlier advanced by Richard
Nixon. The strategy joined the culturally framed sentiments of
alienated southerners with northern blue-collar whites and
suburban Catholics.

Reagan launched his strategy with a bridging frame that
joined issues of race and government excess with criminal
fraud by mocking "welfare queens" and allegedly speaking
on at least one occasion of a "strapping young buck" (Wilenz
2008:180). These stereotypes were used as framing images of
the chronic perpetrators of government-subsidized waste.
However, the most visibly race-freighted signal of the culture
wars agenda Reagan would carry through his presidency occurred in his first presidential campaign speech.

In a deliberate act of frame amplification, Reagan chose to
deliver his first nationally watched postconvention speech in
Philadelphia, Mississippi. This was the site of the 1964 Ku
Klux Klan murders of the civil rights workers James Chaney,
Andrew Goodman, and Michael Schwerner, subsequently
dramatized in the film *Mississippi Burning*. The speech signaled sympathy for the legacy of states' rights and a disregard
for the memory of the three university students who had lost
their lives seeking voters' rights for southern blacks. This was
an unsubtle message about states' rights and civil rights. The
future president and his attorneys general made this kind of

racially tinged messaging an accepted part of the age of Reagan. The linkage of race with drugs later became the most consequential element of this agenda.

Fearful Drug and Sentencing Policies

"Narcoterrorism" and Ineffectual Interdiction

John Kerry is a politician more in the image of the age of Roosevelt than the age of Reagan. He was also a prosecutor before he became a senator. These characteristics may help explain the unyielding investigative approach Kerry took as a freshman senator when he learned in 1985 of a link between a CIA Iran–Contra operation and the smuggling of cocaine into the United States from Latin America. During this period the smuggling of cocaine into the United States was escalating, crack cocaine first made its first appearance in many U.S. cities, and U.S. imprisonment began an upward climb that continued for decades, making the United States the world leader in per capita imprisonment. The role of crack cocaine in rising levels of crime and imprisonment in the mid-1980s is well established. Grogger and Willis (2000:528) note that "in the absence of crack cocaine, the crime rate in 1991 would have remained below its previous peak in the early 1980s" (see also Messner et al. 2005).

It is important for theoretical and empirical purposes to recall the widely publicized charges of U.S. involvement in cocaine smuggling from Latin America in the mid-1980s. In analyzing these charges, it is useful to invoke the analogy Charles Tilly (1985) draws between state-making and organized crime. Tilly argues that leaders of nation-states can act like organized criminals when they contribute to the creation of threats from which they then insist their citizens require protection. This complicity of states in creating threats to their citizens is analogous to the formation of protection rackets in the world of organized crime. Senator Kerry chaired a Senate committee that substantiated the case that Reagan administration policies had contributed to the threat posed by the smuggling of cocaine into the United States in the 1980s. It was not until ten years after Senator Kerry's committee issued its final report that the CIA's inspector general belatedly confirmed its key findings (Central Intelligence Agency 1998). By this time, however, the framing of the cocaine problem was firmly set and resistant to change.

During the 1980s, the Reagan administration surreptitiously supported a dubious rebel group known as the Contras in its efforts to destabilize the Soviet-supported Sandinista government in Nicaragua. The administration charged that the Nicaraguan government was conspiring with Cuba to use "narcoterrorism" in spreading Communist influence in Latin America. The Soviet Union was the alleged source of this narcoterrorism. In a January 1986 speech, President Reagan stoked this fear with an unsubstantiated warning that "the link between the governments of such Soviet allies as Cuba and Nicaragua and international narcotics trafficking and terrorism is becoming increasingly clear. These twin evils—narcotics trafficking and terrorism—represent the most insidious and dangerous threats to the hemisphere today" (cited in Scott and Marshall 1998:23).

However, it would soon become apparent that it was the rebel Contras rather than Cuba or the Nicaraguan government that were more clearly implicated in Central American drug smuggling, and that the CIA was backing the Contras. The covert nature of this support became internationally apparent in October 1986 when an American, Eugene Hasenfus, parachuted from a plane hit by a missile over Nicaragua and later told news reporters he was on a CIA supply operation. The suspicion was that the flight was one of many that under CIA cover were delivering arms to the Contras in Nicaragua and bringing cocaine shipments back to the United States. The following November, Attorney General Edwin Meese conceded that profits from U.S. arms sales to Iran were being funneled, in violation of U.S. law, to the Contras.

The news media primarily framed the Iran–Contra arms scandal as "arms for hostages." The scandal involved an agreement by which the United States paid Israel for weapons shipped to a group in Iran in exchange for assistance in securing the release of six American hostages. As the plan unfolded, Lieutenant Colonel Oliver North involved the National Security Council in diverting some of the funds from the deal to anti-Sandinista and anti-Communist rebels, the Contras, in Nicaragua. How drug smuggling was woven into the Iran–Contra arms episode became more fully apparent when Senator Kerry chaired the above-noted Senate committee, on which Daniel Patrick Moynihan also served. The committee issued a 1989 report titled *Drugs, Law Enforcement and Foreign Policy*.

The report concluded that the U.S. government had underestimated the threat posed by drug cartels in Latin America. The report indicated the administration was prioritizing its opposition to the Soviet-supported Sandinista government and making secondary its efforts to stop the flow of narcotics by the cartels. Criticism also focused on U.S. support of Panama's military strongman, Manuel Noriega, who was facilitating cocaine shipments to the United States from the Medellin cartel in Colombia. The report stated the following:

- The war against Nicaragua contributed to weakening an already inadequate law enforcement capability in the region which was exploited easily by a variety of mercenaries, pilots, and others involved in drug smuggling. . . . There was substantial evidence of drug smuggling through the war zones on the part of individual Contras, Contra suppliers, Contra pilots, mercenaries who worked with the Contras, and Contra supporters throughout the region.

- The saga of Panama's General Manuel Antonio Noriega represents one of the most serious foreign policy failures for the United States. Throughout the 1970s and 1980s, Noriega was able to manipulate U.S. policy toward his country, while skillfully accumulating near-absolute power in Panama. It is clear that each U.S. government agency which had a relationship with Noriega turned a blind eye to his corruption and drug dealing, even as he was emerging as a key player on behalf of the Medellin cartel. (Committee on Foreign Relations 1988:2–3)

The point of the Kerry committee report was how ineffectual U.S. government policy was during this period when the crack cocaine epidemic was spiking in America.

Debate swirled for years about out how deeply the CIA was involved in the drug smuggling that fed the U.S. crack epidemic. Ostensibly for security reasons, the U.S. government blocked opportunities to address this issue in the eventual trial of Manuel Noriega, who had been on the payroll of the United States for more than a decade. A California journalist, Gary Webb, gained national attention in 1996 with assertions that at a minimum, the Reagan administration had tolerated and protected cocaine smuggling by the Nicaraguan Contras. Two internal investigations of this issue by the CIA and Department of Justice in 1998, ten years after Kerry's Senate subcommittee report, found substantial evidence that added weight to the earlier report's conclusions, although none of these reports found that the CIA actively intended or conspired to allow cocaine into the United States.

The highest reaching evidence of overt CIA complicity in cocaine smuggling in conjunction with its support for the Contras came in 1998, when Congresswoman Maxine Waters printed in the *Congressional Record* a 1982 letter of understanding between the CIA and the Justice Department. The letter, from Attorney General Smith, was written at the request of CIA director William Casey. This letter became a foundation for the conclusion of the the CIA inspector general (1998) more than a decade and a half later that "during the years 1982 to 1995, CIA did not have to report the drug trafficking by its assets to the Justice Department." The view of the CIA inspector general in the report finally issued in 1998 was that the CIA during this period had "one overriding priority: to oust the Sandinista Government. . . . [CIA officers] were determined that the various difficulties they encountered not be allowed to prevent effective implementation of the Contra program." More than ten years earlier, in 1986, the International Court of Justice had further found that the United States had violated international law by supporting the Contra rebel forces and by mining Nicaraguan harbors.

The administration's support for the Contras and distraction from the goal of stopping the flow of cocaine into the United States arguably made it unlikely that its interdiction efforts could be successful, and they were not. By the time the CIA inspector general had issued his report confirming much of the Kerry committee's findings, the framing of the cocaine problem was beyond reconsideration. The fear of narcoterrorism and the evidence of a growing crack cocaine epidemic during Reagan's second presidential term increased pressure for a domestic response. Reagan, Meese, and French drew on their earlier experience in California and began a push for a more punitive approach to the sentencing of drug and other crimes associated with minority offenders.

"Law and Order" Sentencing

While the strategic framing of "law and order" politics organized Barry Goldwater's 1964 presidential campaign and subsequently Richard Nixon's 1968 campaign for the presidency, Ronald Reagan first *successfully* used this framing in his 1966 California gubernatorial election. Reagan's gubernatorial campaign demonstrated the powerful potential for law and order reframing of racial politics in America. When Reagan during his California campaign for governor challenged his opponent Pat Brown's unwillingness to impose the death penalty on the African American defendant Aaron Mitchell, he demonstrated how issues of race and crime could be successfully reframed for electoral purposes in America.

The key was to explicitly prioritize protection of the public against the threat of criminal violence. This threat of violence was emphasized over all other competing considerations, notably the protection of race-related civil rights. Following Reagan's success, Nixon gave seventeen speeches spotlighting law and order in his 1968 presidential campaign. A prominent campaign advertisement flashed images of protesters and violence and featured the candidate declaring, "Let us recognize that the first right of every American is to be free from domestic violence. So I pledge to you, we shall have order in the United States." Nixon was quoted after observing the ad that it "hits it right on the nose. It's all about law and order and the damn Negro-Puerto-Rican groups out there" (quoted in Klinker and Smith 1999:292, and Weaver 2007:259).

Murakawa (2006) argues that Reagan and Nixon had simply recognized and found an acceptable way to express a simmering resentment among white northern and especially southern voters over the 1950s civil rights court decisions that began with *Brown v. Board of Education*. These judicial decisions explicitly targeted Jim Crow "separate but equal" practices of segregation in education, housing, and other social sectors.

Conservative politicians fought back by framing these changes more broadly in terms of the alleged threats they posed to citizens who were afraid not only for their homes and schools but also of being victimized by violent criminals. Conservative politicians tapped into public fears that the changes in civil rights–related criminal laws were loosening the very controls that preserved citizens' physical safety and that of their families and neighborhoods. Mississippi senator Richard B. Russell was explicit when he made the following remarks during a session of Congress:

> Mr. President, I say that the extremely high incidence of crimes of violence among members of the Negro race is one of the major reasons why the great majority of the

white people of the South are irrevocably opposed to bring about enforced association of the races. (Russell 1960)

The stark language of these views is notable, but Russell was hardly unique in holding them. The surprise is less that these sentiments were widely shared in the 1950s and early 1960s and more that they received inadvertent support through a legislative alliance in the 1980s of the Reagan administration with northern Democratic senators, including Massachusetts' Ted Kennedy and Maryland's Joe Biden.

Republican Senators John McClellan of Arkansas and Strom Thurmond of South Carolina became co-sponsors with Kennedy and Biden of the 1980s sentencing guideline laws. It is important to understand the sources of their motivations. Like Russell, McClellan believed that desegregation decisions illegally coerced association between racial groups, and that as a result, "serious crime will greatly increase" (cited in Murakawa 2006:485). Similarly, Thurmond argued that "demands for integration of the races" would bring a "wave of terror, crime, and juvenile delinquency" (486). The fear these politicians expressed was that ending Jim Crow separation of the races through the expansion of civil rights would produce chaos and crime.

Murakawa (2006) tracks the movement of these earlier arguments involving the initial Supreme Court *Brown* decision through a transition in the 1970s and 1980s that increasingly focused on an alleged linkage between pressure and protests for civil rights and both communism and crime. Throughout, the attention remained on the role of judges. Thus, as Murakawa points out, "rhetorical attacks on judges as lenient, elitist, and supportive of subversive elements remained stable as the issue at hand slipped from allegedly pro-integration decisions, to allegedly pro-Communist decisions, to allegedly pro-criminal decisions" (486). The latter decisions included, for example, the exclusionary rule about illegally obtained evidence and, notably, drugs.

Many of these Supreme Court decisions were classic criminal law rulings establishing the rights of defendants to remain silent and to have access to legal representation. As with the earlier reversal of Jim Crow laws, these decisions were interpreted as loosening control and raising the specter of chaos and crime in race-related ways. In retrospect, one of the most interesting cases for its implications was *Robinson v. California*. The Supreme Court held in this 1962 case that imprisonment for drug addiction warranted treatment rather than punishment in the form of incarceration. The Court expressed support for the concept of rehabilitation and for alternatives to imprisonment, positions that were to come under steadily increasing attack in the 1980s. Senators like McClellan and Thurmond railed against these decisions as "soft on crime."

An alleged link between civil rights and crime was sometimes implicit and at other times explicit in the reframing of political arguments. Murakawa (2006) indicates that the rhetoric of southern Democrats and Republicans sometimes obscured their racial agenda, so that "the charge of judicial misuse of power transmogrified from 'judges wrongly empower black civil rights' to 'judges wrongly empower (black) criminal rights" (490). Yet as the law and order theme took hold, first in Reagan's 1966 California gubernatorial campaign and then in Richard Nixon's 1968 presidential campaign, even moderate politicians such as Gerald Ford took the lead in a more explicitly fearful bridge framing of racialized images of civil rights protest and crime:

> The War at home—the war against crime—is being lost. . . . The homes and the streets of America are no longer safe for our people. This is a frightful situation. . . . The Republicans in Congress demand that this Administration take the action required to protect our people in their homes, on the streets, at their jobs. . . . When a Rap Brown and a Stokely Carmichael are allowed to run loose, to threaten law-abiding Americans with injury and death,

it's time to slam the door on them and any like them—
and slam it hard! (cited in Weaver 2007:249)

Richard Nixon responded with a law and order "Toward Freedom from Fear" speech that offered only slightly more veiled
connections between demands for an end to poverty, racial
discrimination, and increased crime:

> There is another attitude that must be discarded if we are
> to wage an effective national war against the enemy
> within. That attitude is the socially suicidal tendency—on
> the part of many public men—to excuse crime and sym-
> pathize with criminals because of past grievances the
> criminal may have against society. (ibid. 251)

Few doubted that the "enemy within" referred to poor and
black Americans charged with crimes.

While Ronald Reagan successfully advanced the law and
order frame as governor of California and Richard Nixon
made this frame central to the southern strategy of his presidential campaign, the law and order agenda most lastingly
became the foundation for national law enforcement through
the establishment of a federal sentencing commission and sentencing guidelines at the beginning of President Reagan's second term. Stith and Koh's (1993) legislative history captures
the political paradox of this sentencing law, which was "conceived by liberal reformers as an anti-imprisonment and anti-
discrimination measure, but finally born as part of a more conservative law-and-order crime control measure" (223).

The federal commission and guidelines implemented a shift
to a mandatory approach to sentencing that minimized judges'
punishment options. It is often forgotten today that this
marked a major departure. From the early days of the Republic, judges had exercised wide discretion in sentencing as a
means of individualizing the prospects for rehabilitating offenders (Nagel 1990). The shift was signaled in a short but

widely read book by a prominent federal judge, Marvin Frankel, with the title, *Criminal Sentences: Law without Order* (1972).

Frankel's book captured the attention of Senator Ted Kennedy, who was especially concerned about racial disparities in sentencing. Frankel was a former Columbia University law professor and a widely respected federal judge. He advocated the creation of a new federal agency that would act as a commission on sentencing. Kennedy was intrigued and hosted a dinner for the judge in New York City that included the prominent criminologist and University of Chicago law professor Norval Morris, the senior author of his own well-titled book, *The Honest Politicians' Guide to Crime Control* (1969).

The probable focus of the dinner's conversation was the creation of a system that would result in judges imposing restrained and more consistent sentences in a racially uniform way. Liberal criminologists of this era reasoned that a major source of race and class disparities was indeterminacy in sentencing law that resulted in excessive attention to education and work records. It was thought that this favored white and socioeconomically advantaged offenders with lenient treatment. Senator Kennedy was attracted to the issue of sentencing reform and chose to advance his goals by forging compromises with prominent conservative senators such as John McClellan and Strom Thurmond, who also were interested in more determinate sentencing legislation. Kennedy was increasingly persuaded that determinacy in sentencing law could diminish disparity in race and class outcomes.

Kennedy's thoughts were informed by prominent advisers. As he began to work on a precursor 1978 bill with Arkansas's Senator McClellan, "He brought in as a consultant a man with undoubted liberal credentials, Alan Dershowitz of the Harvard Law School" (Stith and Koh 1993:233). Dershowitz advised Kennedy that the bill could be "a net gain for civil liberties" and to work with it by pressing for "further reforms." However, the latter reforms became less likely as Kennedy brought

South Carolina's Strom Thurmond and West Virginia's Robert Byrd into his efforts.

In the House of Representatives, the African American congressman from Michigan, John Conyers, sounded the first note of skepticism by suggesting that "what happens in the Senate is clearly not a procedural model that ought to be followed" (ibid. 234). Congressman Rodino from New York also expressed concern about the conception of a presidentially appointed federal sentencing commission that was emerging in the Senate, noting that "a presidentially appointed panel can too easily be dominated by political interests. The temptation to seek public approval by appearing tough on crime and therefore to propose standards biased in favor of prosecution and incarceration might prove too great" (ibid. 236).

The fully formed bipartisan politics of the age of Reagan gained force in the 1980s when Delaware's then senator Joe Biden joined with Strom Thurmond to rewrite the 1978 Senate bill into a new and even more unambiguously anticrime measure that included substantially increased and mandatory penalties for drug violations. The 1982 Thurmond-Biden bill was called the Violent Crime and Drug Enforcement Improvements Act of 1982. However, through an odd combination of circumstances and for entirely different reasons, Congressman Conyers and President Reagan both blocked the final 1982 bill, and it did not become law.

Representative Conyers in 1984, foreseeing the likely racial consequences of the emerging sentencing legislation, fought back in the House Judiciary Committee by presenting a sentencing reform measure that would have retained parole and rejected a sentencing commission and guidelines. His bill would have required the sentencing judge to consider and reject all nonprison alternatives before imposing a prison sentence. Conyers explicitly warned that limiting judicial discretion through sentencing guidelines would lead to "an escalation of sentences" due to "political pressure" (ibid. 264).

As would become increasingly clear over time, the sentencing guideline movement was a form of substantive-rational lawmaking that actually increased racial inequality. "While it treated all persons as formally equal," Savelsberg (1992:1348) explained, "it disregarded substantive social inequalities. . . . Under this law, to paraphrase Anatole France, it was forbidden to rich and poor alike to sleep under bridges and steal bread." Of course, it is the poor alone who need to sleep under bridges and steal bread.

Congressman Conyer's bill would have mitigated sentencing inequality, but his was not the legislation that ultimately passed in both the Senate and the House in 1984. The 1984 bill established the Federal Sentencing Commission and the federal sentencing guidelines that followed in 1987, resulting, according to Stith and Koh (1993:281), in "a fundamental transfer of authority over criminal sentencing from an independent judiciary to a politically dependent government agency." They conclude their legislative history of this process by observing that

> To the extent that ideological and political objectives did significantly affect outcomes in both Congress and the Sentencing Commission in the 1980s, it is not surprising that "law and order" concerns dominated. The implementation of more determinate sentencing in Illinois and California has similarly frustrated the liberal reformers who had spearheaded the movement to end indeterminate sentencing and parole. On the state level, and on the federal level, these "due process liberals" had joined with conservative "law and order" advocates to achieve their 'reform' but were disillusioned when the new sentencing regime seemed more responsive to law-and-order concerns than to due process concerns. (285)

A sociologist-criminologist appointed to the Sentencing Commission, Ilene Nagel (1990:892–93), candidly observed that "the Sentencing Reform Act was passed, at least in part, to

make patently clear the rejection of the rehabilitation model . . .
in favor of the new basis for sentencing—to punish, to promote respect for law, to deter, and to incapacitate." The full
implications of this conclusion emerged with development of
the further sentencing provisions that specifically involved the
racial politics surrounding crack cocaine.

From Cocaine to Crack

In 1986, the Boston Celtics talented top draft pick Len Bias
died of a cocaine overdose in his college dormitory. The death
of Bias focused public and political attention on drugs in a
way that captured the attention of the Democratic Speaker of
the House, Tip O'Neill. O'Neill was famous for the aphorism
captured in the title of his memoir, *All Politics Is Local* (1994),
and "local" for O'Neill meant the sports-crazed city of Boston.
O'Neill realized that the Republicans had won the 1984 election with Reagan's law and order politics and speeches and
his endorsement of the 1984 sentencing commission legislation, which he said "was purely political all the way" (cited in
Stith and Koh 1993:265) and which, despite Ted Kennedy's
leading role, was increasingly lauded as "Reagan's bill" (Taylor 1984).

Speaker O'Neill's response was to capitalize on the national
as well as local response to the death of Bias by rushing through
Congress the Anti-Drug Abuse Act of 1986 establishing mandatory minimum sentences. These sentences distinguished between crack and powder cocaine with a 100 to 1 rule that made
African Americans far more liable to imprisonment. The 1986
act required a mandatory minimum sentence of five years for
the simple possession of five grams or more of crack cocaine,
compared to the same sentence for five hundred or more grams
of powder cocaine.

Crack could be sold in smaller amounts that produced faster
and more intense effects than powder cocaine. Its use proliferated at an epidemic rate in African American ghettos during
the later 1980s, while powder cocaine remained the drug of

choice among whites. Any offender who engaged in a "continuing drug enterprise" faced a further twenty-year sentence. The latter charge paralleled the focus on chronic offenders and career criminals in developmental criminology and was much more commonly used against African American defendants than against white defendants. The resulting racial disparities in rates of imprisonment drove the subsequent growth in incarceration rates.

By 1990, the racial inequity of the crack versus powder cocaine distinction had become so suspect that Congress asked the U.S. Sentencing Commission to study the impact of mandatory minimum sentences on African Americans. The commission (1991:82) found that the disparity in sentences between white and black offenders was growing, but the administration did nothing to address this problem. A further study by the commission in 1995 found the crack versus powder cocaine disparity had a differential impact on black offenders. For example, for the year 1993 it was reported that 88.3 percent of the mandatory crack-related sentences were imposed on African Americans.

The Sentencing Commission recommended changes in the guidelines, but Congress refused to pass them into law. Finally, in 2005, the Supreme Court held in *United States v. Booker* that mandatory federal sentencing guidelines violated the constitutional right to trial by jury and that therefore judges must only consider the guidelines as advisory. In 2007, the commission acted on its own to lower the federal sentencing guidelines for crack offenses and made this change retroactive. This allowed some 20,000 inmates to request reduced sentences. It is still unclear how great the impact of this decision on sentencing patterns might be.

What is clear is that the age of Reagan, and more specifically the Reagan presidency, was a time of escalating incarceration. Some of this escalation can be traced to the increase in drug and drug-related crime during the latter half of the Reagan administration, when drug interdiction policies failed and crack cocaine use became epidemic. Yet the escalation in imprisonment had its onset before crack cocaine use became epidemic and continued at a precipitous rate throughout the Reagan presidency, setting a trajectory that has continued into the twenty-first century.

It is important to understand just how punitive this trend has become. Not only does the United States lead the world in incarceration, the forms this imprisonment takes are also literally torturous. For example, the United States today holds at least 25,000 inmates in solitary confinement in the isolation cells of "supermax" prisons. For nearly a century, American prisons rarely isolated inmates. Illinois built the first supermax prison, designed specifically for mass solitary confinement, during the Reagan presidency, in 1983. The former prisoner of war and U.S. senator John McCain has written of his experience of this kind of confinement that "It crushes your spirit and weakens your resistance more effectively than any other form of mistreatment." A California federal court agreed in 1995 that conditions of isolation "hover on the edge of what is humanly tolerable for those with normal resilience" (cited in Gawande 2009). The United States, however, has institutionalized this experience on a massive scale.

Where did the massive increase in punitive incarceration during the age of Reagan lead? Did it succeed in deterring crime, as anticipated by James Q. Wilson (1975:22) when he speculated that "the gains from merely incapacitating convicted criminals might be very large"? Have the concepts of "chronic offenders," "career criminals," and the connected focus on lambda, the distinguishing elements of developmental criminology in the age of Reagan, informed imprisonment policies in ways that have reduced crime in America? Alfred Blumstein, who played perhaps the most central role in advancing a developmental criminology, was agnostic about its policy potential.

By the 1990s, however, Blumstein (1993) had firmly made up his mind. He led a challenge to the massive policy turn toward imprisonment that had escalated in the late 1980s. Blumstein and Wallman (2006) explained how the massive reliance on incarceration in the war on drugs against the crack epidemic in the 1980s resulted in the concentrated imprisonment of older gang leaders and the resulting creation of vacancy chains for new recruits to meet the continuing demands for drugs. This is exactly what an adviser to Nelson Rockefeller had warned decades earlier. New but younger and therefore more inexperienced and violence-prone recruits filled the vacancies created by imprisoning older gang leaders and set off spiraling increases in gun deaths, which in turn led to further subsequent surges in imprisonment in the United States. The street-corner drug dealers sent to prison were simply replaced. Blumstein's analysis did not find the promised benefits of incapacitation and deterrence. The war on drugs produced the worst of several possibilities: an age-based and network-fed process in which mass incarceration led to more violent forms of crime through the 1980s and into the early 1990s.

By 1994, even James Q. Wilson was ready to concede that "very large increases in the prison population can produce only modest reductions in crime rates." Daniel Nagin (1998) offers an interesting explanation for why detection might be a more effective deterrent of crime than severe punishment. He suggests that the public shame that accompanies detection might be of greater deterrent benefit, and furthermore that this shame or stigma might be largest when actual punishment is less common. His intriguing illustration involves the offense of tax evasion, studies of which indicate that the public shame of criminal conviction has a greater deterrent effect than the more private experience of a civil penalty.

Bruce Western (2006:187) offers a comprehensive accounting of the possible costs and benefits of mass imprisonment in the 1990s. He estimates there may have been at most a 5 percent reduction in serious crime from 1993 to 2001, which was purchased at the price of $53 billion. The latter figure raises an interesting question: How could such a large investment in prisons have occurred in the ostensibly austere and fiscally conservative age of Reagan?

From Fearing the Streets to Freeing the Suites: The Deregulated Debt of Imprisonment

Conservatives often frame the age of Reagan as a period of fiscal austerity, but the fearless pursuit of credit and debt during this era was historic. Reagan's views about government were highly selective. As Sam Tanenhaus (2009:82) has recently noted, "Although Reagan is ritually invoked as the enemy of big government, voters in 1966 were attracted by his promise to strengthen the government . . . as the institutional guarantor of 'stability' against student demonstrators and urban rioters."

One of the major oversights of American criminologists is to have treated the historic change in the private settings of America's corporate suites and their links to government during the Reagan era as disconnected from the changes occurring in the more public settings of America's city streets. There were, however, important connections between corporate financial strategies conceived during the age of Reagan and the explosive expansion of imprisonment in the United States during the same period.

Before the age of Reagan, the U.S. government had restricted itself from assuming large budget deficits to times of war or economic emergency, such as World War II and the Great Depression. The Reagan administration encouraged households and governments to take on more debt by loosening the restrictions and freeing up the opportunities to do so in the absence of military or economic emergencies. At the same time that fear and punishment of street crime were reaching unprecedented levels, the Reagan administration was simultaneously sweeping aside cautionary rules and regulations by reducing legal restraint and law enforcement in the corporate suites. The age of Reagan framing was that the marketplace must be set free, both from the fear of debt and from the restraint of regulation. This new freedom was put to many purposes, including the creation of little-known debt instruments to pay for the construction and expansion of imprisonment in America.

Building the new prisons of the 1980s required taking on unfamiliar levels of public debt. In her book *Golden Gulag* (2007), Ruth Gilmore uses the experience of California to explain how many states met their needs for increased prison capacity during the age of Reagan. California is an apt example because since 1982, it has added approximately two dozen new prisons and about an equal number of smaller penal facilities. Each new prison cost between a quarter and a third of a million dollars to build. This expense has required a quadrupling of state spending on corrections.

Ordinarily the new prisons might have been built with state bonds, but California voters in the 1980s were increasingly resistant to approving new bonds, even for projects that were more appealing than prisons. Gilmore explains how well-networked underwriting firms in California helped the California Department of Corrections (CDC) advance a new public-private debt strategy to pay for building new prisons. The key to this scheme was a new debt instrument called lease revenue bonds (LRBs), which increased public debt while avoiding the state's balanced budget rules and the state requirement for ratification of new government bonds by state voters.

The LRBs were an economic framing device that evaded established state regulatory provisions intended precisely to control government debt. We might call this avoidance or evasion a suite misdemeanor. At a minimum, it constituted a kind of innovation that Robert Merton's anomie theory identified as a type of solution to a discrepancy between goals and means. The CDC's goal was to build new prisons, even if it did not have the heretofore legitimate means to do so. LRBs provided a legitimating framing device that redefined the problem in a new economic vocabulary and allowed the construction of new prisons (Gottschalk 2009).

Previously, LRBs were intended for use in situations where the newly funded venture could ultimately generate the revenue needed to make the initiative self-sustaining. LRBs did not require approval from voters because while there was an expectation that the state would assume the risk of compensating losses in the event of default, the state did not explicitly promise its "full faith and credit" as it would for more ordinary state bonds. Of course, the CDC and its new prisons were not going to become self-sustaining in the way other new ventures could. Proponents circumvented this problem by arranging continuing access to funding appropriations from the legislature through the CDC's annual state budget.

California underwriting firms networked with state officials to work out the details, which essentially took funds from one government source, the legislative appropriation for the CDC, and passed it to another government agency, an agency or entity created to construct the prison, which in turn distributed interest payments to buyers of the bonds. Since the bonds were not fully insured by the state, the requirement of voter approval was deemed unnecessary.

Over time, the LRB approach to the expansion of debt for prison construction became common across the United States, so that by 1996 more than half of new prison construction in America was accomplished through LRBs. Because these debt instruments do not provide full state protection against default, they involve added carrying costs, a point that few Americans realize. In less than a decade, California's state debt increased from less than $1 billion to more than $5 billion. At least three citizen groups in California have brought suits charging that the use of LRBs violates the California constitutional requirement that all significant long-term debts must be approved by the voters.

Framing Freedom and Constraint

We began this chapter by recalling Robert K. Merton's classical structural anomie theory, with its emphasis on the disparity between success goals and access to means for their attainment, that was developed during the age of Roosevelt. Merton argued that crime was often a form of innovation used by disadvantaged groups in times of scarcity to overcome the disparity they encountered between goals and means. An implication of this theory was that offenders might be rehabilitated through better access to opportunities to achieve success, for example, by means of educational or employment programs.

The age of Reagan, however, dramatically reconfigured the world of crime and criminal justice by shifting the focus from correctional rehabilitation to incapacitation through incarceration of persons convicted of street crimes. Concomitantly, there was a further move during this period away from the prosecution of white-collar criminals and toward deregulation of the financial industry as an explicit means—indeed, as a legalization of the means—to encourage economic innovation.

Another question therefore urgently presents itself, and is taken up in the following chapter: What if, instead of limitations of means, it is rather the absence of regulations, or in other words *un*limited means, that more notably leads to criminal innovation in the world of high finance? In the deregulated world of finance, "the discipline of the market"—that is, the fear of material loss—is the only presumably efficient, and therefore presumably sufficient, limitation on means to goal attainment. Yet these policies of the age of Reagan may have led Americans to—in contrast to the fearful framing of city streets—fear too little the deregulation of corporate suites. An apposite example is the age of Reagan collapse and bailout in the late 1990s of the Long-Term Capital Management (LTCM) hedge fund.

Simon and Gagnon (1976) argue in an important updating of Merton's structural anomie theory that affluence as well as scarcity can cause criminal innovation. They introduce the concept of the "anomie of affluence" to suggest that "under the changed conditions of affluence, those who have automatically been taught to be conforming . . . are susceptible to deviance" (369). An ironic and perhaps telling illustration of their point may by the story of the LTCM hedge fund and the involvement of Robert C. Merton, the Nobel Prize–winning economist son of Robert K. Merton, the father of structural anomie theory.

Tett (2009:74) writes that Robert C. Merton "passionately believed in the liberating power of derivatives." Merton explains in an autobiographical statement for the Nobel Prize that he took up economics because he believed that macroeconomics could help prevent unemployment and potentially affect millions of people. However, the largely unregulated means for doing this, a hedge fund that in itself is a product of affluence, might not have been imagined by Merton's father. LTCM was one among many hedge funds that, with a new freedom of means provided by the age of Reagan, operated outside the lightly regulated world of investment banking.

Another Nobel Prize-winner, Myron Scholes, joined Merton's son at LTCM. At first LTCM recorded remarkable profits using models based on the ideas of Merton and Scholes. But following the financial crisis in Russia in 1998, LTCM experienced spiraling losses. Scholes was identified in a federal court case as having engaged in innovative tax avoidance schemes to compensate for early LTCM losses. In an e-mail sent to the fund's management committee about tax avoidance, Scholes wrote, "We must decide in the near future . . . how to plan to be able to enjoy the benefits of the use of these losses for the longest period of time. If we are careful, most likely we will never have to pay long-term capital gains on the 'loan' from the Government." Gains were the goal for which the government's "loan" was justified as the means.

Regulators did not sufficiently respond to such warning signs, another of which involved the massive risks posed by the unregulated use of Robert C. Merton's innovative investment ideas. LTCM had leveraged the positions it took on interest-rates by more than 100 times its capital resources. In little more than a month in 1998, LTCM lost nearly $5 billion. The abruptness of this massive loss provoked a sudden loss of confidence in Merton's rational models of risk. Roger Lowenstein (2000:152) ironically writes that "the crisis of fear became a self-fulfilling prophecy, just as Merton's father, who had coined the phrase, had theorized."

Fear may therefore influence not only crime on the streets but also crime in the suites. However, in the financial suites the problem is often too little rather than too much fear. The problem at LTCM began with the fearless framing of the mathematical models of risk that guided its highly leveraged investments and led to enormous losses, both at the fund and through a similar false confidence and systemic application of such models of risk during the larger financial crisis a decade later. Of even greater potential significance, however, was the response of the Federal Reserve Bank of New York to LTCM's losses.

The Federal Reserve Bank of New York responded to the failure of LTCM by insisting that major investment banks provide the capital for a bailout of the fund. The Federal Reserve Bank of New York stressed that the likely effects of LTCM's collapse on worldwide financial institutions required a preventive intervention. Critics, including the Government Accounting Office (GAO), warned that this bailout could encourage large financial institutions to later take on even greater risks in the belief that the Federal Reserve or other government institutions would again intervene to cover their losses. Economists call this problem a "moral hazard." The GAO explicitly warned in relation to the LTCM bailout that "such actions could increase moral hazard and potentially undermine the effectiveness of market discipline."

This discussion of moral hazard was a poignant anticipation of the much discussed "too big to fail" problem of the recent financial crisis. "Too big to fail" has become a common framing of the relationship between excessive freedom from regulation and the escalating risk that led to the recent massive government bailouts of financial institutions. Only one major financial institution that was asked to participate in the

LTCM bailout refused to do so. This was Bear Stearns, and the Federal Reserve Bank of New York declined to assist Bear Stearns when it became a victim of the subprime crisis a decade later (Cohan 2009a).

The age of Reagan framing of the fears and risks of crime on city streets spurred a remarkable growth in rates of imprisonment in America. At the same time, age of Reagan hopes and expectations about the deregulation of financial instruments and institutions fearlessly framed an equally remarkable reduction in the use of legal scrutiny and enforcement in response to crimes in America's business suites. The innovative and underregulated diffusion of the use of lease revenue bonds to build state prisons and incarcerate increasing numbers of street criminals in California and beyond is a provocative example of an unexpected link between the city streets and financial suites of America. Streets and suites form flip sides and sites of the late modern framing of crime in America. The next chapter plunges into the economic trials that bedeviled the nation's health as a result of age of Reagan framing policies.

Chapter 6
Framing the Freeing of the Suites
||||||||||

At the heart of a critical collective framing perspective on the age of Reagan is a realignment in the relative regulation of the streets and suites of America. The shining city on the hill that Reagan rhapsodized about was a city where the streets were highly controlled and the business suites were much less constrained.

Sean Wilentz (2008) speculates that Reagan's frequent capacity to imaginatively recreate scenarios in ways that pleased him was rooted in the darkness of his small-town midwestern childhood and a dysfunctional family life dominated by an alcoholic father. Reagan often spoke in ways that denied such darkness while displaying a well-developed capacity to mix illusion with reality. Wilentz observes that this mixing of illusion and reality increased over time, and concludes that Reagan had "a proven propensity in adulthood to conflate the two—thereby stoking his own desires while turning politics into a realm of dreams" (2008:130).

His later vice president, George H. W. Bush, famously called Reagan's tax policies "voodoo economics" in a primary campaign speech. However, Reagan's rosier picture prevailed. In this picture, the prospect of big government was a threat to the promise of a more laissez-faire form of capitalism. The promise of the "Reagan Revolution" was to get government "out of the way." The dream of Reaganomics was one in which government rules and regulations would be swept aside like unnecessary debris blocking the pathway to the nation's thwarted ambitions. "Restoring the energetic spirit of the past, according to Reaganite myth, was the only way to ensure a prosperous, innovative, secure, communal American future, where a free citizenry could dream big dreams, begin all over again, and make its dreams come true—just as Ronald Reagan did" (Wilentz 2008:137).

This was the free spirit of Reagan-era deregulation. It was proclaimed broadly, applied selectively, and mobilized most dramatically for the people and places at the top of the economic hierarchy. As president, Reagan immediately signed a regulatory order that imposed a hiring freeze on all federal departments, but most pointedly the regulatory agencies. A week later, he issued an order that stopped agencies from issuing new rules. There was little doubt about the economic motivation for these changes. Reagan appointed staunch advocates of economic deregulation to head the Securities and Exchange Commission (SEC), the Commerce Department, the Federal Communications Commission, and even the Department of Interior—where his appointee, James Watt, wasted no time in letting the unregulated mining and drilling for profits begin. Business regulations were primary targets throughout.

The appointment of Alan Greenspan as chairman of the Federal Reserve Bank ensured a longlasting and bipartisan legacy for the age of Reagan. Greenspan, who served U.S. presidents from 1987 to 2006, implemented the free market beliefs of University of Chicago economist Milton Friedman and cited Adam Smith's "invisible hand" to justify deregulation of the financial sector. This use of Smith's writings, however, ignored his warnings about those—especially bankers, traders, and financiers—who would "endanger the security of the whole society . . . and ought to be . . . restrained by the laws of all governments" (Smith 1937:308). Instead, Michael Burry (2010:10), who profited enormously by betting on the oncoming financial collapse, writes that "even when the full extent of the financial crisis became painfully clear early in 2007, the Federal Reserve Chairman, the Treasury secretary, the president and senior members of Congress repeatedly underestimated the severity of the problem."

Suite Freedom

A far-reaching form of deregulation came with the passage in 1982 of the Garn–St. Germain Depository Institutions Act. President Reagan proudly proclaimed it "the most important legislation for financial institutions in the last 50 years." He continued, "It provides a long term solution for troubled thrift institutions." This was the administration's response to a growing scandal in the savings and loan (S&L) industry. Barely containing himself, the president declared, "All in all, I think we hit the jackpot." In a disturbing illustration of intentionally provocative frame realignment, Ronald Reagan called the Garn–St. Germain Depository Act the "Emancipation Proclamation for America's savings institutions" (cited in Thomas 1991:32).

The key player in the passage of the Garn–St. Germain Act was the chair of the House Banking Committee, Fernand St. Germain (Calavita, Pontell, and Tillman 1997). Although he began by advocating reform of the troubled S&Ls, St. Germain wound up radically deregulating them at the behest of the U.S. League of Savings Institutions. He was eventually cited by the House Ethics Committee and the Department of Justice for "serious and sustained misconduct." When St. Germain lost his elected seat in Congress, he became a paid lobbyist for the S&L industry.

St. Germain was aided in his deregulatory efforts by Reagan's appointment of Richard Pratt as chair of the Federal Housing and Loan Bank Board (FHLBB), and the Garn–St. Germain Act became known colloquially as the Pratt Bill. After deregulating the S&Ls with the help of the board and the bill, Pratt took a senior position with Merrill Lynch, where he headed a unit that invested heavily in mortgage-backed securities and junk bonds, including an investment of about $500 million in the infamous Lincoln Savings and Loan operated by Charles Keating. As we will see, Keating and Lincoln Savings are names that echoed through the scandal-plagued years that followed.

The Lincoln fraud and the larger S&L scandal were enabled both by deregulation and lax legal scrutiny. In a signal of larger problems to follow, the SEC had already charged and settled a suit against Keating when he received a charter for the Lincoln S&L in 1984. The Drexel Burnham Lambert firm financed the purchase using the kind of junk (high-risk) bonds that became the basis of a major scandal described below. Keating was a major contributor to candidates of both parties, including to Republican and Democratic senators infamously known as the Keating Five.

Calavita, Pontell, and Tillman (1997:108) describe just how high the Keating Five case reached into the U.S. government:

> The costliest episode in the Saga of Keating's political influence began in early 1987, as Lincoln was being investigated by the FHLB in San Francisco for underwriting of loans and investment irregularities. In April 1987 Senator Dennis DeConcini called Edwin Gray [chair of the FHLB Board] to a now infamous meeting in his office. In attendance at the meeting were Senators John McCain, John Glenn, and Allan Cranston, all of whom had received hefty campaign contributions from Keating.

With the assistance of interventions by these prominent senators from both parties and the future Republican presidential candidate, John McCain, lawyers were soon able to assure Keating that "you have the Board right where you want them."

It is important to emphasize just how broad the responsibility of both the Republicans and Democrats was for the S&L scandal. By 1988, politicians of both parties knew the crisis involved more than one-third of the S&Ls in the United States. Still, the scandal played little role in the 1988 presidential election. Both the Democratic Speaker of the House of Representatives, James Wright, who eventually resigned, and the Republican presidential candidate George H. W. Bush's son, Neil Bush, were extensively investigated for S&L wrong-doings. Calavita, Pontell, and Tillman (1997:110) report that Democratic presidential candidate Michael Dukakis was warned off the topic by party advisers because, as one account of the scandal put it, "too many officials from both parties had their fingerprints all over it" (Lowy 1991:216).

The significance of the Garn–St. Germain Act, which was implemented with the help of Democratic Speaker Wright, was that it set the foundation for the S&L scandal and was furthermore a forerunner of the subprime mortgage crisis. This act removed restrictions dating from the age of Roosevelt that required significant down payments by home buyers. Fear of the undercapitalized risks of debt and default among homeowners dominated the age of Roosevelt, while the age of Reagan fostered a freer and more fearless approach to credit and risk-taking. Reaganomics fearlessly placed its bets on a "magic of the marketplace" that would flourish when it was set free by the removal of regulation and restrictive government rules.

Like the subprime crisis that followed later, the S&L scandal involved the undercapitalization of bad loans that led to government-funded bailouts. Wilentz (2008:203) writes that "one trouble with this spurt of unrestrained free enterprise was that it twisted the bracing, acquisitive, get-ahead elements in the American psyche—and the genuine economic improvements of the Reagan era—into crasser, sometimes callous, and reckless impulses." In what has proven to be a substantial understatement, Wilentz observed that "at the top of the financial ladder, a considerable portion of the new wealth was built on insubstantial paper transactions, overleveraged credit, and sharp dealing that from time to time crossed over into illegality." This new wealth was fearlessly pursued with new freedom.

Freed for Greed?

An iconic example of this acquisitive reframing came with Ivan Boesky, the real-life model for the ruthless fictional financier Gordon Gekko portrayed by Michael Douglas in the film *Wall Street*. The real Boesky famously said in a speech given at Berkeley in 1986, "I think greed is healthy," providing the precedent for the memorable Michael Douglas film proclamation that "greed, for lack of a better word, is good!" His line earned Boesky acclaim at the time. He became a short-lived role model for a new no-holds-barred approach to the economy. However, Boesky's image changed when he was later prosecuted with Michael Milken, sometimes known as "the junk bond king," for insider trading in debt instruments that included the poorly regulated "anything goes" world of high-risk bonds. This prosecution illustrated some of the challenges of the alternative framings of street and suite crimes for law enforcement in the age of Reagan.

The insider trading operation that Boesky and Milken constructed struck at the core of public and investor confidence in Wall Street and the financial sector of the economy. Their cases also exposed the ways in which white-collar criminals can use corporate organizations and the trust placed in persons occupying high leadership positions to frame their crimes in obscure ways that prevent easy detection and punishment (Shapiro 1984).

Wheeler and Rothman (1982) cogently observe that the corporation "is for white-collar criminals what the gun or knife is for the common criminal—a tool to obtain money from victims." A key part of the problem is an absence of cultural framings or beliefs that discourage these corporate crimes (Geis 1962). Thus, C. Wright Mills (1956) classically commented that "it is better, so the image runs, to take one dime from each of ten million people at the point of a corporation than $100,000 from each of ten banks at the point of a gun."

Milken and Boesky worked through the firm of Drexel Burnham Lambert. This firm specialized in hostile takeovers through leveraged buyouts of targeted companies with capital raised from high-yield debt or junk bonds. Junk bonds were named for the high risks of default, which in turn commanded high returns or yields in the absence of default. Milken became known for illegally creating markets with manipulated bids for these junk bonds, which in turn were used in business takeovers. The SEC ultimately sued Drexel Burnham Lambert for insider trading, stock manipulation, defrauding its clients, and "stock parking," or the practice of secretly buying and manipulating stocks in the names of others. Milken's department in the Drexel firm was the site for this activity.

The Drexel Burnham Lambert operation aptly illustrates the ways in which individuals such as Milken and Boesky use corporate organizations to leverage their criminal profits. In an intriguing study that documents this criminal leveraging of corporate profitability, Wheeler and Rothman (1982) categorized white-collar offenders into three groups: (1) those who commit offenses alone or with affiliated others using neither an occupational nor an organization role (individual offenders), (2) those who commit offenses alone or with affiliated others using an occupational role (occupational offenders), and (3) those who commit offenses in which both organization and occupation are ingredients (organizational offenders). They found that the median take across the same four kinds of offenses for individual offenders was $5,279, for occupational offenders $17,106, and for organizational offenders $117,392 (all figures in 1980 dollars).

The deregulated age of Reagan enabled white-collar offenders like Boesky and Milken to leverage their gains even more dramatically, while the corporate organization of their acts further shielded them from easy detection or prosecution. Because of the organizational complexity and opacity of much white-collar crime, it is often necessary to develop evidence of the crimes by playing offenders like Boesky and Milken off one another through plea bargaining. A plea agreement can be used to reward the development of evidence and testimony. An enforcement cost of the bargain is that it can also lead to a reframing of the rewarded participants as "cooperative" and "remorseful" to justify their lesser penalties. The story of the prosecution of Boesky and Milken is told in a number of books, most notably in James Stewart's *Den of Thieves* (1991).

Boesky and Milken jointly initiated crimes by using companies and partnerships to obtain and trade confidential financial information. They used the information to manage blocks of secretly and illegally parked securities with their firm and to profitably manipulate share prices. However, because the charges were ultimately plea bargained, the cases never went to trial, and the full details of the actual crimes were not revealed. Despite the publicity surrounding these crimes, this meant that the framing of the actual insider trading practices as criminal remained vague and obscure. This is a recurring pattern seen throughout the accounts of crimes presented in this chapter.

Boesky's own undercover work was used to obtain the evidence needed to convict Milken of conspiring in the complex insider trading scheme. In exchange for pleading guilty to only one felony, Boesky agreed to arrange a face-to-face meeting with Milken and to wear a body microphone. The information collected provided indirect evidence of an underlying crime. Yet a depiction of the actual crime could not be developed in full detail.

> Nothing Milken said would be a "smoking gun" at any future trial, but the tape would be useful probative evidence. Milken had never denied the existence of their scheme; he'd never denied that Boesky owed him money. The discussion of the payment, and how it could be characterized as an investment banking fee, plainly suggests a cover-up. The whole discussion made little sense unless Boesky's version of the conspiracy were, in fact, true. (Stewart 1991:336–37)

Still, the exact nature of the conspiracy was not revealed. Boesky's plea bargain allowed him to serve only eighteen months in jail.

Milken had nobody more important than himself to turn in, and he therefore faced ninety-eight counts of racketeering and security fraud. He served three years in jail and was fined $1 billion. Nonetheless, Stewart concluded that this left Milken with an extraordinary fortune, "one that would place him high on any list of the [then] richest Americans" (524). Milken spent much time before and after his prosecution reframing his own image as a philanthropist, while Boesky studied Judaism and emphasized his religious devotion.

The House of Morgan and the Age of Roosevelt

Corporate complexity and a trust of persons in high corporate positions worked hand in glove with policies of deregulation to set the foundation for an increasingly free and fearless pursuit of risks and profits during the age of Reagan. Prosecutions such as those of Boesky and Milken were of limited effectiveness in countering the excesses of this era. Financial scandals abounded throughout the 1970s, 1980s, and 1990s: the S&L scandals, the Bank of Credit and Commerce International (BCCI) affair, Long-Term Capital Management, and Enron are well-recognized names and only a few of the most egregious of these scandals that preceded the recent subprime collapse. Nonetheless, the deregulation frame has largely held sway through most of the last half century. The free and fearless pursuit of risk seemed to grow in waves and crests that were impervious to fundamental change.

Thus, no adversarial frame could effectively challenge and contain the deregulation frame of the age of Reagan. Yet there is historical precedent for such a challenge in the now nearly forgotten hearings of the Senate Banking and Currency Committee, held during the waning months of the Hoover presidency and the early days of Roosevelt's New Deal. These hearings are instructive in suggesting how an adversarial framing can occur and even succeed in a time of crisis.

These long-neglected hearings involved perhaps America's most famous banking family, colloquially known as the House of Morgan. Before the Great Depression, the public standing of the Morgan family's activities exemplified a "normal" framing of banking as a highly respected profession and institutional enterprise. Ron Chernow's (1990) account of the House of Morgan includes a statement by Jack Morgan to the Senate Banking and Currency Committee in 1933 that captures the personification of this framing of the occupational life of the private professional banker before the Depression:

> The private banker is a member of a profession which has been practiced since the middle ages. In the process of time there has grown up a code of professional ethics and customs, on the observance of which depend his reputation, his force and his usefulness to the community in which he works. . . . [I]f, in the exercise of his profession, the private banker disregards this code, which could never be expressed in any legislation, but has a force far greater than any law, he will sacrifice his credit. This credit is his most valuable possession; it is the result of years of faith and honorable dealing and while it may be quickly lost, once lost cannot be restored for a long time, if ever. (cited in Chernow 1990:363–64)

Jack Morgan was chagrined when he was called before the Senate committee in 1933. He was rightly worried about what was to follow.

The Senate Banking and Currency Committee was dominated by its chief counsel, Ferdinand Pecora, a former assistant attorney from New York. Pecora was Sicilian-born, and his photograph from the period reveals a man with a knowing grin, a strong chin, and a full head of black- and gray-flecked hair. "Smoking a blunt cigar, his shirtsleeves rolled up," Chernow writes, "the hard-bitten Pecora captured the public's attention" (355). He had a reputation for being fearless and incorruptible, and by the time he finished his work for the committee he had produced 10,000 pages of testimony collected together in eight large volumes. Pecora gained so much favorable publicity that Roosevelt made him an otherwise unlikely choice as a commissioner of his newly created Securities and Exchange Commission.

One of the shocking revelations of Pecora's hearings was that major bankers who earlier had been credited with heroically trying to stem the 1929 stock market collapse were revealed as actually having used their organizational positions (which mixed commercial and investment banking) to sell off failing Latin American loans to unsuspecting investors as bonds. Such revelations had two effects. First, it led a Montana senator to label Morgan and his colleagues "banksters" and to suggest that, as with the infamous "gangsters" of the era, "the best way to restore confidence in the banks would be to take these crooked presidents out of the banks and treat them the same way we treated Al Capone when he failed to pay his income tax." Second, the revelation that savings and speculative operations were being mixed together led to the passage of the Glass-Steagall Act, which separated these two sides of banking and intended to prevent the creation of banks "too big to fail." The deregulation of the age of Reagan swept this separation of deposits and speculative investments aside.

Pecora was especially unsparing in his questioning of Jack Morgan before the committee. Chernow describes the confrontation as typifying the contrasting images of "the imperturbable Bourbon and the assertive immigrant." (363). He continues: "His black hair swept up in a pompadour, his chin jutting, Pecora jabbed the air and posed aggressive questions; sometimes he even pointed his cigar at Jack" (364). Pecora reduced Morgan to sputtering responses, leading Morgan to whiningly lament, in a most un-Bourbon way, "I am not used to this form of examination, Mr. Pecora, and I do not get my words quite straight always." Morgan later complained that "Pecora has the manners of a prosecuting attorney who is trying to convict a horse thief" (368). This was, of course, the kind of criminal framing or stigma probably intended by Pecora as a former prosecutor from the criminal courtrooms of New York.

There were junctures when Pecora may have taken advantage of Morgan in somewhat misleading ways, but also to great public effect. Morgan and his colleagues had legally avoided paying taxes in several years when they had incurred large stock losses. The admission that they had paid no taxes, even if legally, caused an uproar when the newspapers blared this avoidance as "tax evasion." The response was much like the reaction to excessive executive salaries and bonuses for bankers today.

A third revelation from the hearings was that the Morgans had been following a practice of offering shares of stocks to "friendly individuals" at a discount the public did not receive. The preferred list of highly placed friends confirmed Main Street's framing of Wall Street as a place of easy money and loose morality. "For Morgan critics," Chernow writes, "this was at last the smoking gun, the tangible proof of corruption." (370). The former president, Calvin Coolidge, headed the list of "friends."

Roosevelt had to this point been agnostic about the form that new banking regulations should take, but the stream of revelations and especially the friends list made for a major scandal that the president could not ignore. The result was the passage of the Glass-Steagall Act on June 16, 1933. The private banks would now have to choose between their roles as savings and investment businesses. That is, they could take deposits and make loans or they could sell securities, but they could not do both. The elimination of this legislated restriction in 2000, with the support of Bill Clinton's treasury secretary and former Citibank CEO Robert Rubin, assisted by current

Obama economic adviser Larry Summers, is a possible factor in the recent subprime crisis.

Pecora's hearings retain a contemporary resonance. The intent was to restore a confidence in American financiers and their banking institutions. The hearings themselves provided a crisis framing of the post-Depression finance sector. Chernow notes that "In the 1920s, the banker had gone from a person of sober rectitude to a huckster who encouraged people to gamble on risky stocks and bonds" (375).Congress responded with both the hearings and new legislation. The abuses revealed by the hearings led to passage of the Securities Act of 1933 and the Securities Exchange Act of 1934, as well as the Glass-Steagall Act of 1933.

Recovery from the subprime crisis and financial collapse of 2008–9 might benefit from a similar reframing of financial affairs in America. Roosevelt called the elite malefactors "economic royalists," and chastised their practices of "entrenched greed." Although there is evidence of his hesitancy and reluctance, Roosevelt was finally forced by the revelations of Pecora and others to lead an oppositional reframing that demanded indictments, prison terms, and essential New Deal reforms. In the aftermath of the current crisis, Congress has allocated $8 million for an uninspiring Financial Crisis Inquiry Commission to undertake a comparable task in 2010.

From Savings and Loans to "Subprime"

David Leonhardt (2006) in a *New York Times* article prophetically suggested in advance of the most recent financial crisis that there was an unsettling regularity to contemporary economic emergencies. He noted that the global financial system has suffered a crisis roughly once every three or four years over the past several decades. Such events include the stock market crash of 1987, the Asian and Mexican meltdowns in the 1990s, the dot-com implosion of 2000, and the aftermath of September 11, 2001.

Thus, although white-collar crimes and scandals are often thought to be unusual, unrelated, and even random events, this is probably not the case. It certainly was not true of the junk bond and S&L scandals of the 1980s, which were directly connected. The framing that enabled deregulation of credit and debt is a clear connecting link between these earlier scandals and the subprime mortgage crisis. Recent estimates are that while the S&L crisis cost taxpayers about $300 billion in 2009 dollars, the financial crisis that began in 2008 will cost much more. For example, while banks have been able to repay much of the Treasury Department's bailout, the Federal Reserve Bank still holds more than a trillion-dollar portfolio of mortgage-backed securities of unknown and doubtful market value.

The age of Roosevelt was a world apart from the age of Reagan in its framing of the concepts of credit and risk. The economists Philippon and Reshef (2009) argue that the shifting frames involve three eras of the twentieth century. The first era lasted from the beginning of the twentieth century until the Great Depression. It featured explosive growth in banking, bankers' earnings, and household debt. The collapse of this financial system marked the onset of the Great Depression and brought on the age of Roosevelt, the Pecora congressional hearings, regulatory reforms, reduced earnings for bankers, and a contraction in household debt. This second era lasted until the age of Reagan and the 1980s. The third era has featured extensive deregulation, a new expansion of banking, a renewed explosion in bankers' earnings, and a return to household debt levels last seen in the lead-up to the Great Depression.

Simon Johnson (2009) calls this age of Reagan expansion "the quiet coup" in which the financial sector reached unprecedented economic dominance. Over the past thirty years, the ten largest financial institutions increased their control from about 10 percent to more than 60 percent of U.S. financial assets (Kaufman 2009). In the midst of the recent economic collapse, the four biggest banks in America—Citigroup, Bank of America, J.P. Morgan Chase, and Wells Fargo—got bigger rather than smaller. The financial sector grew from about 16 percent of U.S. domestic corporate profits between 1973 and

1985 to double this figure in the 1990s, peaking at more than 40 percent of these profits in the current decade. Many of these profits derived from what Tett (2009:chap. 1) calls the "derivative dream." Before discussing the derivative dream, however, I introduce the securitized mortgages on which so much of this dream recently has been built.

Securitized Debt, Subprime Mortgages, and the Derivative Dream

Subprime mortgages are household loans usually provided to less credit-worthy borrowers at higher than prime rates. Similar loans are used for cars, student borrowing, and other forms of debt, much of which is charged to credit cards. "Securitizing" debt involves pooling loans into investment instruments that generate a flow of payments. In recent years, subprime mortgages were increasingly bundled together in this way. Theoretically, a bundling of the combined debts of many borrowers should have reduced the risks of individualized lending by spreading or distributing the risk, thereby lowering the costs of borrowing.

The payments from securitized mortgages were further "sliced and diced" into tranches, which were then ranked in terms of their assumed levels of risk. This involved a further reestimation and presumed reduction of the repackaged risk for resale to new investors. Again, the ostensible value added by the initial securitization and the further repackaging of the tranches was to reduce the risks involved in the original sources of the debt.

The financial industry used derivatives to take another step presumed to reduce risk. The tranches of mortgages were additionally bundled together for use in derivative contracts. The point was to buy insurance through these contracts against the risk of mortgage defaults. The derivative contracts were not just for subprime mortgages but also for corporate bonds and other kinds of loans. Credit default swaps were a forerunner of these derivative contracts. These swaps involved trading risks on the ownership of various kinds of assets, such as foreign currency or gold, as a hedge against possible losses.

The investment bank of J.P. Morgan spearheaded the development of derivatives contracts from the earlier use of credit default swaps, and its derivatives business grew from $512 million to $1.7 trillion in value between 1992 and 1994. Derivatives generated half of J.P. Morgan's trading profits by 1994. Tett (2009:9) defines a derivative as follows:

> As the name implies, a derivative is, on the most basic level, nothing more than a contract whose value derives from some other asset, such as a bond, a stock, or a quantity of gold. Key to derivatives is that those who buy and sell them are each making a bet on the future value of that asset. . . . At the heart of the business is a dance with *time* [emphasis in original].

Derivatives can become complicated when the underlying assets or the way in which they are combined is unclear, and this lack of clarity can be used to create power and profit for those who form and trade these financial instruments. Nonetheless, the basic idea of a derivative is as prosaic as the buying and selling by farmers of futures on their soybeans or pork bellies to insure against changes in prices between production and market.

When the futures, for example, are in subprime mortgages, the process can become more opaque because of the financial elaboration and jargon involved. Bankers called the derivatives made out of securitized mortgage loans "collateralized debt obligations" (CDOs). These CDOs were not made from individual mortgages but rather from the tranches of "asset-backed securities" (ABS), or the above-noted "securitized mortgages":

> The pyramidlike structure of a collateralized debt obligation is a beautiful thing—if you are fascinated by the

intricacies of financial engineering. A banker creates a CDO by assembling pieces of debt according to their credit ratings and their yields. The mistake . . . was believing that the ones with the higher credit ratings were such a sure bet that the companies did not bother to set aside much capital against them in the [presumably] unlikely event that the CDO would generate losses. (Sorkin 2009:158)

Traders also used derivatives to insure against and bet on defaults using "synthetic CDOs of ABS" that did not require owning the CDOs.

Banks innovated further by creating quasi-shell entities to hold the CDOs of ABS. These companies were referred to as special-purpose vehicles (SPVs) or structured investment vehicles (SIVs). SIVs allowed banks to avoid rules about capital reserves and to evade bank regulations more generally. These vehicles moved the mortgages off the books of the banks and also repackaged and resold the securitized mortgages. As Tett (2009: 97) explains, "they were thus a bit like the garage of a house: a useful place for banks to park assets they did not want inside their home banks." Figure 6.1 illustrates the application of the credit default swap and derivatives concepts to housing loans.

The Growth of the Derivative Dream

The trade in derivatives became remarkably lucrative. As these and earlier profits from other parts of the financial sector grew, so also did the financial sector's influence and involvement in the nation's politics. The movement of investment bankers back and forth between Wall Street and Washington became extensive and expected. Not coincidentally, this co-occurred with financial deregulation. Deregulation enhanced the freedom and power of the banks, for example, by ending the Depression-era Glass-Steagall Act's separation of commercial and investment banking.

Deregulation boosted the "leverage" of investment banks by decreasing the capital required to back up the new risks

The Risky Business of Mortgage Derivatives

"Collateralized debt obligations" [CDOs] are forms of credit derivatives used by banks to manage risks as well as produce profits. They played a major role in the recent financial crisis.

Banks made mortgage loans to clients, who in turn made interest payments to banks. The banks offset the risk of defaults in these interest payments by selling the risk in the form of "credit default swaps."

The banks sold the risk by entering into credit default swaps with "special purpose vehicles" (SPVs), to which banks paid insurance fees for assuming the risks of paying the costs of mortgage loan defaults.

The SPVs funded their insurance obligations by dividing and repackaging the risks into classes called tranches, differentiated by the degree of risk, and then sold the tranches to investors. Banks also invested their own capital in some of the highest-risk tranches. Money managers, accountants, and brokers often misled investors with marketing materials that did not disclose the risk.

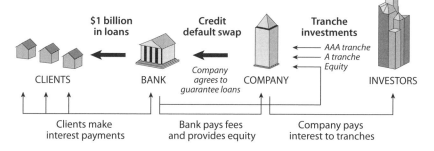

The financial crisis ensued in part because even though the banks received compensation for insured defaults, the banks also lost their investment capital in high risk tranches. As defaults increased, investors in lower-risk tranches also realized losses. Eventually investors and banks created a new instrument to bet against mortgage-backed securities that did not require actual purchase of these securities. This new instrument was called a synthetic CDO, the subject of the 2010 SEC complaint against Goldman Sachs in the highly publicized Abacus deal.

Figure 6.1 Explaining credit derivatives. After *New York Times* (March 10, 2009, D4).

they increasingly and then voraciously pursued. Passage of the Commodities Futures Modernization Act in 2000 further established that derivative contracts were not futures or securities and therefore did not fall under the control of any specific regulatory agency. The growth in derivatives also took on global dimensions with the increased speed and international movement of money (see Cassidy 2009). These instruments have even been used by Goldman Sachs and other U.S. investment banks to help mask and stabilize national economies such as Greece's (Story, Thomas, and Schwartz 2010).

The growth of digital technology and the Internet did not in itself create financial irregularities but did increase their scope and spread. The more fundamental problem was that banks were set free to earn greater profits but also ultimately losses by increasing their risk-taking with highly leveraged investments. This was the freer and less fearful approach to credit and risk-taking embraced in the age of Reagan, with its faith in the "magic of the marketplace" unencumbered by regulation and restrictions. It was a faith advanced by not just the Reagan administration but through the above-noted carryover influence of figures like Alan Greenspan as chairman of the Federal Reserve Bank in the Clinton and Bush administrations as well. Clinton's chief economist, Laurence Summers, called the head of the Commodity Futures Trading Commission when she pushed for regulation of derivatives to say, "I have 13 bankers in my office and they say if you go forward with this you will cause the worst financial crisis since World War II" (cited in Johnson and Kwak 2010:9). Enthusiasm for deregulation reached a near-term peak when top government regulators in 2003 staged a telegenic photo opportunity in which they used garden shears and a chainsaw to cut up bundles of paper representing bank regulations.

Along the way, there were warning signals about the risks presented by extensive trading in derivatives. In the mid-1990s, the treasurer of Orange County, California, invested heavily in derivatives, and the county went bankrupt after losing $2 billion (see also Morgenson 2010). The Government Accounting Office (1994) issued a report warning about the scale of potential losses and the possibility of a repetition of the S&L crisis. Nonetheless, legislation reining in derivatives trading failed in Congress. Tett (2009) concludes that "self-policing had won the day. . . . And in the absence of regulatory oversight, the eventual innovation frenzy would later fuel a boom beyond all bounds of rational constraint—or self-discipline" (40). The age of Reagan theory of self-control, as discussed in the context of street crime in chapter 4, remained as the default government policy for the financial suites. This assumed, of course, that there was self-control.

An entire shadow banking system that was largely unregulated by government grew up around capital markets based
on the packaging of debts, and especially subprime mortgage
debt, using SPVs and SIVs. Tett (2009) describes the scramble
for the profits that were now widely foreseen in the subprime
sector:

> Mortgage lending had become an assembly-line affair in
> which loans were made and then quickly reassembled
> into bonds immediately sold to investors. A bank or bro-
> kerage's ability to extend a loan no longer depended on
> how much capital the institution held; the deciding factor
> was whether the loans could be sold as bonds, and the
> demand for those was rapacious. (95–96)

It is now recognized that mortgage securitization and the use
of derivatives based on these mortgage securities set in motion
the cycle of lending and borrowing that inflated the bubble in
housing prices that ultimately collapsed. Perhaps at its peak,
the Goldman Sachs trader Fabrice Tourre wrote a fevered
e-mail saying, "more and more leverage in the system. The
whole building is about to collapse" (cited in Norris 2010:B4).
    There were even profits to be made from the collapse.

Underlying Insecurities

A key problem in the securitization of mortgage debt involved
predicting when and where the defaults on mortgages would
occur. The assumption was that the risks of individual losses
could be reduced by spreading the risks of defaults across a
large number of mortgages. But what if the risks of default
inside the collection of mortgages, despite the assumed dispersion, were interconnected or strongly correlated? These relationships, which remain poorly understood, had the potential to minimize or multiply risks and losses, depending on the
directions they took. For example, one approach to slicing and
dicing the mortgages mixed mortgages from different regions,

assuming that problems of employment and housing would
be localized and that diversifying across regions would spread
the risks. However, when the housing bubble burst nationwide, the risks and losses were amplified instead of reduced.

At the next higher level of derivative contracts on the securitized mortgages, the risks and losses were even harder to
predict. The largest institutional player in these derivative contracts, American International Group (AIG), became the biggest loser in the ensuing financial debacle. Again there were
warning signs. The team inside AIG that was created to develop a capital markets business in derivatives turned out to
be a group of traders who had previously worked for Drexel
Burnham Lambert, the firm that years earlier Milken and
Boesky had made infamous in the junk bond scandal (Tett
2009:62). AIG imported thirteen former Drexel employees.

The triple-A credit rating of AIG gave the former Drexel
group enormous capital to leverage in their trading of derivatives. These trades went disastrously bad, and in February
2008 AIG's auditor forced it to acknowledge a "material
weakness"—"a rather innocuous euphemism for a host of
problems . . . in its accounting methods" (Sorkin 2009:160).
Warren Buffett called the AIG derivatives "weapons of mass
destruction." The AIG trades were massively threatening because they involved counterparty exposure around the world
notionally valued at $2.7 trillion, with $1 trillion of the exposure concentrated in twelve major financial institutions.

Another financial insurance company, MBIA, also lost heavily in layered derivative contracts of "secured collateralized
debt obligations" that defied notions of transparency. MBIA
literally was dealing in "collateralized debt obligations secured by collateralized debt obligations secured by collateralized debt obligations that were secured by mortgage-backed
securities" (Norris 2009:B1)—known in the financial industry
as "C.D.O. cubed." At issue is who acted negligently if not
fraudulently in authorizing these highly structured and leveraged transactions. "By early 2007, MBIA was issuing insurance
for hundreds of millions of dollars worth of mortgage securi-

ties within less then two weeks of first being told of the pending transaction" (ibid. B8). MBIA relied on assurances it received from firms like Merrill Lynch, Countrywide Financial, and IndyMac Bank, as well as credit rating agencies such as Moody's and Standard & Poor's, about the underlying instruments. None of the assurances proved trustworthy, leaving courts and lawyers to settle who was responsible and therefore liable.

Our interest, of course, is ultimately in questions about crime. Was the promise of spreading risks through securitization of debt actually a massive fraud? Did the financial engineers of securitization understand they were actually increasing risks rather than reducing them, for example by creating a bubble in housing prices that would collapse and contribute massively to a financial crisis?

The economists George Akerlof and Paul Romer (1993) argued in the aftermath of the S&L crisis of the 1980s that private investors actually engage in "looting" when they take advantage of government in ways that they know will ultimately leave government and taxpayers to pay for the losses. They argued that the S&L managers displayed a "total disregard for even the most basic principles of lending," such as gathering and verifying information about borrowers. In the current collapse, the SEC concluded, for example, that the mortgage lender New Century knowingly "misled investors by implying that virtually all . . . borrowers had considerable equity in their homes, whereas, in fact, nearly one-third of New Century's borrowers had no equity in their homes whatsoever" (Kouwe 2009b:B4). The motivations for the deception were clear: the high-risk instruments backed with highly leveraged and borrowed capital generated enormous short-term profits and extraordinary personal bonuses. Akerlof and Romer hold that in such circumstances, executives have defrauded investors and have "acted as if future losses were somebody else's problem."

Of course, the "somebody else's problem" created by the S&L and more recent subprime crises were losses the government paid for with taxpayer-financed bailouts. The government deemed the S&Ls, and later the largest banks, too big to fail, and therefore covered their losses with government debt (Sorkin 2009). I noted in the last chapter the problem that the Government Accounting Office warned could result from the role of the New York Federal Reserve Bank in its orchestration of the bailout of the Long-Term Capital Management hedge fund. In the case of the S&Ls and then with the subprime crisis, the "looters" transferred the losses to the taxpayers, but before doing so the banks made high fees and the money managers received huge bonuses. Economists refer to this encouragement of the transfer of losses as creating a "moral hazard." Was this hazard resulting from the spreading of risk the consequence of fraudulent conspiracy or innocent optimism?

The innocence-of-optimism framing may be a latter-day version of Sutherland and Cressey's explanation of white-collar crime, which dates to the age of Roosevelt and their differential association theory, discussed in chapter 3. Cressey's more specific version of this theory was that embezzlers take other people's money only after they first rationalize their guilt. The institutional belief in spreading risk through securitizing mortgages may have been a similar kind of framing that could neutralize guilt and in this way excuse the claim of fraudulence against the bank managers. The "too big to fail" rationalization for the bailouts may be a similar kind of rationalization from the government's side. The question is whether these are causes or justifications of the practices involved. Part of the answer involves the subprime mortgages that were securitized.

Origins and Consequences of Subprime Mortgage Practices

There is an argument that the subprime crisis originated in efforts by the Clinton administration to increase home ownership among the poor. This administration made changes in 1995 to the Community Reinvestment Act of 1977, which rated banks on how much lending they did in low-income neighborhoods. Fannie Mae and Freddie Mac, government-initiated ventures in home lending, were encouraged to become involved in the securitization of subprime loans. The investment firm of Bear Stearns joined with Freddie Mac to launch the first $385 million securitization of these loans in the fall of 1997. One motivation was the expectation that increased home ownership would stabilize neighborhoods and reduce crime.

As noted earlier, the latter part of the 1990s was also a period of falling violent crime rates in the United States. There is important recent evidence from research conducted by Ruth Peterson and Lauren Krivo (2009) on more than 9,000 U.S. urban neighborhoods that indicates that increased residential investment in home ownership lowered violent crime rates, especially in African American neighborhoods in 1999–2001. Based on research in Chicago neighborhoods in the 1990s, Sampson and Wikstrom (2009) similarly argue that concentrated disadvantage and low levels of homeownership depress neighborhood levels of social control, social trust, and collective efficacy, which in turn increases rates of violence. The hope was that increasing home ownership would reduce neighborhood instability, including that attributable to neighborhood violence.

Peterson and Krivo (2009) are quite precise. They estimate from their large sample of neighborhoods that a one standard deviation increase in the amount of housing loan dollars in the 1990s resulted in a nearly 9 percent lower rate of criminal violence. They note that although the association of residential loans with crime has received little attention in previous research, "outside investments should shore up neighborhoods in ways that reduce violence." Of course, they make this observation on the assumption of a stable housing market in which families can benefit from a strengthening of the housing stock in their neighborhoods. The deregulated proliferation of subprime lending practices challenged the foundation of this assumption.

Peterson and Krivo's data come from the early years of sub-prime mortgage lending, before problems proliferated in this financial sector. George W. Bush added an ironically named Dream Downpayment Initiative in 2003 that extended the growth of mortgage lending in low-income communities. Although Bear Stearns in particular received a great deal of good publicity as it moved ahead with its mortgage securitizations, there were questions about what would happen if and when house prices fell below the value of the mortgages that were being issued to persons with limited resources to sustain them.

A landmark along the path to financial calamity was the merger of the U.S. mortgage lender Household Financial with the London-based international bank HSBC. Household Financial was already a huge lender to homeowners with credit problems and had a bad reputation for its aggressive collection tactics. Michael Lewis (2008) called this kind of "non-bank financial institution" the "lower class of American finance." The merger with HSBC came after Household Finance reached a settlement of nearly a half billion dollars in response to claims about its predatory practices.

The theory of the merger was that HSBC could use its better reputation to borrow money more cheaply and in turn benefit by giving its Household partner higher profit margins from expanded lending. William Cohan in *House of Cards* (2009a) explains that "the idea of these . . . acquisitions was to become a fully integrated mortgage factory capable of originating mortgages, servicing them, packaging them into marketable securities, and selling them off" (314).

This is a kind of advantage that is often sought in the vertical integration of industries and markets. To maximize advantage in a housing market that was already beginning to slow, HSBC heavily bought and securitized loans that others besides Household Finance had originated. The pressures exerted from the top down in this kind of expansion can create what has been called a criminogenic market structure (see Farberman 1975). The point is that top-down pressures can lead to unethical practices, such as steering customers into disadvantageous credit arrangements. A further advantage at the top level of the vertical integration is the distancing of the leadership from the responsibility of direct knowledge about the effects of the application of pressure and the resulting practices at the bottom. The chairman of the Federal Reserve Bank, Ben Bernanke, has conceded that "In the area where we had responsibility . . . we should have done more" (quoted in Andrews 2009:B1).

Problems became apparent at HSBC in 2007, when Household Financial revealed that the pattern of defaults it had begun to observe contradicted the predictions of its risk models. The mix of "bad" loans with "good" loans became increasingly costly, and HSBC ultimately had to close many of its recently acquired Household offices. Before the dust had settled, however, HSBC had played a major role in popularizing the subprime securitization model.

The vertical integration of the mortgage securitization industry was profitable and rapacious in its growth, as illustrated by the expansion of Merrill Lynch's CDO operation:

> Creating and selling CDOs generated lucrative fees for Merrill, just as it had for other banks. But even this wasn't enough. Merrill sought to be a full-line producer: issuing mortgages, packaging them into securities, and then slicing and dicing them into CDOs. The firm began buying up mortgage servicers and commercial real estate firms, more than thirty in all, and in December 2006, it acquired one of the biggest subprime mortgage lenders in the nation, First Franklin, for 1.3 billion. (Sorkin 2009:144–45)

Merrill just as rapidly began to implode in 2008 and was acquired in turn by Bank of America.

Lehman Brothers was the top-ranking loan originator on Wall Street, and its leadership exerted intense pressure downward through its mortgage-origination arm, Aurora Loan

Services. Aurora assembled 400-person sales teams to stock-pile high-risk, high-cost mortgages for repackaging through the firm's financial division. The top-down growth imperative led supervisors to lower Aurora's pricing and credit standards, for example, encouraging "no-doc loans" for borrowers with undocumented incomes. A senior vice-president reported the pressure to approve these loans: "Anyone at our level who had a different view from senior management would find themselves going somewhere else quick . . . you are not paid to rock the boat" (Story and Thomas 2009:B7).

Because institutions resold, mixed, and traded so many sub-prime mortgages in the secondary securitization market, it became difficult for homeowners or anyone else to be certain who owned their loans. This is a crucial point at which digital technology became an enabling part of the story. A national data system, Mortgage Electronic Registration Systems (MERS), was designed to facilitate this secondary market and today holds sixty million mortgages on American homes. This system now makes it difficult for either homeowners or regulators to track predatory lenders (McIntire 2009:B1; see also Morgenson 2009c). Mortgage brokers worked extensively with MERS and often steered their clients to high-priced loans of the kind noted above. A recent report indicates that borrowers who used brokers paid added interest payments ranging from $17,000 to $43,000 for every $100,000 they borrowed (*New York Times* 2009). Who are the borrowers victimized by these predatory practices?

The NAACP charged in a class action suit that more than a dozen of America's largest banks used expensive and onerous loan products, including subprime loans, in systematically discriminating against African American and Latino American homeowners. The NAACP charges that this is a new form of housing discrimination. In the 1960s, many banks drew red lines (the origin of the term "redlining") on maps around black neighborhoods where they refused even to make home loans (Satter 2009). The NAACP charges these same banks now targeted many of the same black neighborhoods for subprime loans, even including black middle-class homeowners who did not need these types of loans. Mortgage lenders recognized that blacks who were historically redlined from receiving home loans might now be susceptible, ready-made customers for the new manipulative mortgages.

In a series of articles, the *New York Times*'s Michael Powell (2009a, b, c, 2010) exposed the extent of these practices. He reported that even black households in New York City making more than $68,000 a year were almost five times more likely than whites with similar or lower incomes to hold high-interest subprime loans. The loans victimized both middle- and working-class blacks and Latinos. People of color are three times more likely to have subprime home loans, and more than half of the home loans held by people of color are high-cost loans. Advocacy groups estimate that black homeowners lost from $71 to $93 billion in home wealth even before the subprime crisis and that Latinos lost a similar amount (Rivera et al. 2008). The resulting defaults and foreclosures paradoxically pose new risks to the prior stabilization of minority neighborhoods that accounted for violent crime reductions identified by Peterson and Krivo. "You drive through our neighborhoods and it's just palpable," observed the mayor of Memphis. "You see a strong emerging black home-owning community that's gone" (quoted in Powell 2009c).

In Baltimore and Memphis, Powell (2009b, c) reported on lawsuits against Wells Fargo Bank. This bank was alleged to have a "ghetto loans" program and "an emerging-markets unit" that specifically targeted black churches because "it figured church leaders had a lot of influence and could convince congregants to take out sub-prime loans." An affidavit in the Baltimore suit quotes a Wells Fargo loan officer as saying that in 2001, the bank "created a unit in the mid-Atlantic region to push expensive refinancing loans on black customers" (Powell 2009b). The allegation is that Wells Fargo profited from a minority ill-founded belief in the promise of the American dream of home ownership. A federal judge dismissed the initial comprehensive suit, but he also said Baltimore officials could still file neighborhood-specific claims. A lawyer for the city said, "We are not saying Wells is responsible for . . . all the deterioration of the neighborhoods . . . we are simply saying that they are engaged in illegal conduct" (quoted in Powell 2010).

The national growth in subprime mortgage lending was pernicious. As Friend (2009:36) writes, "In 2006, two of five first-time home buyers in California put no money down, relying on a variety of 'loan products' whose nicknames foretold trouble, at least in retrospect: 'liar loans'; 'piggyback loans'; 'neg am loans'; 'Ninja loans' (No Income, No Job or Assets); and 'exploding' or 'suicide' loans." Two years later, more than a quarter of these loans nationwide were in default or foreclosure, placing the entire banking system in jeopardy (Overbye 2009).

Foreclosures on these loans represent a serious threat to neighborhood stability, as evidenced by the research of Peterson and Krivo (2009). The scenario is grim:

> In West Philadelphia, Councilman Curtis Jones Jr. . . . watched his neighborhood consumed by foreclosure, as the homes of working families—their porches once lined with flower pots—were boarded up with plywood. . . . "It becomes a blight on your entire community," Mr. Jones said, "It creates an environment that fosters everything bad, from prostitution to drug dealing. . . . One house becomes 10, and 10 becomes the whole block." (Goodman 2009:A26)

This story rippled through American low-income and minority neighborhoods.

Probably America's most prestigious investment bank, Goldman Sachs, paid $60 million to end an investigation by the state of Massachusetts into its subprime practices. Goldman Sachs itself issued more than $33 billion in mortgage-backed securities that packaged subprime mortgages. Beyond this, Goldman Sachs financed other subprime lenders, including Option One, which is cited in the NAACP suit for systematically discriminating against black homeowners (Buckley 2009; Wayne 2009). A prominent Wall Street analyst (Zuckerman 2009) claims Goldman further created specialized collateralized debt obligations that it propitiously sold in anticipation of the housing collapse. Goldman Sachs may have used a similar strategy to bet on a default by the government of Greece on its international debt (*New York Times* 2010).

In the United States, investigations of Goldman Sachs have focused on whether this powerhouse Wall Street firm actually created synthetic CDOs, named Abacus, that were sold with the expectation that they would lose rather than make money, and often very quickly. The charge is that in violation of securities laws or rules of fair dealing, Goldman may have "sold these mortgage linked debt instruments and then bet against the clients who purchased them" (Morgenson and Story 2009; see also Lewis 2010). Since Congress deregulated derivatives in 2000, such deceitful practices may actually have been legal. The "bets" consisted of the purchase of insurance that guaranteed Goldman would receive payments in the event of defaults on the CDOs that the firm created for its clients. Goldman was allegedly able to structure "some Abacus deals in a way that enabled those betting on a mortgage-market collapse [i.e., including Goldman] to multiply the value of their bets, to as much as six or seven times the face value of those CDOs." Goldman was certainly far from alone in "shorting" securitized mortgages by betting on their collapse with purchases of insurance (Zuckerman 2009). In probably the single biggest short of this kind and period, a Deutsche Bank trader turned an $11 million position into $3.7 billion (Lewis 2010). The effect may have been to amplify the broader collapse in mortgage-backed securities. Lewis Sachs, a senior adviser to current treasury secretary Geithner, led a firm called Tricadia that created these instruments.

Are these business practices by America's financial institutions criminal? Mortgage fraud is an elusive term, and suits like those described above are usually filed in civil courts in an attempt to gain compensation for homeowners instead of seeking to impose the stigma of criminal convictions. Yet Edwin Sutherland (1949) regarded distinctions between civil and criminal jurisdictions as largely irrelevant for the purposes of criminologists, who are more interested in the actual behaviors than in the prosecutorial choice between kinds of courts and charges. A growing number of court decisions indicate that some banks are liable for civil if not criminal fraud.

Gretchen Morgenson (2009b) has traced several of these cases. Probably the best known is a jury trial involving the aggressive home lender First Alliance and its principal source of capital investment from Lehman Brothers. Both firms have since failed, but at their peak they represented a vertically integrated "joint enterprise" of massively costly proportions. Morgenson writes that "More than 7,500 borrowers had successfully sued First Alliance for fraud, and in 2003 a jury found that Lehman, which had lent First Alliance roughly $500 million over the years to finance its lending, 'substantially assisted' it in its fraudulent activities. Lehman was ordered to pay $5.1 million or 10 percent of damages in the case, for its role."

Morgenson refers to a further 2004 case involving Wells Fargo Bank acting as the trustee in financing a similar kind of abusive lending operation. The case was eventually settled under terms that identified Wells Fargo as having acted in a "joint venture" with the originator of the loans and therefore as being responsible for the results. "Joint criminal enterprise" is a legal concept that earlier was advanced by the criminologist Donald Cressey to reflect and prosecute the kind of vertically and horizontally structured crimes perpetrated by organized crime groups. Morgenson concludes that "eager for the profits generated by originating these loans, big firms bought subprime lenders to keep their securitization machinery humming," and that "this could expose the firms' liability."

A narrow 5–4 U.S. Supreme Court decision in June 2009 involving the Clearing House Association, a consortium of national banks, gave states authority over national lenders. Since then, state attorneys general have pursued a prosecution theory that banks perpetrated massive frauds on borrowers by offering exotic loans that the borrowers in the long term could not afford to pay back. This did not deter the lenders, because they did not retain these mortgages but repackaged them for resale as securitized mortgages. Illinois attorney general Lisa Madigan used this prosecution theory to file a civil rights case alleging Wells Fargo of predatory lending. This case was already in preparation before the Clearing House Supreme Court decision, but the decision made the path to prosecution less difficult, and more difficult for Wells Fargo to evade with national protection from state regulation. The Bush administration comptroller of the currency had issued rule changes in 2004 that protected national banks against state regulation and prosecution under predatory lending laws (Streitfeld and Rudlof 2009).

The Case of Angelo Mozilo

One of the highest-profile cases yet filed involves charges against Angelo Mozilo, the CEO of Countrywide Financial, for securities fraud and insider trading. The charges in this case were filed in a civil case by the SEC and did not initially include criminal charges by the Justice Department—but these may follow. While criminal law requires proof "beyond reasonable doubt," civil law relies on a less burdensome "balance of probabilities." Again, as Sutherland emphasized, social science is based on behavioral probabilities and does not demand legal certainty. Sutherland helped us understand that criminology is concerned with establishing and explaining systematic patterns of criminal behavior rather than with convicting individuals of crimes.

Mozilo is an important figure in the age of Reagan for several reasons: because he was so prominent in the secondary markets of securitized mortgages, because the evidence of his fraudulent behavior in these markets is so compelling, and because he exemplifies so well the role framing processes can play in defending and explaining how financiers of massive frauds often remain free to commit their crimes.

The prominent business magazine that is aptly called *Fortune* played a significant role in elevating Angelo Mozilo from a faintly disreputable financier to lofty status in the mortgage industry. It did so with a story in 2003 titled "Meet the 23,000% Stock," which celebrated Mozilo's Countrywide Financial Corporation as having "the best stock market performance of any financial services company in the Fortune 500, measured from the start of the Great Bull Market over two decades ago."

Fortune lionized Mozilo for accomplishing his financial goals despite being a relative outsider to the financial elite, and for advancing the previously underappreciated money-making potential of home loans. Buck (2009:46) writes that "by 2003 Wall Street had become addicted to home loans, which bankers used to create immensely lucrative mortgage-backed securities and, later, collateralized debt obligations, or C.D.O.s—and Countywide was their biggest supplier. Suddenly, Mozilo seemed almost an insider." One indication of his insider status was Mozilo's friendship with Democratic senators Chris Dodd, chairman of the Senate Banking Committee, and Kent Conrad, chairman of the Senate Budget Committee. Both senators were put into a special category of customers called "friends of Angelo" and received favorable financing for their homes (Hernandez 2009:A12). A senate ethics committee chastised both Dodd and Conrad for failing to avoid "appearances of impropriety" (Herszenhorn 2009:A9).

The fraud involving Mozilo in the Countrywide case is that although he publicly portrayed the company as a prime quality mortgage lender with high underwriting standards, in his private e-mail communications he acknowledged the reckless nature of the risks he was increasingly pursuing in developing the company's loan products. For example, in 2006 Mozilo informed his Countrywide colleagues by e-mail that loans had been written without regard for the company's guidelines. He described as "poison" subprime second mortgages that Countrywide had issued with no down payments by the borrowers. Mozilo explicitly described such practices in his e-mail as so risky that "the bottom line is that we are flying blind on how these loans will perform in a stressed environment of higher unemployment, reduced values and slowing homesales" (Morgenson 2009a:A3).

These e-mails make explicit what otherwise would need to be inferred and could therefore be denied about practices by Countrywide and other subprime lenders. Although the concept of criminal fraud is uncertain in definition and proof, *Black's Law Dictionary* places its emphasis on gaining advantage by false suggestions or suppression of the truth. Mozilo's e-mails offer unusually explicit and compelling evidence that he knowingly manipulated the truth in just this way. Yet Mozilo's public image was framed quite differently by himself and others.

Mozilo's personal biography was framed as an exercise of entrepreneurship in the service of home ownership for all. In thousands of speeches, Mozilo described himself as the son of a Bronx butcher whose family was too poor to own a home (Buck 2009). Mozilo's public mission was to find ways of lowering the barriers for minorities and others to gain access to home ownership by broadening access to loans. As we have noted, this was a theme emphasized in the Clinton and Bush administrations as well.

Mozilo argued that extending home ownership could be simultaneously altruistic and profitable. He insisted that "he wanted all of Countrywide's employees to feel that mortgages were not just loans but a way of improving people's lives" (Buck 2009:49). Countrywide designed commercials specifically for prospective black homeowners. It was no accident that some of the most prolific buyers of Countrywide's mortgages in the secondary market were government agencies such as Fannie Mae, Freddie Mac, and Ginnie Mae. Mozilo's practices had effects that radiated far beyond Countrywide.

The Financial Crisis Hits

Countrywide was the largest independent mortgage broker in America when it revealed in August 2007 that rates of defaults and foreclosures were hitting high levels and that it was having difficulty selling its mortgage-backed bonds. At last, and in the face of the signs of growing problems, observers of the banking industry were beginning to ask questions and express doubts. Citibank, which had grown dramatically in size, had established seven shadow banks, or structured investment vehicles, which held $100 billion in assets. However, by the fall of 2007 the problems of the banking sector had extended far beyond Citibank to include redoubtable institutions such as Merrill Lynch.

At first it seemed that foreign funding for a financial sector bailout might merely involve an embarrassment to America's sense of national sovereignty. The Abu Dhabi Investment fund injected capital into Citibank, and a Chinese government fund invested in Merrill Lynch. Yet these investments from abroad were not enough to stem the tide of mounting losses and a growing panic. Tett (2009:210) explains that a pernicious feedback loop was developing: "The essential problem was that the system was becoming trapped in a vicious spiral. The more that the banks revealed losses . . . the more scared investors became, causing the prices of the assets to fall still further, which forced the banks to make more write-downs." The business press and its readers were coming to realize that the "derivative dream" of the age of Reagan—namely, that investment risks had been spread and vastly diminished if not eliminated through the magic of the market and its models—was highly flawed. Rather, risks and losses aggregated and multiplied.

Bear Stearns was caught in the middle of these events in March 2008 by its concentration on mortgage debt and its reliance on short-term credit markets for operating capital. The strategy, which worked well until lenders observed the growing weakness in the mortgage securitizations and derivatives, involved borrowing huge sums in low-cost short-term capital markets to finance longer-term mortgage obligations. As Reinhart and Rogoff (2009:145) persuasively demonstrate, "The implosion of the U.S. financial system during 2007–2008 came about precisely because many financial firms outside the traditional and regulated banking sector financed their illiquid investments using short-term borrowing."

Because it was not a commercial bank, Bear Stearns did not have access to capital loans from the Federal Reserve Bank of New York to cover its shortfall in capital. Perhaps also as a result of the refusal of Bear Stearns to cooperate a decade earlier in the rescue of Long-Term Capital Management, the New York Federal Reserve Bank was not sympathetic to Bear's plight (Cohan 2009a:chap. 21). Bear Stearns was known in the industry for its fierce aggressiveness and competitiveness. If the "greed is good" and "survival of the fittest" mantra of the junk bond era endured anywhere in the world of investment banking, it was at Bear Stearns. Now entirely on its own, Bear was sinking instead of swimming. Tim Geithner as head of the Federal Reserve Bank of New York developed a heavily subsidized plan for acquisition of Bear Stearns by J.P. Morgan, led by the increasingly influential Jamie Dimon.

In September 2008, the government allowed Lehman Brothers to collapse without a government bailout. It later became apparent that Lehman Brothers had used a highly dubious accounting procedure called Repo 105 under the eyes of SEC officials and with the help of the New York Federal Reserve Bank to disguise the demise of its toxic assets (Sorkin 2010). Sorkin's (2009) chronicle of this sequence concluded, however, that after the Bear Stearns bailout, Treasury Secretary Paulson felt he could not be seen as "Mr. Bailout" (282) and instead "needed to make it clear to all the other banks that there would no handouts, no more 'Jamie Deals'" (286). Lehman's collapse rocked financial markets beyond expectations. AIG, the giant insurer of many of the derivative trades that were going bad throughout the banking world, was now also near default.

Under the collective weight of these problems, stock markets around the world faltered and financial institutions began to freeze up, refusing to take on any new debt. The combined effect was the largest economic breakdown since the 1929 Wall Street crash.

Soon the federal government had to step in and finance the series of bailouts that staved off the collapse of AIG, Citibank, Bank of America, and a number other financial institutions. Part of the bailout of Bank of America involved it taking over the failing Merrill Lynch. This part of the government bailout wound up exposing one of the many objectionable executive compensation arrangements that became public knowledge during the financial collapse.

When the SEC announced the Bank of America takeover of Merrill, the representation to stockholders was that executives at Merrill would receive no year-end bonuses. Yet lawyers had actually drafted a schedule of "exceptions" for billions of dollars in bonuses. The lawyers, however, did not attach the schedule to the proxy materials. One Bank of America director e-mailed another that "Unfortunately, it's screw the shareholders!!" (Story and Dash 2009).

The deal exemplified a contemporary Wall Street aphorism called IBG—"I'll be gone"—about short-term reward strategies that in the longer term could lead to bankruptcy. Bank of America later explained that its lawyers advised its executives not to disclose the bonuses, and paid a fine in a settlement with the SEC. A *New York Times* opinion piece suggested that "although the deal was probably necessary to help get us through the financial crisis, everything about it has seemed a little fishy" (Nocera 2009:B2). SEC rules explicitly prohibit acts or omissions that result in fraud or deceit in relation to the purchase or sale of a security (Cohan 2009b:65). An appeals court judge subsequently voided the settlement in an apparent rebuke of both Bank of America and the SEC (Kouwe 2009b).

Two financial institutions seemed to have survived and even fared well when the dust began to settle: J.P. Morgan and

Goldman Sachs. This too raised questions. Jamie Dimon, head of J.P. Morgan, had said that good government relations were his firm's "seventh line of business." To illustrate the potential influence of this business strategy, Gillian Tett (2009: 245) describes a cocktail party hosted by Dimon for 200 key clients and contacts at the 2009 World Economic Forum in Davos, Switzerland: "As J.P. Morgan's guests nibbled on canapés in the Piano Bar, Al Gore, an adviser to the bank, could be seen mingling in the crowds. So could Tony Blair, another well-paid new adviser." Dimon also nurtured relationships from his Chicago banking days with William H. Daley, the former commerce secretary and Obama campaign strategist, and with Rahm Emanuel, who, after serving in the Clinton administration and before returning to Congress and to be President Obama's chief of staff, is said to have made $16 million in two years of investment banking.

It was therefore worrisome that in an article about Morgan's government-leveraged acquisition of Bear Stearns, a business writer drew a parallel to the politics of the S&L scandal. The *Barron's* article speculated that "Jamie Dimon appears to have pulled off the coup of his career. The best analogy for the Bear Stearns deal could be the government-orchestrated takeovers of savings and loans in the late 1980s that turned out to be windfalls for well-connected buyers" (cited in Cohan 2009a:125).

The Deregulated Freedom of Higher Responsibilities

How high does the responsibility for the financial collapse reach? The age of Reagan argued that the free market could impose necessary restraint on financial services and that little further government regulation was needed. In the age of Reagan, regulators largely left individual borrowers and the investment institutions to their own protection. As for the latter institutions, Lawrence Summers, when he was deputy secretary of the treasury in the Clinton administration, opined that "the parties to these kinds of contract are largely sophisticated financial institutions that would appear to be eminently capable of protecting themselves from fraud and counterparty insolvencies" (cited in Lanchester 2009:85). The financial crisis thoroughly tested this optimistic age of Reagan assessment and found it seriously deficient.

For example, most financial experts now agree that a major source of the economic collapse was the Clinton-era extension of age of Reagan deregulation that exempted derivatives trading from regulatory oversight. Derivatives became the monsters that devoured Wall Street: they not only threatened to bring down huge financial institutions like AIG, they also created a node interconnecting major institutions worldwide in ways that threatened the world system.

Neither the SEC nor the Department of Justice took serious responsibility for monitoring the explosive growth of the financial sector and the mortgage industry during the age of Reagan. The SEC notoriously failed to detect the $50 billion Ponzi scheme executed by Bernard Madoff until late 2008, despite five investigations over sixteen years and one prominent and detailed tip by a private fraud investigator in 2000. The inspector general of the SEC confirmed in 2009 congressional testimony that Madoff had told investors his fund must be credible because it successfully endured repeated SEC investigations.

The SEC also overlooked problems in the private ratings services such as Moody's and Standard and Poor's that evaluated the quality of the new investment instruments and institutions. The investment institutions paid the fees that supported the ratings agencies, in a transparent conflict of interest. These agencies gave high ratings to many institutions such as Countrywide Financial Corporation in the lead-up to the subprime debacle, exposing the ways in which conflicts of interest undermined the independence, objectivity, transparency, and therefore protective benefit of this kind of self-regulation. Cohan (2009a:332) quoted a Bear Stearns partner as remarking "it would be like cattle ranchers paying the Department of Agriculture to rate the quality and safety of their beef." The same partner completed this metaphor by concluding that "subprime credit has become the mad cow disease of structured finance."

The SEC released a 2007 e-mail exchange between two Standard and Poor's analysts, Rahul Shah and Shannon Mooney, as further evidence of the disturbing practices of the ratings agencies. The exchange began with Shah writing Mooney, "By the way, that deal was ridiculous." Mooney replied, "I know right—[the] model def[initely] does not capture half of the risk." Shah responded, "We should not be rating it." Mooney nonetheless answered, "We rate every deal. It could be structured by cows and we would rate it" (Cohan 2009a:331–32). The agencies rushed to correct their ratings when their inadequacy became fully apparent.

Thus the ratings agencies rapidly downgraded their estimates of subprime products as the financial collapse began, and this further fueled the collapse. James Surowiecki (2009:25) calculates that "In the space of just a few months between late 2007 and mid-2008 (after the housing bubble burst), the agencies collectively downgraded an astonishing $1.9 trillion in mortgage backed securities: some securities that had carried a AAA rating one day were downgraded to CCC the next." Regulations on holdings of low-rated securities based on the ratings now forced the major institutional investors to sell them while preventing other institutions from buying them, even at low valuations. The regulations were counterproductive, accelerating the crash in subprime securities by relying on a badly flawed ratings system. Surowiecki concludes that "working with a fake safety net is more dangerous than working without any net at all" (25).

Several state attorneys general in Ohio and California are pressing lawsuits against Moody's Investors Service, Standard & Poor's, and Fitch ratings agencies, which frequently gave triple-A ratings to bonds based on securitized mortgages that often proved worthless, or nearly so. Ratings agencies, in a blatant conflict of interest noted earlier, receive fees from the issuers of the securities they appraise. "Given that the ratings agencies did not receive their full fees for a deal unless the deal was completed and the requested rating was provided," Ohio's attorney general concluded, "they had an acute financial incentive to relax their stated standards of 'integrity' and 'objectivity' to placate their clients" (Segal 2009a:B6). Connecticut's attorney general threatened a "coalition of states" would sue the ratings agencies (Segal 2009b:A20). The ratings agencies argue they merely issue "opinions" protected under the First Amendment, but this protection is a dubious defense against deliberate financial manipulation that otherwise could be called fraud.

A further example of flawed regulation brings us full circle to the S&L scandal. This case involves Darrel Dochow and his role in the Office of Thrift Supervision (OTS), which oversaw the IndyMac Bank that failed in California in 2008. Dochow had improperly allowed IndyMac to plug a hole that its auditors had belatedly found in its financial reserves. IndyMac's problems went unregulated until its takeover by the Federal Deposit Insurance Corporation with an accumulated loss of nearly $9 million. Years earlier, Dochow had played a central role in voiding a recommendation to seize Lincoln Savings and Loan, the institution owned by Charles Keating that became the infamous focal point of the S&L crisis.

The events of the financial crisis and the age of Reagan raise many questions. In particular, they raise questions about the ability of powerful interests to frame important policy issues and determine their outcomes. This capacity for Congress and enforcement agencies to become pawns of the financial industry they are supposed to oversee is known as "regulatory capture." An illustration of this risk is the record of contacts that occurred between the Bush administration secretary of the treasury and former CEO of Goldman Sachs, Henry Paulson, and his successor as CEO of Goldman Sachs, Lloyd Blankfein, during the mid-September 2008 peak of the financial crisis. Because of his prior role in Goldman Sachs and because he still was slated to receive pension benefits from this firm, Paulson signed and then later obtained a waiver from an agreement not to consult with Goldman as treasury secretary. Sorkin (2009:424) reports that Paulson had hoped to keep this waiver secret.

According to *New York Times* reporting (Morgenson and Van Natta 2009), the phone records during the week of the AIG bailout include twenty-four calls between Paulson and Blankfein. Paulson had appointed Blankfein as his replacement after the announcement of his nomination as treasury secretary in 2006. At Treasury, Paulson surrounded himself with former colleagues from Goldman Sachs, including Dan Jester and Ken Wilson. The government transmitted almost $13 billion to Goldman Sachs through AIG following its bailout, in addition to $10 billion from the Troubled Assets Relief Program (TARP) and other guarantees and borrowing benefits. Jester spearheaded the shift in use of the TARP funds from acquisition of troubled assets to direct capital injection into the banks, including Goldman (Sorkin 2009:500). Wilson came up with the recommendation of Ed Liddy, a former Goldman board member, as the new CEO of AIG (ibid. 397).

The $700 billion TARP legislation, drafted as the largest one-shot expenditure in the history of the federal government, was crafted and implemented by Neil Kaskari, a former investment banker with Goldman Sachs. The TARP legislation was so brief and open-ended in the unchecked authority it gave to Treasury Secretary Paulson that Tom Brokaw asked him on *Meet the Press*, "If you were in your old job as Chairman of Goldman Sachs and you took this deal to the Partners they'd send you out of the room and say, 'come back when you've got a lot more answers,' wouldn't they?" (Sorkin 2009:471).

Treasury Secretary Paulson worked closely with his successor and the then president of the Federal Reserve Bank of New York, Timothy Geithner, on the AIG bailout. A Special Inspector General's Report (Barofsky 2009) revealed that the Federal

Reserve Bank of New York "refused to use its considerable leverage" with the counterparties to AIG, such as Goldman Sachs, "because FRBNY was acting on behalf of AIG as opposed to in its role as a regulator" (29). The report went on to say that "these policies came with a cost—they led directly to a negotiating strategy with the counterparties that even then-FRBNY President Geithner acknowledged had little likelihood of success" (29).

The report also notes that Federal Reserve Bank of New York refused to release the identities of the counterparties—with Goldman Sachs receiving the largest amount (nearly $13 billion) in what the report calls a "backdoor bailout"—until Congress forced their disclosure by AIG. Throughout, then Federal Reserve Bank of New York president Geithner insisted that Goldman Sachs did not need the backdoor bailout because its potential losses were otherwise "hedged." When asked if he had closely examined Goldman's hedges, he said he had not: he had relied on the assessment of Goldman's chief financial officer relayed to him in a phone conversation (Morgenson 2009a:B6).

A spokesperson for Goldman Sachs explained the phone contacts with the treasury secretary in the following way: "Lloyd Blankfein, like the C.E.O.'s of other major financial institutions, received calls from, and made calls to, Treasury to provide a market perspective on conditions and events as they were unfolding." Yet Treasury Secretary Paulson's contacts with CEO Blankfein were far more frequent than his contacts with other Wall Street executives.

The point is that Paulson's framing of the bailout, which materially benefited Goldman Sachs with taxpayer money, was at a minimum well informed by the input of the CEO of Goldman Sachs. When the Democratic Obama administration's Tim Geithner replaced the Republican administration's Paulson, the pattern did not change much. Geithner's daily calendar revealed that in the first half of 2009, his contacts were highly concentrated with Goldman Sachs, Citigroup, and J.P. Morgan (Apuzzo and Wagner 2009).

The Power and Control of the Feared and the Free

The age of Reagan featured a frame realignment process that simultaneously advocated more severe punishment of U.S. street crimes and the deregulation of American financial practices. The result was an institutional redistribution of risk and regulation. American minorities and the poor lost out in two ways: they were prosecuted and incarcerated for street crimes at massively increased rates, and they were victimized by evolving forms of financial manipulation, including subprime mortgages and similar kinds of lending arrangements for credit cards, cars, and related loans.

The age of Reagan imposed a realignment of conceptions of the "good" and the "bad" in American life. The Reagan administration vilified risk-taking on our city streets even as it valorized risk-taking in our nation's financial suites. The consequences played out in growing evidence of socioeconomic inequality. When we simultaneously appraise the consequences in the streets and the suites, the full redistributive effects of the age of Reagan reframing of American life become apparent.

In the preceding chapter, I traced the political and racial roots of the realignment of the regulation of street and suite crimes to the early years of the age of Reagan and the election campaign of Ronald Reagan for governor of California in 1966. Many of the policies and consequences of the age of Reagan that realigned the criminal control of city streets and simultaneously deregulated the financial suites remain in place today. I have also shown that the age of Reagan had perhaps surprisingly robust sources of bipartisan political support. Furthermore, the implications of the age of Reagan extend well beyond the shores of the American continent.

Sometimes explicitly and sometimes implicitly, this and the preceding chapter have posed questions about possibilities and responsibilities that extend beyond an age of Reagan. The age of Roosevelt challenged narrow ideas about "gangsters" with broadened images of "banksters," and it is notable that bankers during the Depression faced both criminal and civil prosecutions when their banks failed. Now as then, it is possible to reframe our understanding of the feared and the fearless, and I have argued that a key step in doing so is to emphasize the link between the two. A new cycle of reform can rebalance the ledgers of the twenty-first century by reconsidering our conceptions of the feared and the fearless. A critical collective framing perspective is an explanatory pathway toward this goal.

Chapter 7
Crime Wars, War Crimes, and State Crimes

It is not in the Sudanese culture
or people of Darfur to rape.
It doesn't exist. We do not have it.

—President of Sudan Omar al-Bashir

I can't sit down and remain silent
when it is said
that an Iraqi woman was raped. . . .
This couldn't happen
while Suddam Hussein is alive.

—Former President of Iraq Saddam Hussein

I've said to the people that we don't torture,
and we don't.

—Former President George W. Bush

We also have to work, though,
sort of the dark side, if you will. . . .
It's going to be vital for us to use any means
at our disposal, basically, to achieve our objective.

—Former Vice President Richard Cheney

THE FRAMING PROCESSES discussed so far have ranged widely across America's social landscape, from the nation's streets to its business suites. This chapter looks beyond the demonization of our city streets and the deregulation of our corporate suites to the international landscape of war, state crime, and international law. The expanded view casts into relief a framing competition between the *denial* and *deflection* of responsibility for war crimes by state perpetrators and an opposing *denunciation* by international legal bodies. Although war crimes are discussed broadly, for purposes of illustration, the discussion primarily addresses the responsibility of states for torture and the more specific crimes of sexual violence and rape, including what I call state rape.

|||||||||||

Although much of the age of Reagan involved the war against street crime in America and a concomitant deregulation of U.S. financial suites, the Reagan administration also, of course, aggressively pursued international agendas. For example, the Iran–Contra arms scandal linked narcoterrorism to the perceived global threat of Communist aggression, while the deregulation of the corporate suites linked American Reaganism to the like-minded influence in Europe of British Thatcherism.

So, when the 9/11 attackers struck, the Bush administration's continuation of the Reagan administration's domestic war on street crime expanded with ease and alacrity into an international war on terrorism. The smoothness of the transition was as predictable as the successive and lasting popularity of Clint Eastwood's domestic *Dirty Harry* movies in the 1970s and the international exploits of Kiefer Sutherland's Jack Bauer in *24* after 9/11. Much of the logic of the war on street crime reappeared, magnified, in the war on terrorism. Thus, the skepticism and disregard for legal due process that characterized the war on terrorism mirrored the earlier age of Reagan disdain for the legal rights of street criminals. This taken-for-granted dismissal of legality was so much part of the rush to war after 9/11 that it obscured the realization that a militaristic framing excluded other important considerations. While commentators often compared 9/11 to Pearl Harbor, few observed that the victims of the former were nearly all civilians, whereas the Pearl Harbor victims were overwhelmingly soldiers. This difference could have led to a further framing of 9/11 as a widespread and systematic attack on civilians constituting an international crime against humanity.

Wesley Clark, the U.S. general turned politician who led the NATO forces in Bosnia, advanced an international law framing of attacks on civilians in global conflicts in the Democratic Party primaries in the run-up to the 2004 election (Clark 2001), and John Kerry alluded to this rule-of-law framing as the candidate. General Clark's wartime experience symbolized an effort to combine military and legal priorities. However, the Bush administration characterized this kind of legal concern as "pre 9/11" thinking and insisted that the urgency of war superseded international law.

The Bush administration adopted an exclusive adversarial frame of retribution and incapacitation through war. This allowed the Bush administration to rush into the war on terrorism at a pace that rivaled the deregulation of financial practices during the age of Reagan. This war framing included Richard Cheney's move to "the dark side," indicated in the epigraph at the head of this chapter and in Sean Wilentz's analysis:

> In the continuing War on Terror, [Vice President] Cheney remarked that it was sometimes necessary to go to the "dark side." The Bush White House did so, but in unprecedented ways; Bush authorized the detention of thousands of suspects in secret CIA prisons around the world, where they were denied legal due process. He ended the United States adherence to the venerable international Geneva Conventions outlawing torture—provisions that the White House legal counsel (and later attorney general) Alberto Gonzales dismissed as "quaint." In 2006,

Bush derided as "vague" Common Article Three of the
Geneva Conventions, which spelled out the prohibition
of torture. (Wilentz 2008:442)

The Bush administration added a preemptive logic for its war
on terrorism:

> Under what became known as the Bush Doctrine, the
> United States would now assume the right to embark uni-
> laterally on preventive war against any nation it deemed
> a potential threat, while also placing a special emphasis
> on extending democracy, free markets, and security to
> "every corner of the world." (ibid. 442)

The Bush administration thus subordinated the option of in-
tervening in Iraq on grounds of Saddam Hussein's mass atrocities and violations of international humanitarian law and
instead staked urgent plans for war on false claims about
the existence of weapons of mass destruction, including the
presumed threat of Iraq's "soon-to-be-mobilized" nuclear
weapons.

Eventually, however, concerns about war crimes and the
rule of law reclaimed their place in debates over the war on
terrorism. In this chapter, I take up these concerns in relation
to war crimes and international criminal law in two international settings, pre-invasion Iraq and Sudan. American involvements in these two settings, of course, have varied, and
the settings themselves differ not only in political and economic development but also in the social organization of the
crime problems they have confronted, such as torture, sexual
violence, and rape.

The Bush administration selectively employed international
criminal law to call the mass atrocities that peaked in 2003–4 in
the Darfur region of Sudan genocide. It did so at approximately the same time that the United States was leading the
invasion and occupation of Iraq. This chapter focuses on the

rapes and sexual violence in President Omar al-Bashir's Darfur and in the pre-invasion Baathist regime of Saddam Hussein in Iraq, but I focus first on the postinvasion U.S.-led torture and sexual violence at Abu Ghraib prison. The Bush administration's denials and deflection of responsibility for torture and sexual violence in postinvasion Iraq involved disclaiming the migration of outlawed torture techniques from Washington to the prison and interrogation camp at Guantánamo Bay, Cuba, and on to the Abu Ghraib prison in Iraq.

Scenes from Abu Ghraib Prison

Abu Ghraib, on the outskirts of Baghdad, was the most important prison of Saddam Hussein's pre-invasion Baathist regime. High-level political prisoners shared space in this prison with thousands of other Iraqis. It was a factory for terror, torture, and executions, with the latter scheduled twice weekly. After removing Saddam's portraits and rebuilding Abu Ghraib, the United States resumed operation of this prison, with its unfortunate lingering symbolism. The U.S. military called the prisoners at Abu Ghraib "security detainees" to emphasize that they were "unlawful combatants," the war on terrorism framing that denied its enemies the provision of Geneva Convention protections. Amnesty International first reported abuse of prisoners at the refurbished and U.S.-run Abu Ghraib prison in June 2003, but conditions soon worsened.

The commander of the Guantánamo Bay prison, Geoffrey Miller, visited the Abu Ghraib facility in September 2003 to discuss what he called "the current theater ability to rapidly exploit internees for actionable intelligence." The administration was disappointed and impatient with the intelligence coming from the detainees and wanted to employ "harsh interrogation" if not torture (Sands 2008).

The techniques the administration imported into the Iraq theater astonishingly included a chart of "coercive methods" unknowingly adapted from an article written by Albert Biderman (1957) about "brainwashing" during the Korean War.

This is the same Albert Biderman who later pioneered crime victimization surveys. His earlier article was embarrassingly, for the U.S. military, titled "Communist Attempts to Elicit False Confessions from Air Force Prisoners of War." The U.S. military had inadvertently embraced Communist Chinese torture tactics (Shane 2008).

Geoffrey Miller recommended importing from Guantánamo Bay the use of stress positions, isolation for up to thirty days, removal of clothing, twenty-hour interrogations, use of dogs, and many other measures authorized in a memo by Defense Secretary Rumsfeld (Sands 2008). Within a month, Military Intelligence had obscured and confused matters by authorizing up to five different versions of interrogation rules for Abu Ghraib (Gourevitch and Morris 2008:53):

> There was no way to keep up, and the more prisoners there were, the more the demand for intelligence grew. "People were on edge and under pressure," Colonel Warren said. "General Sanchez," he said, "was under intense pressure." Warren was told about calls coming in from Washington, and the message was: produce, produce. Everybody wanted to know: What was the Intelligence? Where was the intelligence? So what MI [Military Intelligence] wanted at Abu Ghraib, MI got. (ibid. 55)

This account unveils a parallel with the same kind of top-down, vertically organized, and deniable sources of pressure described in the last chapter as building criminogenic market structures for financial crimes (Farberman 1975).

In the case of postinvasion Iraq war crimes, analysts trace the chain of political and military command from Abu Ghraib in Iraq back through Guantánamo Bay in Cuba to the Department of Defense in Washington, and ultimately to the White House. For example, Seymour Hersh (2004) and Philippe Sands (2008) trace this chain through Defense Secretary Donald Rumsfeld to the president, based on the infamous Justice

Department "torture memo" and an earlier memo presented to the president by Douglas Feith. Feith (1985) had written an article that was the basis for his memo titled "Law in the Service of Terror" years earlier while in the Reagan administration. President George W. Bush signed a February 7, 2002, order in which he stated, "I accept the legal conclusion of the Department of Justice and determine that none of the provisions of Geneva apply to our conflict with al Qaeda in Afghanistan or elsewhere throughout the world" (cited in Ambos 2009:406). This order indicated that the treatment of al Qaeda detainees did not violate Common Article 3 of the Geneva Conventions. The Bush administration had officially entered a legal netherworld of its own creation.

The highest-level lawyers in the U.S. military disagreed with the Bush administration's position on the Geneva Conventions. This finally became fully apparent in testimony before the U.S. Senate Armed Services Committee in 2006:

> The Judge Advocate General for each of the four services attended: Major General Scott Black of the Army, Rear Admiral James McPherson of the Navy, Major General Jack Rives of the Air Force and Brigadier General Kevin Sandhuhler of the Marine Corps. They were also joined by General John Hutson, former Navy Judge Advocate General, and General Tom Romig, former Army Judge Advocate General. . . . "Would you agree that some of the techniques that we have authorized clearly violate Common Article 3?" Senator Lindsey Graham asked Major General Rives. Rives barely paused. "Some of the techniques that have been authorized and used in the past have violated Common Article 3," he answered. "Does everyone agree with that statement?" Senator Graham asked the other five. There was a common murmur, a positive murmur. The transcript for the hearing recorded: "Affirmative response by all concerned." (Sands 2008:175)

The view of Hersh (2004), Sands (2008), and others is that it would have required willful ignorance by the president and defense secretary to misjudge the consequences of the messages they sent about the Geneva Conventions to and through their subordinates.

The results of the open-ended messaging were a mixture of violence, intimidation, humiliation, and, not least, sexual degradation:

> Mostly what interrogators wanted when they asked for "special treatment" was punishment: take away his mattress, PT him; keep him awake; take away his clothes. "It was normal procedure for MI to say, This guy wears panties for a day, or wears panties for three days, or until he decides to cooperate with us." (Gourevitch and Morris 2008:97)

In a further tactic adopted by the U.S. military and referred to as "invasion of space by females," women soldiers were included in interrogations. These actions became famous through photographs of "leash lady" Lynndie England and of "pile-ups" by Sabrina Harman:

> What better way to break an Arab, then, than to strip him, tie him up, and have a "female bystander," as Graner described Harman, laugh at him? American women were used on the MI block in the same way that Major David DiNenna spoke of dogs—as "force multipliers." (Gourevitch and Morris 2008:113)

Army investigators received photographs of the sexual humiliation and abuse of prisoners, and CBS News first broadcast these images on *60 Minutes II*.

> They arrived on Tier 1A around ten, and by the time they were shown to their cells three and a half hours later, they

had been thrown in a pile, jumped on, punched, stripped, written on with a magic marker, stacked atop one another in a human pyramid, posed to simulate oral sex, lined up against a wall, and made to masturbate—and none of the MPs who took part in this unhinged variety show could come up with an excuse for it. (Gourevitch and Morris 2008:187)

Gourevitch and Morris conclude in their aptly titled book, *Standard Operating Procedure*, that "Abu Ghraib was the smoking gun" of U.S. war crimes in Iraq (171).

Evidencing War Crimes

When torture occurs in the form and on the scale that it did in Abu Ghraib, the essential evidence of criminality is difficult to ignore. International criminal law acknowledges this point with regard to the higher levels in the military and political chain of command by requiring less direct forms of evidence of criminal responsibility than in conventional domestic crimes. Prosecutors in international criminal cases, increasingly with the help of social scientists, have the potential to demonstrate the joined roles of lower-level physical perpetrators of crime acting together in horizontal relationships, with these in turn linked to higher-level leaders in a chain of command through their indirect participation in vertical relationships of "superior responsibility."

Legal scholars have recognized the latter hierarchical forms of participation as "indirect co-perpetration," "perpetration-by-means," "perpetration by another person," and "control over an organization" (van der Wilt 2009). This kind of reasoning about "joint criminal enterprise" came to international criminal law through the work of U.S. Department of Justice lawyers using their experiences with American RICO statutes—the Racketeering-Influenced and Corrupt Organizations Act—to prosecute organized crime (Hagan 2003). The American sociologist-criminologist Donald Cressey spearheaded adoption of the U.S. RICO statutes in the 1970s (Matsueda and Akers 2005).

The forms of knowledge evidencing criminal responsibility in international prosecutions of war crimes ultimately involve the "superior responsibility" invoked by the legal philosopher Hugo Grotius. Writing centuries ago, Grotius observed that "we must accept the principle that he who knows of a crime, and is able and bound to prevent it but fails to do so, himself commits a crime" (1615 [1964]:523).

Thus, the former International Criminal Court judge Navi Pillay (2009:8) notes that participation "refers to any individual who plans, instigates, commits, orders or abets the execution of crimes. It does not require the direct hand or the physical participation of the accused in the perpetration of the criminal act. Rather, it applies when this individual participates in criminal conduct with a plurality of actors." Pillay emphasizes that "The responsibility lies not just with the military leaders, but with their political masters as well."

Yet denials are often an effective adversarial framing device that in practice successfully immunize military and political leaders from criminal prosecution in domestic and international courts. There is much evidence of such denial as a successful framing device to avoid legal accountability for crimes in pre- and postinvasion Iraq as well as Darfur. In postinvasion Iraq, the Bush administration advanced a framing strategy that partially deflected the prospect of high-level prosecution of those responsible for torture and sexual violence at Abu Ghraib prison by diverting attention to the crimes of torture and sexual violence of the former Baathist regime of Saddam Hussein.

Thus, on the last day of February 2004, U.S. Major General Antonio Taguba (2004) finalized his official report on postinvasion torture and sexual violence by American soldiers at the Abu Ghraib Correctional Facility in Iraq. This was a month and a half after Donald Rumsfeld had informed President Bush about activities at Abu Ghraib. Taguba briefed his superior officers on March 3 and submitted his final report on March 9. Three days later, President Bush chose to speak about sexual violence in *pre*-invasion rather than postinvasion Iraq.

President Bush reminded his audience about sexual violence during Saddam's Baathist regime, observing that "Every woman in Iraq is better off because the rape rooms and torture chambers of Saddam Hussein are forever closed" (Bush 2004a). The following month, Secretary Rumsfeld similarly deflected questions about Abu Ghraib by reporting that he had not yet read the Taguba report (CNBC 2004). A month and a half after the delivery of Taguba's report, the president ignored Abu Ghraib and instead proudly told an audience in Iowa that

> Our military is . . . performing brilliantly. See, the transition from torture chambers and rape rooms and mass graves and fear of authority is a tough transition. And they're doing the good work of keeping this country stabilized as a political process unfolds. (Bush 2004b)

Two months after the Taguba report and more than three months after Rumsfeld first informed him, the president finally spoke to Arab news reporters about the Abu Ghraib "issue." He belatedly and dubiously reported that "when an issue is brought to our attention on this magnitude, we act—and we act in a way where leaders are willing to discuss it with the media" (Bush 2004c).

Throughout this period, President Bush spoke frequently about Saddam Hussein's "rape rooms" and "torture chambers," and the Bush administration lauded the creation of the Iraq High Tribunal to punish the crimes committed in these places. "We know about the mass graves and the rape rooms and the torture chambers of Saddam Hussein's regime," President Bush's press secretary remarked, "we welcome their decision [the Iraqi Governing Council's] to move forward on a Tribunal to hold people accountable for those atrocities" (McClellan 2003). As we report later in this chapter, the Iraq

High Tribunal placed Saddam Hussein on trial in 2005 for crimes against humanity in Dujail and in 2006 for the Anfal genocide.

Yet at this writing, neither the United States' nor Iraq's courts have held a high-ranking government official responsible specifically for sexual violence in Abu Ghraib, Anfal, or anywhere else in pre- or postinvasion Iraq. The absence of a prosecution for rape by the Iraq High Tribunal might seem especially surprising, since the Bush administration spoke so frequently about the "rape rooms" of the Hussein regime and about the role of the tribunal during the period of revelations about sexual violence by American soldiers at Abu Ghraib. Yet we argue that the absence of rape cases before the tribunal should not be surprising because international as well as domestic courts also have a long and unfortunate record of ignoring and only relatively recently recognizing sexual violence in international conflict zones. This common situation illustrates how framing processes of denial have blocked the development of criminological theory, research, and policy about rape and sexual violence, even in highly publicized circumstances such as in Iraq.

A Long History of Denial

History provides much evidence of the severity and extent of rape and sexual violence during armed conflicts. For example, historians estimate that Russian soldiers raped nearly two million women in eastern Germany during World War II (Mandl 2001). Japanese occupiers raped, assaulted, or killed about 20,000 women in Nanjing during the first months of 1937, and Japan kept approximately 200,000 Korean and other women in sexual slavery from about 1931 to 1945 (Gardam and Jarvis 2001; Pritchard and Zaide 1981). Yet the charters for the international military tribunals for Germany and Japan that followed World War II did not explicitly include rape in their charges of crimes against humanity (Askin 1997:163, 2009; Zanetti 2007:219).

International criminal law's failure to recognize sexual violence has left its victims without redress or remedy. Instead, states have long treated rape as among the "spoils of war." Zanetti writes that "Not only was it not condemned with the same severity as other equivalent violations of rights, but it was long considered as a 'side effect' of war or even, more cynically, as a bonus to soldiers, regardless of allegiance" (2007:219). Denial, neglect, allowance, instigation, organization, and cover-up all played their roles. Social science offered little compensation, with neither sufficient data collection nor theoretical conceptualization to expose state responsibility for sexual victimization in armed conflicts. This situation has only recently begun to change.

International tribunals did not prosecute wartime rapes separately or as crimes against humanity or genocide until after rape was explicitly included in the charters establishing the International Criminal Tribunals for the Former Yugoslavia (ICTY) and Rwanda (ICTR) in 1993 and 1995. Judges in the 1994 ICTR *Akayesu* decision acknowledged the role of rape as an instrument of power and domination in international conflicts. They did so by observing that rape is a form of aggression and a component of genocide, although they offered no specific physical or mechanical description of rape (United Nations [UN] 1998). The ICTY *Furundzija* case provided an explicit judicial definition of rape as sexual penetration by coercion or by force or the threat of force (UN 1999a, b). This decision included within the meaning of rape acts perpetrated on both male and female victims.

Despite this physical and mechanical explicitness in defining rape in international case law, international institutions more generally still lag in recognizing the role of state participation in and state responsibility for protection from rape and sexual violence in armed conflicts. The United States, of course, was unwilling to acknowledge its high-level responsibility for torture or sexual violence at Abu Ghraib. Yet the United States officially repudiated state-led sexual violence when it presented a resolution in October 2007 at the United Nations. The UN resolution condemned government-led organized sexual violence and rape to achieve political or military objectives.

The United States had little fear that the UN would actually use such a resolution to investigate, much less prosecute, its leaders for war crimes at Abu Ghraib or elsewhere. Since its historic role at the Nuremberg Tribunal after World War II, the U.S. relationship with international courts has been intermittent. In 1984, the Reagan administration refused to acknowledge the finding of the International Court of Justice that it had violated international law by mining the port of Managua in Nicaragua. However, the United States subsequently played major roles in establishing the ICTY, the ICTR, and other ad hoc (i.e., time- and place-bound) international tribunals and special courts to try mass atrocities and war crimes. The United States also played a major role in negotiating crucial parts of the 1998 Rome Treaty that determined the parameters of the permanent International Criminal Court. However, the U.S. Senate has never ratified the Rome Treaty, and the Obama administration shows no signs of joining the International Criminal Court.

Other states and their leaders, especially in Africa, were concerned for their fates when the United States proposed at the UN to condemn the political use of sexual violence and rape for state purposes. Their response to the U.S.-sponsored resolution temporarily succeeded in removing references to government responsibility (Warren 2007:A10). In June 2008, the UN Security Council finally adopted a follow-up U.S.-sponsored resolution that *implied* the role of states by asserting that "sexual attacks in conflict zones may be considered war crimes" (AFP 2008).

The role of states in promoting sexual violence still was not explicit, but the organizing role of governments in sexual violence during war making became more difficult to ignore. Finally, in response to state practices that deny the existence and responsibility for rape, international criminal law is at last beginning—but only beginning—to frame serious forms of this sexual violence as what I call "state rape." This step represents an adversarial framing of rape in conflict zones with the potentially important force of international criminal law behind it. The challenge is to apply this with the force of law.

The adversarial framing tactics of diversion and deflection used by the Bush administration were nuanced and subtle compared to the denial frames employed by other states. Heads of state such as Saddam Hussein of Iraq and Omar al-Bashir of Sudan did not merely discount problems of rape and sexual violence, they completely denied their entire existence. Yet sexual attacks in Saddam's Iraq and Bashir's Sudan were frequent, highly organized, and state-led.

Comparative Overview of Sudan and Pre-invasion Iraq

In the case of Bashir's Sudan, state-led racial dehumanization played a role in denying rights of protection to rape victims as persons and citizens. In Saddam Hussein's pre-invasion Iraq, police and court practices were used to undermine victims and as the means of denying state responsibility for crimes of rape. In both Sudan and Iraq, distorted policies of state protection and security were sources of the perpetration and denial of rape victimization. State structures and framing processes of victim denial used techniques of neutralization of the kind discussed in chapter 3 (see also Alvarez 1997). These neutralizing frames can, however, be exposed and opposed through international criminal law, and state leaders can be held responsible for using systematic patterns of rape and sexual violence as instruments of war and repression.

A starting point is Charles Tilly's work, "War Making and State Making as Organized Crime" (1985), in which he observes that collective efforts to create and defend states can involve the use of methods analogous to those used by organized crime. State-led rape and sexual violence are organized crimes of war.

State involvement in rape and sexual violence varies in important ways that a comparative analysis of Sudan and Iraq helps reveal. However, there are also underlying similarities in the collective state framing of these crimes. In both Sudan and Iraq, the collective framing is a process by which the state denies victims of sexual violence protection, and crimes of sexual violence receive legal impunity.

The framework for this comparative analysis is presented in table 7.1. The role of President Bashir's Sudanese state in rape and sexual violence has been loosely organized and diffusely undertaken through paramilitary forces, often called Janjaweed militia. In contrast, the role of the state in rape and sexual violence in Saddam Hussein's Iraq was tightly organized and compartmentalized within the government's General Security Directorate. We need a better understanding of the forms state rape and sexual violence can take.

Further, dehumanization based on racial epithets formed a framing mechanism of denial that allowed rape and sexual

TABLE 7. 1

Comparative Analysis of State Rape in Darfur and Pre-invasion Iraq

Parameter evaluated	Darfur	Iraq
Structural schemas	Loosely coupled and diffused	Tightly coupled and compartmentalized
Organizational perpetrators	Janjaweed militias	Security Directorate
Framing mechanisms	Racial dehumanization—racial epithets	Legal proceedings— arrests, trials, confessions
Victimized groups	Black Africans: Fur, Masaleit, Zaghawa	Kurds and Shi'ites
Judicial response	Rape without genocide charge	Genocide without rape charge

violence as part of genocidal attacks in Omar al-Bashir's Darfur. In Saddam Hussein's pre-invasion Iraq, legal proceedings involving arrests, trials, and confessions were used to deny protection to victims of rape and sexual violence and to create judicially framed rationalizations that facilitated these crimes. In both settings, a systematic framing process based on state-led denial played an essential role in the intentional targeting of the victimized groups.

In both Sudan and pre-invasion Iraq, rapes and sexual assaults were part of regime strategies for subordination, intimidation, and terror, with the larger exploitative purpose to privilege and protect advantaged groups against members of less advantaged groups. It is attention to the latter purpose that makes the perspective applied in this chapter a *critical* collective framing approach. Supporters of the Arab-dominated government in Sudan and the Sunni-based government in pre-invasion Iraq empowered and enriched themselves through state-organized strategies of criminal intimidation and subordination.

The use of violence for the exploitation and protection by privileged groups against the anticipated threats of disadvantaged groups is at the core of Tilly's organized crime theory of war-making and state-making. The protected groups in the Darfur region of Sudan were Arab groups and the victimized groups were black African, whereas in pre-invasion Iraq Sunni tribal groups were protected and Kurdish and Shiite tribal groups were victimized.

The international legal responses that were presumably intended to impede crimes against humanity such as rape and sexual violence in the Darfur region of Sudan and pre-invasion Iraq differed. However, it is extremely important to explain the variable ways in which states have criminally organized and collectively framed the perpetration of rape and sexual violence. This is a point that is central to this book: the framing of crime and criminals, by and of individuals and by and for states, can never be taken for granted, and this statement applies to the United States as well as to Sudan and Iraq.

State Rape as a Crime against Public Health and Humanity

The personal harm of rape is easily recognized in the forms of physical and reproductive trauma, sexually transmitted diseases (including HIV), pregnancy, as well as the feelings of personal helplessness and humiliation that persist as posttraumatic stress disorders. Victims are physically traumatized, for example, by medical problems such as traumatic fistula or the urinary incontinence that is often caused by rape. Halima Bashir's *Tears of the Desert* (2009) graphically documents these traumas that individual victims in Darfur must confront in their daily lives.

These harms have highly consequential social dimensions as well. When rapes are targeted against groups, they can be used to intimidate and terrorize these groups as methods of exploitation and subordination. Families and communities often treat victims of rape as dishonored, and victims are stigmatized and ostracized. Small amounts of sexual violence can create havoc in households and communities. Sexual violence is a uniquely terrifying crime that can be an extraordinarily powerful and efficient instrument of domination and control.

The injuries to female victims of rape often physically and socially isolate them from others, and this alters gender relationships within the population and can have detrimental consequences for family formation and fertility. Sexual violence can threaten the physical reproduction and survival of whole groups. Thus, intergroup rape can be used as a means of controlling reproduction and targeted by states and their leaders to destroy entire victimized groups and to empower and enrich perpetrator groups.

The role of states in the perpetration of sexual violence is especially important. States are responsible for sexual violence in at least three ways. The first and most direct kind of involvement is through acts of sexual violence perpetrated by state agents and forces. The second and more indirect involvement is through proxies, such as state-linked paramilitary forces and militias that engage in sexual violence. The third kind of involvement is the potentially much wider-ranging neglect of the responsibility of states to protect citizens and residents from sexual violence by state and non-state actors, such as invading or internal rebel groups. All three forms of state involvement in sexual violence are evident in the recent history of Darfur and Iraq. Of course, these are only selected national examples, and we need to be mindful of our own U.S. state responsibility for sexual violence as already discussed in postinvasion Iraq.

Several aspects of international criminal law should be kept in mind in this discussion. First, individuals, not states, are tried in international criminal courts. Second, whereas individuals at all levels of a political and military chain of command may engage in rape and sexual violence as war crimes, international criminal courts devote their resources to prosecuting leading perpetrators at higher levels in the command chain. At issue in these cases is how political and military leaders use the apparatus of the state and its official and unofficial armed forces as instruments of criminal organization and joint criminal enterprise that lead to sexual violence.

The full force and potential significance of this kind of international legal recognition are expressed in the collective responsibility of nation-states, through international criminal courts of law or other lawful means, to provide protection to victims against crimes of sexual violence. While this collective responsibility too often in the past has been merely an aspiration of international criminal law, it may today be coming closer to actualization. A specific example explored in this chapter is the prospective arrest and prosecution of Sudan's president Omar al-Bashir for his responsibility for the targeting of state rape in Darfur (Office of the Prosecutor 2008).

I turn next to the challenge of explaining the role of states in the use of rape and sexual violence as war crimes. Critical criminologists from the age of Roosevelt, such as William

Chambliss, Stanley Cohen, and Austin Turk, played important roles in reframing states and their agents as potential criminal offenders, and this premise is a starting point for contemporary genocide researchers. Savelsberg (2010) points out that it was more common for classical criminology, and now in the age of Reagan for the public, to frame the role of the state—for example, in the war on terrorism—simply as a bulwark against crime, and not as a perpetrator itself.

Thus, modern criminologists as well as the public often give credence to Thomas Hobbes's framing of the state as a Leviathan that protects citizens from harms they would otherwise do to one another if left entirely free to do so. This view was encouraged by the historical declines in violence and killing associated with civic life in modern states. Yet this progress is hardly uninterrupted or without exception. This is the point made by Charles Tilly (1985) in his analogy of state-making with organized crime.

States have a capacity to fail as well as succeed, and when states fail, they often become massively destructive of life and property. Yet both failing and prevailing states historically demonstrate an impressive capacity to kill, rape, pillage, and plunder. Political scientists, historians, and sociologists, such as Raul Hilberg (1985) and Irving Louis Horowitz (1980), document the devastation even presumably modern states can bring upon humanity.

An Organized Crime Theory of War-Making and State-Making

Across eras and nations, it sometimes makes more sense to think about states as coercive criminal organizations than as protectors of social contracts, free markets, shared norms, or human security. This is the logic of Charles Tilly's (1985) analogy between war-making and state-making as organized crime. He argued that states often develop policies that are similar to the smooth-running protection rackets of organized crime, provoking and perpetuating false or exaggerated threats involving both external and internal enemies from which state leaders then frame their actions as protecting their citizens.

For Tilly, "banditry, piracy, gangland rivalry, policing and war making all belong on the same continuum." State-making may require less naked aggression than war-making, but Tilly maintains that both nonetheless can require violence, which characteristically is invoked under the guise of citizen protection. He noted that in the name of security and protection, some groups, external or internal, are privileged and advantaged relative to others, who are intimidated and subordinated if not eliminated.

In his work, Tilly describes how state-making often takes up where war-making leaves off. For example, he explains that "the organization and deployment of violence themselves account for much of the characteristic structure of European states" (181). The point for our purposes is that states expand their bureaucracies, such as a ministry of foreign affairs, as well as domestic institutions, such as the police and the courts, to justify external and internal coercion as mechanisms of selective security and protection.

Tilly most provocatively argues that domestic protection often requires eliminating or neutralizing the enemies of those who are privileged and advantaged by this protection, so that "from the relative predominance of state making [springs] the disproportionate elaboration of policing and surveillance" (184) with the consequence that "state making actually reduces the protection given some classes" (181).

Tilly developed his ideas about war-making and state-making to explain the historical development of modern European nation-states, but he also applied these ideas contemporaneously to colonies and less developed nations that often act as proxies for modern states' international purposes. He argues that organized criminality has characterized the modern client states not only of Central Europe but also of the United

States, China, and Russia. This focus on client states brings us to late modern states, and more specifically to Omar al-Bashir's Sudan and Saddam Hussein's Iraq. Tilly wrote about these issues nearly a quarter century ago, during the age of Reagan, when both Sudan and Iraq were still the Reagan and Bush administrations' covert allies.

Later, Sudan and Iraq turned to China and Russia for protection and defense against perceived internal and external threats to their security. Tilly (1985:186) remarked in one of his most frequently quoted and ironic passages:

> To the extent that outside states continue to supply military goods and expertise in return for commodities, military alliance or both, the new states harbor powerful, unconstrained organizations that easily overshadow all other organizations within their territories. To the extent that outside states guarantee their boundaries, the managers of those military organizations exercise extraordinary power within them. The advantages of military power become enormous, the incentives to seize power over the state as a whole by means of that advantage very strong. Despite the great place that war making occupied in the making of European states, the old national states of Europe almost never experienced the great disproportion between military organization and all other forms of organization that seems the fate of client states throughout the contemporary world. A century ago, Europeans might have congratulated themselves on the spread of civil government throughout the world. In our own time, the analogy between war making and state making, on the one hand, and organized crime, on the other, is becoming tragically apt.

This is why Charles Tilly probably would be unsurprised by state-led organized sexual victimization as one among many forms of coercion in Sudan and Iraq. He saw such client states as prone to massively repressive forms of criminal abuse, especially when they are failing and vulnerable, as during the final stages of Saddam's pre-invasion Iraq, and this repressive abuse unfortunately can also include sexual abuse.

State Rape and the Protection of Privilege in Sudan and Iraq

Tilly's theoretical insights can take us only so far. He tells us little, for example, about variation among states in how they organize their criminality. A starting point is to note that states obviously vary in their forms and resources, and that this will likely influence the organization of their war crimes. Criminal states share the need to repress some groups as a means to ensure the privileging of others, but they vary in the resources they have available to do this.

Sudan and Iraq differ in many ways, including in their societal circumstances and resources. For example, Iraq's population is more concentrated in urban areas and its population is more highly educated (Tripp 2002). Still, a key similarity is that both Omar al-Bashir and Saddam Hussein came to power by undemocratic means and stayed in power with the force of brutal authoritarian regimes. Both used rape and sexual violence as instruments of subjugation and oppression, and both found ways to collectively frame and deny this violence by means that made it more pervasive. The rationalization or framing of sexual violence in a society can conceal even from the constituency of the perpetrator group the enormity of their crimes, which is crucial to their perpetuation. Sudan's and Iraq's leaders, however, differed in how they did this.

While the role played by Omar al-Bashir's Sudanese state in rape and sexual violence was loosely organized and diffuse, Saddam's Iraqi state was much more tightly organized and compartmentalized in perpetrating its crimes. Thus these regimes mobilized sexual violence in different ways to impose disfavor and disadvantage on targeted groups. A process of explicit dehumanization using racial epithets played a crucial role in forming and framing the intentions of sexual violence in Darfur, while legal proceedings formed a judicial rationalization or framing of this behavior in Iraq.

To set the stage for our comparative analysis, it is important to recall that the two waves of most intense rape and killing in the western Darfur region of Sudan began with attacks in the spring of 2003 and continued through the fall of 2004 (Hagan and Rymond-Richmond 2009). This was during the early phases of the U.S.-led invasion and occupation of Iraq (Hashim 2006). During the Bush administration, crucial events in these two countries at least temporally and possibly strategically overlapped. It is likely that the leadership of Sudan concluded that the United States was too busily engaged in Iraq to become directly involved in Darfur. In this highly fraught and complicated period, the world's collective responsibility to prevent rape as a war crime received little attention in Sudan, Iraq, or elsewhere.

Surveys of Human Rights Victims in Darfur and Pre-invasion Iraq

We draw on two sources for a comparative analysis of Darfur and pre-invasion Iraq. The first source is the U.S. State Department (2004) Atrocities Documentation Survey conducted in the summer and fall of 2004 with a sample of 1,136 Darfur refugees who fled to neighboring Chad. The second source is the Iraq History Project (Rothenberg 2008). This project involved 6,982 persons interviewed in 2007–8 in displacement camps and communities who reported human rights abuses from the time Saddam Hussein entered Iraq's government in 1969 until the 2003 invasion.

Saddam could draw on a highly developed bureaucracy in Iraq that included an extensive security apparatus and a coordinated police and court system (Makiya 1989). As discussed further below, the latter justice system was paradoxically used to legally frame and rationalize sexual violence in Iraq. In contrast, in Darfur, Bashir had to enlist civilians from a variety of local Arab militia groups and incite them with a unifying ideological framing that mixed ideas about Arab supremacy with racism (Harir 1992). The differences between these regimes and their implementation of sexual violence provide insights into mobilization and implementation of state rape in repressive states.

State Rape in Omar al-Bashir's Darfur

Observers usually trace the Darfur conflict to several highly publicized attacks by rebel groups on Sudanese forces in early 2003 (Flint and de Waal 2005). In response, the Sudanese state cast black African civilians in Darfur as an insurgent threat from which the government and local Arab groups required protection. From Charles Tilly's perspective, the government exaggerated the rebel threat as justification for repressing black African groups who peacefully supported rebel demands for more state resources.

Sudan sent a deputy security minister, Ahmad Harun, to Darfur to organize and encourage attacks by Arab militias on black African civilian populations he associated with the rebels (Office of the Prosecutor 2007). Harun said in a public meeting that the militias must "kill three-quarters of Darfur in order to allow one-quarter to live." When he was asked to defend this policy, Harun said the "rebels infiltrate the villages" and thus that the villagers "are like water to fish." Harun wanted to "drain the water" from Darfur by displacing the African villagers. He regularly encouraged taking from "all the Fur and what they had," which he characterized as "booty," and he more broadly identified the targets of the attacks as three black African tribes, the Fur, Zaghawa, and Masalit.

The state portrayed the security threat as immediate and urgent, although the conflict was more deeply and diffusely rooted (Harir 1992). The polarization dates to at least the mid-1980s and conflicts between Arab nomadic herders and black African farmers. Desertification and famine intensified the conflict, which is why war crime in Darfur involved crops and livestock, as well as killings and rapes.

The Arab-dominated Sudanese government that is led from Khartoum has historically refused to invest resources in Darfur. Omar al-Bashir assumed the presidency of Sudan following a military coup in 1989 and advanced a policy of brutally excluding black Africans from their land and villages in Darfur. Bashir's government incorporated the nomadic Arab groups that operated as militias into Sudan's loosely controlled Popular Defense Forces. The government armed and trained the local Arab groups who wanted greater access to water and pastures to graze their herds on lands farmed by the black Africans. This amounted to outsourcing much of the government policy of repression to Arab militias as proxies (Hagan and Rymond-Richmond 2009).

Journalists reported from militia camps on the salience of race in the training regime of new Arab recruits. The militia leader Musa Hilal played a prominent leadership role, promoting the idea among Arab recruits that the black African groups were farming land that originally belonged to Arabs. *Washington Post* reporter Emily Wax (2004) described how before an attack in April of 2004, Hilal and the troops sang war songs proclaiming, "We go to the war. . . . We are the original people of the area."

Another journalist reported from a camp that "Mr. Hilal made a speech in which he told them all Africans were their enemies" (Vasagar 2004). An interview with a defector reported that men paraded around singing songs degrading local Africans and proclaiming, "We are lords of this land. You blacks do not have any rights here" (Power 2004). Hilal did not just convert individuals to his cause; he built local militias around a collective framing designed to support attacking and killing black Africans.

Bashir's Sudanese government increasingly urged the Arab groups to take land for their herds by terrorizing and displacing the black African farming settlements. The government's approach required only providing the Arab groups with training, weapons, and strategic air and ground support from government military forces during attacks. Alex de Waal (2004:15) called this a state policy of "counter-insurgency on the cheap."

The growing scarcity of water and grazing opportunities aggravated a herder-farmer dichotomy and divisions between the "Arab" herders and "non-Arab" or "black African" farmers. Although both groups were predominantly Muslim, the conflict was increasingly expressed in terms of differences in livelihood and language, which were linked to perceived skin tone and defined as racial.

The government training of the Arab militias included encouraging the use of racial epithets. The epithets dehumanized and degraded non-Arab Zaghawa, Fur, and Masalit groups (Hagan and Rymond-Richmond 2008). These epithets became distinguishing features of the most violent attacks on black Darfur villages. Refugees reported hearing shouts involving tropes of slavery and subhumanity like the following during the attacks:

- "They called her Nuba [a derogatory term for blacks] dog, son of dogs, and we came here to kill you and your kids."

- "You donkey, you slave, we must get rid of you."

- "You blacks are not human. We can do anything we want to you. You cannot live here."

- "You blacks are like monkeys. You are not human."

- "Black prostitute, whore, you are dirty—black."

These dehumanizing epithets played a major role in denying the ways in which those targeted in the attacks were persons and victims with rights and deserving protection.

Dehumanization is a collective framing mechanism that degrades both individuals and entire groups (Fein 1979). This process of dehumanization had the effect of stripping black

Darfurians of their individuality and membership in Sudanese society, justifying attacks and denying the moral or normal protections of citizenship. Racial and ethnic epithets conveying contempt and denying rights to targeted groups were the mechanisms of dehumanization that make it easier for ordinary people to participate in mass atrocities.

The first of two major offensives involving Sudanese government forces in Darfur began in 2003. As noted, attackers often shouted racial epithets designating the Zaghawa, Fur, and Masalit groups as the targets for attacks as black Africans. Such explicit evidence of racial intent is a foundation for the charge of genocide. Judges in the Rwandan leader Jean-Paul Akayesu genocide case (UN 1998) decided "the use of derogatory language toward . . . the targeted group" provides "sufficient evidence of intent," and judges in the Bosnian Jelisi genocide case cited "words" and "remarks" as evidence of racial intent (UN 1999b). Data from the Atrocities Documentation Survey indicate that Sudanese forces joined with Janjaweed militia in using racial epithets that targeted African villagers for violence that included sexual victimization, while at the same time sparing Arab settlements from these attacks.

Map 7.1 portrays variation in the proportion of respondents in each settlement cluster reporting epithets, with circles of increasing size ranked in quartiles. About half of the respondents in the top quartile heard racial epithets during the attacks. Thus, 45 percent of the respondents heard racial epithets in Kebkabiya, where the militia leader Musa Hilal was reported as beginning his attacks, and from 43 to 50 percent of respondents heard these epithets in settlements in southwestern Darfur, in al Geneina, Masteri, Habilah, Garsila, Foro Burunga, and Bendesi—the sites of attacks reportedly led by other Janjaweed leaders. The latter sites are located in the more fertile and densely settled areas of Darfur.

Respondents also heard the racial epithets more often when the Sudanese government forces joined with the Janjaweed militias in attacks and in areas of high settlement density. This

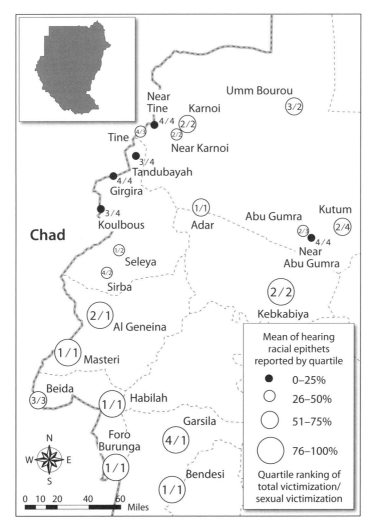

Map 7.1 Settlement cluster map of racial epithets and total victimization and sexual victimization.

finding, which reflects both the effects of state military organization and the opportunities and incentives provided by land-based resources, is summarized in figure 7.1. As the figure indicates, when Sudanese and Janjaweed forces attacked together, in the more fertile areas of elevated population density, the hearing of racial epithets increased. Sudanese and Janja-

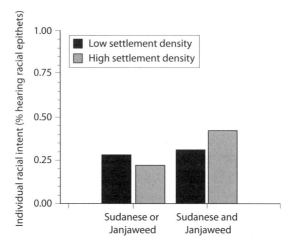

Figure 7.1 Effects of separate and/or combined forces with settlement density on hearing of racial epithets.

weed forces operated together in about two-thirds of the attacks. This combination of forces in the right-hand side of the figure, representing settlements with higher population densities, approximately doubled the hearing of racial epithets from about 20 percent to more than 40 percent. This constitutes compelling evidence that the Sudanese state intensified the expression of racial intent in a process of racial dehumanization by joining its forces with the Janjaweed militias in attacks on densely settled areas of Darfur.

The violent impact of the racial epithets is further documented in map 7.1. This map shows that reported racial epithets were most often used in the Kebkabiya area, where the notorious militia leader Musa Hilal launched his attacks, and in the more densely populated southwestern settlements of Darfur, where several other militia leaders were reportedly active. The circles on map 7.1 reflecting these elevated reports of racial epithets also present the quartile ranks of an overall victimization score, as well as a sexual victimization score. The racial epithets and victimization clearly coincide.

Overall, the evidence indicates a pattern in which state rape is organized and carried out as a tactical part of a more general strategy of subjugation and subordination of black African groups. As Tilly's organized crime theory of war-making and state-making explains, the Arab-dominated state created a security problem—in this case by withholding investment of resources from Darfur. It then used the small rebellion to justify widespread and systematic repression of the black civilian population through rapes, killings, property destruction, and displacement.

The racial framing of the conflict denied the humanity of being recognized as a crime victim in the attacks on black Africans. Rape is an especially terrifying tactic that is increasingly recognized as a strategic weapon of war in international conflict zones. In Darfur, the Sudanese government was clearly implicated in this use of rape as an instrument of war and as a crime against public health and humanity (Hagan, Rymond-Richmond, and Palloni 2009).

State rape was practiced in pre-invasion Iraq as well, but in Saddam Hussein's Iraq the state organization and carrying out of rape was different in its organization and perpetration.

State Rape in Saddam Hussein's Iraq

Saddam Hussein's regime policies changed radically in the aftermath of the First Gulf War in 1991 (Zubaida 2003). His regime was at serious risk of upheaval, and security concerns reached new heights. Saddam ended secular reform programs and reintroduced Islamic traditions to increase his support from Sunni tribal and religious groups. The UN Special Rapporteur estimated in 2001 that 4,000 women and girls died as a result of a brutal reinforcement of traditional gender roles, which included a resurgence of "honor killings" (Hashim 2006). A presidential decree exempted men from prosecution and punishment for these killings. The power of presidential decrees reflected the centralized control Saddam imposed through a tightly structured set of security agencies. The regime enlisted the courts in collectively framing women as scapegoats rather than as victims of crimes such as rape.

Saddam's security regime bureaucratized torture through arrest and court authorized investigations, using torture to extract confessions (Marashi 2002). In court proceedings, two Baathist Party military officers and a civilian president presided. Judges conducted trials without right of appeal to higher courts. The regime used the legal system, and especially confessions, as a way to frame victims as offenders and thereby to deny the crimes of rape and sexual violence against them.

Following the conclusion of the war with Iran and the defeat of Iraq in the First Gulf War in Kuwait, serious uprisings broke out in the Shiite south and the Kurdish north regions. The United States encouraged but did not militarily support these uprisings. The Kurdish north had already suffered through the atrocities of the Anfal Campaign, in which Saddam Hussein's government brutally prevailed. However, the United States and Great Britain finally provided protection in the aftermath of the post–Gulf War uprisings. Since that time, the Kurds in relative terms have prospered in three effectively autonomous governorates. In October 1991, Saddam Hussein withdrew the central government administration from the north (Tripp 2002).

However, Saddam retained control in the south of Iraq until the U.S.-led invasion and occupation. Saddam's security forces arrested, tortured, and executed Shiites in southern Iraq throughout the post–Gulf War period. By 1994 the government had institutionalized its repression with a series of state decrees that established branding, amputation, and execution as traditional punishments for more than thirty crimes, many of which were minor offenses. In Tilly's terms, war-making gave way to a kind of state-making that legitimated its brutality with arrests, confessions, and trials before courts in which the UN reported "the judiciary is wholly subservient to . . . the RCC [Revolutionary Command Council] and the President."

Saddam Hussein's government increasingly relied on a vast, multifaceted, and constantly domineering security apparatus that involved numerous agencies that both competed and overlapped in a tightly structured, multilayered fail-safe system of repression (Boyne 1997). The security apparatus was under Saddam's direct control and was centralized and compartmentalized. This apparatus worked outside the military chain of command and the regular army

Although each of the security agencies had its special function, Hussein relied in particular on a special General Security Directorate to ensure his own personal safety and to direct the other security and intelligence services. The General Security Directorate managed an enormous system of personal files and a huge network of spies and informants, insinuating itself into the everyday lives of Iraqi citizens. It coordinated operations with the civilian police force and maintained a unit in every police station with branches in every Iraqi governorate. It maintained its own set of detention facilities, including Abu Ghraib.

In Tilly's terms, the General Security Directorate was a highly specialized agency that represented in ideal type the culmination of state-making as organized crime. It legitimated its use of torture to extract confessions and under the cover of summary court proceedings. It justified its activities as protecting the presidency and the Iraqi state, fused in the image of The Leader, Saddam Hussein (Makiya 1989). The state included the systematic and highly organized use of rape among its most feared methods.

Data from the Iraq History Project, conducted at the DePaul University College of Law, Chicago, under the direction of Daniel Rothenberg, confirm the patterns I have described. Rothenberg's data show that the repression of Shiite and other women markedly intensified in the post–Gulf War period. As shown in figure 7.2, rapes were highly concentrated in the project data, with Shiite victims accounting for 82.7 percent of all the rapes reported. Kurdish and Sunni victims accounted together for less than 16 percent of the rapes.

The bar graphs in figure 7.3 mark more specifically the shift over time in Saddam Hussein's regime from targeting Kurds

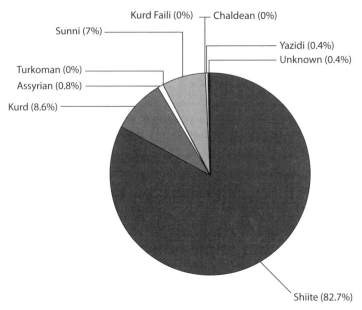

Figure 7.2 Ethnic backgrounds of victims of forcible rape (N = 698). After Iraq History Project (Rothenberg 2008).

to targeting Shiites. The regime increasingly targeted Shiites for rapes and torture during the Iran-Iraq War and after the defeat of Iraq in the First Gulf War. The proportions of those who reported torture and more specifically rapes who were Kurds peaked in the period from 1974 to 1979, and continued at high levels from 1980 to 1988. The latter period includes the Anfal attacks against the Kurds in northern Iraq. However, by the final reporting period following the First Gulf War, from 1992 to 2003, the proportions of respondents reporting torture and rape who were Kurds declined substantially. The pattern is reversed for Shiites. The proportions of those who reported torture and rapes who were Shiites peaked later and at even higher levels from 1989 to 1991 and from 1992 to 2003.

Figure 7.4 further indicates that a wide array of state actors employed and directed by the regime were in some degree involved in perpetrating rapes. However, more than 80 percent

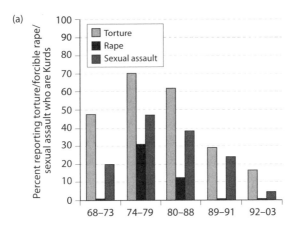

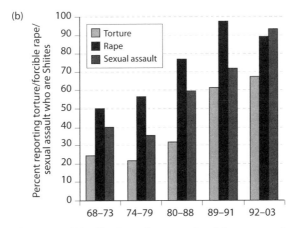

Figure 7.3 Distribution of torture, forcible rape, and sexual assaults by period, 1968–2003. After Iraq History Project (Rothenberg 2008).

of those who were reported to be perpetrators of rape in figure 7.4 were reported to be employees of the General Security Directorate. About a quarter of the perpetrators were also Baathist Party members, but this is a categorization that overlaps with being in the General Security Directorate. It is clear from these data that General Security personnel were the driving force in the reported rapes. Meanwhile, it is also noteworthy how relatively little part regular army forces were reported to have

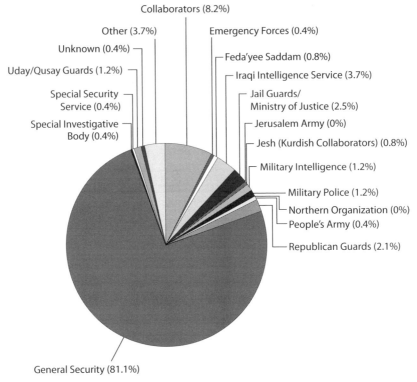

Figure 7.4 Affiliations of perpetrators of forcible rape (N = 6,982). After Iraq History Project (Rothenberg 2008).

played in perpetrating rapes. Few of the rapes involved regular army personnel.

The role of the state in the organization of sexual violence in Saddam Hussein's regime involved a linkage of the General Security Directorate with the police and courts in the perpetration of rapes and sexual assaults. Table 7.2 presents a cross-classification of the association of the police and courts through arrests and trials with General Security Directorate personnel in the reported sexual violence. An arrest and trial were more likely to be involved when General Security Directorate personnel were reported to be the perpetrators of the rapes compared with other forms of abuse (42.6 percent versus 28.2 percent). Thus, the use of arrest and trial procedures was especially common in rape cases.

TABLE 7. 2

Use of Arrest and Trial Procedures by General Security Perpetrators in Forcible Rape and Other Rights Abuse Cases, Iraq History Project (N = 6,982)

| | Arrest/trial | | | | | |
	No	Yes	N	χ^2	df	P
Forcible rape	57.4% (−2.4)	42.6% (2.4)	197	5.761	1	.010
Other abuse	71.8% (−15.6)	28.2% (15.6)	1016	222.414	1	.000

Several of the interviews offer insights into the ways in which perpetrators linked the use of investigation procedures with the perpetration of sexual violence even without sufficient evidence for arrests. For example, a woman explained how a series of rapes by a man was justified by asserting in court that she had insulted Saddam Hussein. Subsequently, after each rape he would tell her, "Put your clothes back on, bitch! You insulted the President and the Party. This is what you deserve! . . . The same thing happened every night for four months."

As indicated, in some cases the rapes occurred before the arrest and trial to coerce a confession, while in other cases the rapes took place after the arrest and trial as a form of presumed punishment. In both cases, the legal procedure denied the innocence of the victim and therefore the occurrence of the crime. Elizabeth Wood (2006:330) calls this kind of procedure or practice in the context of rape and sexual violence an "enabling norm." When the innocence of the target of the sexual attack is denied, it enables the perpetrator to commit the rape with impunity. There is no "victim" and therefore no crime. We come back to the use of this kind of framing mechanism again after presenting a final analysis of the different forms of rape practiced in Saddam's Iraq.

Table 7.3 involves a distinction between more common individual rapes and even more serious forms of rape that involve sexual enslavement and humiliation through multiple rapes, group or gang rapes, and rapes in the presence of families. The outcome in table 7.3 is whether the respondent was a victim of each of these different kinds of rape. If the organized and state-led intent is to use rape as an instrument of terror against a specific targeted group such as the Shiites, then in pre-invasion Iraq we should see the more serious and damaging kinds of rape being reported by Shiite respondents even more often than individual rapes.

The coefficients in table 7.3 indicate the change in likelihood of a respondent reporting being the victim of one of the kinds of rape. The escalating size of the coefficients in table 7.3 indicates that although single rapes were reported much more often by Shiite respondents than by others, the even more serious and damaging kinds of rape involving sexual enslavement and humiliation were especially likely to be reported by Shiite respondents. That is, Shiite respondents were especially likely to report being victims of multiple rapes, gang rapes, and rapes in the presence of families. The rapes in front of family members were intended and experienced as extreme forms of degradation that often mixed intense humiliation with forced confessions. A male victim explained, "They tore down my wife's clothes and burned her in front of my eyes and she confessed to whatever they wanted and I was crying, and she was crying also. I signed blank pages for them and told them to write whatever they wanted on the papers but to leave my wife alone and not to harm her." The rapes in this way mixed family dishonor with an insistence on confession of guilt as legal legitimation.

The legal proceedings used in conjunction with rape and sexual violence in Saddam's regime provided both tactical and moral leverage. Perpetrators were able to frame both the actions of the victims of these crimes and the meaning attached to their victimization through their control of the state's legal apparatus.

TABLE 7.3
Binary Logistic Regression of Reported Forcible Rapes, Iraq History Project (N = 6,982)

Predictor variables	Common Rape	Sexual Slavery and Humiliation		
	Single rapes (N = 62) logit (SE)	Multiple rapes (N = 67) logit (SE)	Gang rapes (N = 60) logit (SE)	Rapes in presence of families (N = 23) logit (SE)
Young child	−16.103 (2143.459)	−.124 (.742)	−.783 (1.024)	.481 (1.048)
Child/adolescent	.285 (.341)	−.774 (.475)	−.436 (.441)	.542 (.516)
Gender	1.677 (.264)***	1.944 (2.262)***	2.066 (.284)***	1.346 (423)***
1980–88	.359 (.326)	.481 (.334)	.083 (.349)	.533 (.552)
1989–91	−.576 (.356)	−1.235 (.414)**	−1.427 (.467)**	−.969 (.641)
1992–2003	.918 (.333)**	.504 (.344)	−.327 (.391)	.144 (.579)
Shiites	2.090 (.344)***	3.016 (.394)***	2.746 (.363)***	3.350 (.757)***
Constant	−8.695	−9.528	−9.129	−10.129
−2 log likelihood	599.265	596.002	554.534	259.865

State-Making and State Rape

At the heart of Charles Tilly's (1985) organized crime theory is the analogy he draws between war-making and state-making, and the claims about protection involved in both. The very enlistment of the Arab Janjaweed in the Sudanese Public *Defense* Forces and the Iraq General *Security* Directorate reflects this protective theme. Tilly's point is that war- and state-making bureaucracies parallel the methods of organized crime by creating threats to security, which the state then claims the privilege and responsibility to eliminate. Both in organized crime and in nation-states, this "protection" can prove far more criminogenic than the projected security threat.

Tilly's theory is especially prescient when he uses it to more fully and specifically consider the nature of the relationship of powerful nation-states, such as the United States and China, with allied and militarily dependent states. It is often forgotten that during the 1980s and the age of Reagan, the United States nurtured such a relationship with Saddam Hussein's Iraq as a strategic means of containing the perceived threat posed by the Islamic revolution in neighboring Iran. Donald Rumsfeld, the U.S. secretary of defense who in 2003 would oversee the American invasion and occupation of Iraq, was sent twenty years earlier by President Reagan to establish "direct contact between an envoy of President Reagan and President Saddam Hussein," while emphasizing "his close relationship" with the president. Rumsfeld and Hussein famously posed for photographers shaking hands and they discussed mutual interests in the safe transportation of Iraq's oil during the Iran-Iraq War. They agreed to meet again the following year.

Much more recently, China has protected itself against the threat of insufficient access to oil to fuel its economic growth by forming an alliance and military dependency relationship with Sudan. Tilly's point is that for such purposes, powerful nation-states often allow if not encourage militarily dependent states to combine powerful and unconstrained political leadership with criminally repressive practices to subordinate competing groups and organizations within their territories. The coercive control and exploitative benefits of such power can become enormous, and Tilly emphasizes that the temptation is intense for protected and dependent states in such situations to exercise this opportunity for subjugation and subordination of rival groups. Unconstrained power corrupts client states in ways that often mimic and exceed organized crime, using generic forms of coercion, including rape and sexual violence, framed as providing security and protection.

We have further seen in this chapter that variation in structural forms and resources diversifies how states achieve this domination over rival groups. The structure of Omar al-Bashir's domination of black African groups in Darfur was loosely organized and diffused through an outsourcing of sexual and other forms of violence based on the recruitment of Janjaweed militias into Sudan's Popular Defense Forces. The structure of Saddam Hussein regime's domination of Shiite groups in the south of Iraq was more tightly coupled and compartmentalized through a centrally controlled Security Directorate that imposed sexual and other forms of violence using its agents in local settings.

The framing mechanisms that enabled sexual victimization in these regimes similarly denied the status of crime victim to targets of rape, but again in somewhat different ways. In Bashir's Darfur, the mechanism of denial was the use of racial epithets to dehumanize the targets as criminal victims of rape and sexual violence. The perpetrators of the rapes rationalized their acts by defining their victims in racial terms that were less than human. In Saddam's Iraq, the mechanism of denial involved using the legal procedures of arrest, trials, and confessions to degrade the targets of rape and sexual violence and their prospective claims of criminal victimization. The courts allowed the confessions as a tool of rationalization for the rapes. These framing mechanisms are important to consider in relation to their prosecution and punishment respectively by the International Criminal Court and the Iraqi High Tribunal.

In July 2008, the chief prosecutor of the International Criminal Court, Luis Moreno Ocampo, sought judicial approval of an arrest warrant in Darfur charging President Omar al-Bashir of Sudan with genocide, rape, and other war crimes (Office of the Prosecutor 2008). In the months leading up to the March 2009 issuance of an arrest warrant for President Bashir by the court, Prosecutor Ocampo continued to publically charge the Sudanese president with responsibility for ongoing rapes in and around internal displacement camps in Darfur. The prosecutor's point was clear: he held Sudan's president criminally liable in "real time" for allowing these rapes to persist and proliferate.

Prosecutor Ocampo followed the *Akayesu* decision from the Rwandan tribunal in reasoning that rape is often an element of genocide. However, the International Criminal Court in its pre-trial chamber ultimately issued a warrant charging rape and crimes against humanity, including extermination and rape, but not the crime of genocide. The decision by the judges not to charge genocide removed the focus of this charge on "protected groups." That is, it took attention away from the dehumanizing framing process that used racial epithets to enable the widespread raping and killing to occur in Darfur. By doing so, the court lost an important opportunity to enforce international norms about the protection of targeted groups from the practice of sexual violence. In February 2010, the court's appeals chamber reversed the earlier decision not to charge genocide and remanded the case for reconsideration.

Several years earlier, in 2007, the Iraqi High Tribunal had announced its *Anfal* decision to convict six of the highest officials responsible for the killing and raping of Iraqi Kurds in 1987–88. The Iraqi High Tribunal is based on the same Rome Statute as the International Criminal Court, so the same kinds of charges were available to the former as the latter. The Iraqi High Tribunal invoked the liability indicated in the concept of "joint criminal enterprise" to hold higher officials responsible with one another and together with subordinates for crimes that were foreseeable even though committed by others.

As noted by the Center for Global Justice's (2007) analysis of the *Anfal* case, "The tribunal's decision on joint criminal enterprise allows tribunals to prosecute not only the individual rapists, but also the architects of a system that left women obviously vulnerable to rape." This aspect of the *Anfal* decision upholds the precedent of arguments earlier applied by the International Criminal Tribunal for the former Yugoslavia (Hagan 2003) and extends the organizational foundation for the concept of state rape applied to Omar al-Bashir and Saddam Hussein in this chapter.

The Center for Global Justice report goes on to explain why it is so important in the context of states like Iraq and Sudan—which poorly protect and often allow persecution of rape victims, while also rarely prosecuting perpetrators of rape—to have decisions invoking international legal norms about rape. The center's explanation focuses on the collective framing process in Iraq that still today denies the status of victim to women who are subjected to rape and sexual violence. The center says the following about the *Anfal* decision:

> This view of rape is remarkable in its stark contrast to Iraqi domestic penal law, which treats rape as an issue of family honor or a loss of a woman's body as property. As it stands, Iraq's domestic penal code calls for monetary compensation for virginal rape victims, not for the crime itself but only for the loss of the hymen. If the accused rapist marries his victim, "any action becomes void and any investigation or other procedure is discontinued, and if a sentence has already been passed in respect of such action, then the sentence will be quashed." This often results in women being forced by their families to marry their attackers. Given that this law clearly blocks a woman's access to justice, it is essential to find a way to shift the thinking on rape away from proprietary interests and family honor and change Iraqi penal law so that it reflects the advances made by the IHT and international law.

Yet there is also a serious problem recognized by the center's analysis of the *Anfal* case. In contrast to the International Criminal Court judges' initial decision to issue a Darfur warrant for rape but not genocide, in the *Anfal* case the Iraqi High Tribunal prosecuted and punished genocide but, despite hearing and accepting evidence about rape, it did not charge a single defendant in *Anfal* with rape.

The Iraqi High Tribunal decided after hearing testimony to leave rape off the list of charges against the defendants, even though the prosecutor in the case explicitly argued in favor of including rape. Instead, the judges chose to recognize rape simply as a form of torture. I have argued that rape was a form of torture in Iraq, and I have further argued that this torture was a crucial tool used to elicit confessions as a framing mechanism that enabled the perpetration of this crime. Yet if social and legal practices with regard to rape in Iraq are going to be meaningfully influenced by the Iraqi High Tribunal, it is essential that this court explicitly treat rape as a crime that is specifically prosecuted and punished by charging defendants with rape itself. Stanley Cohen (2001) aptly refers to this process as necessary to break the "wall of ideological normalization," which is the framing process that refuses to acknowledge rape as a war crime.

The message of this book is that we cannot simply take framing processes for granted. Framing processes have the power to both deny and denounce criminality, and in this important sense, they have the capacity to both cause and deter crime, depending by whom and how they are used. This is an argument for why the United States should apply the principles of international law to the conduct of its own leadership in relation to the war crimes of sexual violence at Abu Ghraib prison in Iraq, and in relation to the war on terrorism more generally.

Epilogue
The Age of Obama?

A 2008 *TIME* MAGAZINE COVER portrayed the newly elected President Barack Obama looking like Franklin Roosevelt, a cigarette holder jutting skyward from his jaw, riding in an open-top car down Pennsylvania Avenue toward the White House. The cover heralded "The New, New Deal," and the accompanying story was titled "The New Liberal Order." The story recalled Obama's earlier election-night celebration in Chicago's Grant Park and contrasted it to the night forty years earlier, when 10,000 people gathered in the same park to protest the Democratic Convention's ratification of Lyndon Johnson's Vietnam War and the convention's ill-fated nomination of Hubert Humphrey. A commission later concluded that the Chicago police rioted that night when they charged and beat the demonstrators.

Many fearful television viewers, recalling the images of ghetto and campus riots, likely approved of that night's rough "law and order" tactics. The *Time* story argued that Grant Park in 1968 was the symbolic turning point marking the end of the age of Roosevelt and the beginning of the age of Reagan, with Republicans going on to win seven of the next ten presidential elections.

In his postelection story, *Time*'s Peter Beinart (2008) argued that Obama promised a new era of order and stability: "The coalition that carried Obama to victory is every bit as sturdy as America's last two dominant coalitions: the ones that elected Franklin Roosevelt and Ronald Reagan." He continued, "the

Obama majority is sturdy for one overriding reason: liberal-
ism, which average Americans once associated with upheaval,
now promises stability instead."

This is a story about conservative compromise as much as
liberal change. It posits an electorate that is newly fearful of
the risks posed by the banks and Wall Street and a public still
fearful of violence on ghetto streets as well as international terrorism. I noted in the last chapter the limits of Obama administration support for institutions of international law such as
the permanent International Criminal Court. This leads to the
question of whether an Obama administration will overcome
the sturdy resistance to domestic changes posed by American
public opinion and financial interests.

Will "Obama's majority" be able to change the massive
shifts in the direction of downward social control and upward
financial deregulation that have resulted from fear of the
streets and freeing of the suites? Will this majority reform the
criminal justice system and re-regulate the banks and corpora-
tions? Time will tell, but there are reasons to consider how
great the break from the age of Reagan is likely to be.

||||||||||

The first African American attorney general to head the Department of Justice, Eric Holder, is a strong ally of the first
African American president of the United States. The attorney
general (Holder 2009) provocatively commented just after his
confirmation and during Black History month that America
was "essentially a nation of cowards" for its silence about racial problems, notably including crime. President Obama was
even more provocative in saying the Cambridge police behaved "stupidly" in handcuffing and arresting his friend,
Henry "Skip" Gates, the African American Harvard professor,
on his own front porch. However, the media and public resistance to these statements was so strong that the newly elected
attorney general and president soon reframed their remarks.

Still, policies can be more important than pronouncements. Two policy areas I have emphasized in my critical collective frame analysis are those concerning prisons and markets, and the reform and regulation thereof. Changing the direction of a system as massive and decentralized as America's prisons is like changing the course of a large ship—in this case, the ship of state. Sociologists call this the problem of path dependency. The policy path of mass incarceration is solidly entrenched. At a minimum, a phase of institutional reframing is likely necessary to shift this past- and path-dependent trajectory.

Neither Obama nor Holder has yet explicitly indicated support for a major change in America's world leading rate of imprisonment, which at the beginning of 2010 amounted to 2.4 million Americans imprisoned. Yet there are signs in the last year or two that the expansion of the prison population may have peaked. Some state initiatives, such as those in California, New York, and Michigan, promise to reduce correctional populations. The sheer fact that about one-third of the national prison population will be older than fifty years of age by 2010 points to an expensive geriatric imperative toward selective decarceration. Michigan, conscious of its strained resources, has reduced its prison population by nearly 10 percent. New York State has reduced it inmate population by nearly 20 percent by modifying its Rockefeller-era drug laws. On the other hand, New York still sends about 10 percent of former inmates back to prison each year for minor parole violations such as missing a scheduled appointment.

Meanwhile, the national imprisonment of immigrants is growing, with immigration cases making up more than half of all criminal prosecutions by the federal government in 2009. The point person on immigration detention is Homeland Security Secretary Jane Napolitano. Secretary Napolitano has said that the "paradigm" of enforcement in the preceding Bush administration that increased immigration imprisonment was wrong. The Homeland Security Administration estimates that the United States still detains nearly half a million undocumented immigrants annually, more than double the number in 2003. Secretary Napolitano has said she expects the current number to stay the same or even grow slightly.

As of January 1, 2010, state prisons held nearly 6 percent fewer inmates than the year before, while the population in federal prisons had increased by nearly 7 percent. Because state prisons hold more inmates, overall there is a marginal net decline in the U.S. world-leading rate of imprisonment (Pew Center on the States 2010). The challenge is to get both the federal and the state systems to reduce imprisonment.

The Obama administration has extended a Bush administration program that deputizes local police so they can act as immigration officers on their street patrols and in city jails. A jail fingerprinting program called Secure Communities has identified more than 100,000 "criminal aliens." This has resulted in the detention of several thousand serious offenders, but also the detention of many undocumented immigrants for traffic violations and other minor infractions, including technical visa violations. One effect is to make immigrant crime victims afraid to engage the police in community law enforcement. Secretary Napolitano wants to direct resources toward the more serious criminal offenders among the detained immigrants, but about half of those detained in 2009, the first year of the Obama administration, had no criminal record, and only about 10 percent had committed a violent offense. A paradox of the immigration detention initiative is that immigrants identified as criminal defendants frequently remain in U.S. prisons through lengthy periods of prosecution and sentencing before being deported.

The federal government and the states subcontract the detention of many immigrants to rented and private facilities built with the financial instruments called lease revenue bonds (LRBs). The number of immigrants in private prisons doubled from 2000 to 2008. U.S. Supreme Court decisions hold that detention of immigrants is not punishment and therefore detained immigrants do not require access to lawyers. Officials frequently transfer detainees between overcrowded facilities without notice, making it difficult to maintain contact with families or retain legal assistance. More than half the detainees face deportation without legal counsel. Prosecutors typically process immigration cases in several days, while white-collar and narcotics cases average about a year. The Obama administration nonetheless promises to improve detention conditions, increase access to lawyers, and build model detention centers to replace substandard facilities, but there is little further prospect that the extensive imprisonment of immigrants or others in America's overcrowded penal system will radically change in the near term.

The Obama administration apparently hopes to diminish opposition to work and citizenship programs in the United States by dampening objections with a punitive system of imprisonment for undocumented immigrants. The goal is to frame an immigration policy that promises a "tough and fair pathway to earned legal status." Yet in advancing this bridge framing of the immigration debate, the administration risks pursuing a policy compromise that perpetuates a tension if not a contradiction with its ultimate goals. Too many of the same people being locked up are potential candidates for legal work and citizenship. This encourages the public to confuse the aspiration to immigrate and work with the desire to commit crimes, and some of the policies could ultimately do more harm than good. The policy of immigrant detention is an "add-on" to past policies of mass incarceration.

Senators James Webb and Arlen Specter have joined with many members of Congress in proposing a national criminal justice commission that would offer an alternative framing of U.S. reliance on imprisonment. It is important that the mandate of this commission be framed in terms of criminal justice rather than merely crime. Webb directly addresses the imprisonment issue, observing that "America's criminal justice system has deteriorated to the point that it is a national disgrace." He continues, "With five percent of the world's population, our country houses twenty-five percent of the world's prison population. Incarcerated drug offenders have soared 1200% since 1980. And four times as many mentally ill people are in prisons than in mental health hospitals. We should be devoting precious law enforcement capabilities toward making our communities safer" (Webb 2009). Senator Webb's co-sponsor, Arlen Specter, lost his bid to be re-elected as a Democratic Senator from Pennsylvania, and the other proponents of the criminal justice commission may fare no better.

Uncertainty similarly clouds the administration's plans for financial reform and regulatory enforcement. Much of this uncertainty involves the sources and victims of the economic collapse. So far, the bank and non-bank sources of this collapse have received far more financial assistance than have the recipients of subprime and related kinds of lending, and larger reform and regulatory efforts remain more aspiration than achievement. More than a year after the economic collapse, there is growing reason to believe that individuals and institutions engaged in the vertically integrated strategies to aggressively market subprime mortgages have committed civil and criminal financial fraud.

The top-down bailout of the banks may have stabilized these institutions, but the economy remains weak, and there are continuing problems in the housing sector. For example, after already having bailed out the mortgage lenders Fannie Mae and Freddie Mac with a government investment of $96 billion, the Federal Housing Administration (FHA) continues to experience rising foreclosures. For the past two years, about one in every four FHA borrowers has faced serious problems, including foreclosure. There is a fundamental debate over whether the FHA should tighten its lending practices, and over assistance for borrowers. Yet lenders defrauded many of these borrowers. The FHA had former employees sign secrecy agreements before giving them severance payments, and this impaired investigations of their loan practices.

In light of the evidence presented in chapter 6 that increased residential loans in the years leading up to 2000 produced reductions in violent crime rates in African American and Latino neighborhoods, it makes sense to consider how the collapse of mortgage lending and the escalation in frequently fraud-induced defaults and foreclosures may now be affecting the stability of neighborhoods in America. Effective mortgage assistance, such as mandated in the $75 billion Making Homes Affordable Program (MHAP), promised to be an effective bottom-up age of Obama housing policy.

Yet six months after the economic collapse, the Obama administration acknowledged its disappointment with the use made by major mortgage-holding banks and non-banks of this program. The MHAP offered these institutions several thousand dollars for each loan they modified and maintained for up to three years. The program targeted up to four million foreclosures but reached less than 5 percent of this goal in the first half year. The secretary of the treasury called major institutional representatives to Washington and implored them to triple this outcome in the following six months. Although lenders met this goal, foreclosures continued to mount faster than the modifications.

Critics charged that by keeping homeowners in default and foreclosure rather than modifying their mortgages, the lenders could keep the homes on their books at full value and profit from the fees they charged homeowners for being delinquent in making payments. As well, the modifications were initially for only three trial months, and the vast majority of the modifications did not lower the loan balances. This meant that most of the borrowers still owed more than the market value of their homes. This gave the borrowers less reason to care for their homes or to keep making the temporarily modified payments. Many of the borrowers have credit card and other debts that are not considered in the loan modifications. Elizabeth Warren, the Harvard law professor chairing a congressional oversight panel, estimated that foreclosures were outpacing modifications by two to one.

The cornerstone of the Obama administration's efforts to reform and regulate financial institutions is its promise to create a consumer financial protection agency. Such an agency could, for example, insist on transparent loan and credit instruments and enforce their legal use. The goal is to centralize regulatory and policing responsibilities in one agency so that institutions could not "shop around" for the least intrusive regulator to report to, and to facilitate the monitoring of the new regulatory agency to ensure that it exercises its enforcement powers. The further goal is to recreate for consumers a framing of finance that encourages trust and confidence in the marketplace.

The naming of the proposed consumer financial protection agency is in itself an attempt at institutional reframing and competes with adversarial frames that seek to derail its actualization. There is an array of opposing frames advanced by the lobbying efforts of the financial industry that thrived on deregulation. These include arguments that deregulation is an already remedied problem, that the regulatory issue is of much lower priority than other more pressing matters, that there are already more regulatory bureaucracies than we need, and that the financial world is too vast, complicated, and rapidly changing for government regulation. The challenge is whether the public as well as the administration is sufficiently engaged to make a fully independent consumer financial protection agency the realization of an age of Obama.

Lobbyists for the financial industry invested $200 million in 2009 in weakening the legislation to create this agency. They succeeded in exempting 8,000 community banks among the nation's 8,200 banks from regulatory oversight, so that only the largest banks and other lenders would be included. Foresight Analytics, a banking research firm, estimated that more than a quarter of these "runaway banks" exceeded risk thresholds that would ordinarily call for greater scrutiny from regulators. Lobbyists oppose state regulation that would lead state attorneys general to police and prosecute the large national banks more aggressively than federal laws. A major concern with the largest financial institutions is to regulate trading in the derivatives that were central in the economic collapse.

Lobbyists are trying to keep some derivatives in the dark by creating legislative exceptions from oversight for large fee-producing forms of these trades.

A key to the new agency is that its single mission would be to protect consumers. Existing regulatory agencies are primarily concerned to make sure the financial institutions are sound, which requires institutions to raise capital. Practices that harm consumers, such as teaser rate mortgages and credit card penalties, increase capital and thus help meet regulatory requirements of solvency. This makes it optimistic, for example, to believe existing regulatory agencies will work single-mindedly to impose plain vanilla lending practices that meet a meaningful standard of reasonableness in the creation and use of transparent financial instruments and practices. The Obama administration reinforced this concern when it hired an executive from Goldman Sachs as the chief of the enforcement unit of the Securities and Exchange Commission. By the second quarter of 2009, Goldman was moving ahead with a "value at risk" (i.e., calculated as VaR) strategy that was the most aggressive in its history.

A protection agency institutionally devoted to consumers is more likely to reframe practices according to tightened standards. As a result, the financial industry is lobbying hard to limit and weaken powers of the protection agency and other reforms. Citigroup's chairman, Richard Parsons, hired Richard Hohlt, a former lobbyist for the U.S. League of Savings Institutions discussed in chapter 6. Former members of the Reagan administration credit Hohlt and the league with having successfully persuaded Congress to deregulate savings and loan institutions, setting off the 1980s S&L crisis that led to more than 2,000 bank failures and anticipating today's collapse.

The prognosis for the age of Obama is therefore unclear. The age of Reagan's deregulation of America's corporate suites contributed to a massively costly and counterproductive policy response to problems of crime in America's streets. Unregulated financial innovations advanced the prison construction necessary for the policy of mass incarceration, and other forms of deregulation spurred the mortgage manipulation creating the foreclosure crisis that destabilized housing in disadvantaged neighborhoods.

The prospect of a new age of Obama in crime policy depends heavily on reversing the incarceration and financial crises in the United States. The age of Obama, for example, could bring a national commission on criminal justice and a new consumer protection agency with the promise of imposing important institutional reforms and reframings of crime control in America. These efforts have the potential to be "frame-changers" in the path-dependent directions of the crime policies of the age of Reagan. They are promising but unproven steps toward rebalancing the overcontrol of the streets and the undercontrol of the suites.

The story of under control in the suites spread from the big banks to big oil as this book went to press. The story again was about the under regulation of risk. Environmentalists already knew British Petroleum (BP) was a company that underestimated safety risks in pursuing profits when the Deepwater Horizon explosion killed eleven workers and spewed hundreds of thousands of barrels of oil into the Gulf of Mexico. A prior explosion at BP's Texas oil refinery killed 15 workers in 2005, and BP was responsible for an oil spill in Alaska's Prudhoe Bay a year later. Americans learned after the Gulf spill that Congress in a 1990 post–Exxon Valdez law had legally capped cleanup costs at $75 million. Even though BP agreed to exceed this cap in the Gulf, the point is nonetheless clear. Threats of civil or criminal penalties did not deter BP from devising slipshod Gulf drilling plans, and preliminary investigations revealed that BP's planning was both shoddy and sparse. The Minerals Management Service (MMS) exempted big oil companies in 2008 from even filing plans for cleaning up major oil spills that BP argued would not happen in the Gulf.

The modeling and the markets that promised to minimize risks were no more effective in the oil industry than in the banking sector. MMS was in a conflict of interest in the Gulf and elsewhere because it collected royalties from the same companies it regulated. An Inspector General report for the Interior Department revealed that during the Bush Administration MMS was a captured regulator whose officials negotiated rigged contracts, worked part-time as private oil consultants, received illegal drugs, and had sexual and other compromising relationships involving oil company employees.

As the BP oil spill in the Gulf unfolded, President Obama fired his new Director of MMS, Elizabeth Birnbaum. Reports by the *New York Times* and other news organizations indicated that Ms. Birnbaum had done little or nothing to reform MMS, including ignoring the tendency of agency employees to dismiss and neglect safety and environmental risks in off-shore drilling plans.

It is common for commentators to frame oil and banking activities as highly complex and as posing high-cost but low-probability risks. This may explain some of the public tendency in the past to fear the threats posed by practices of the oil and banking industries less than conventional street crimes, and this may also be one reason we treat dangerous corporate practices more like suite misdemeanors than street crimes. Yet the same low-probability/high-cost framing also applies to homicide compared to more common crimes, and the complexity frame applies equally well to the mass atrocities of genocide. The challenging question is whether a new awareness of the enormity of the damages and costs to life and environment associated with corporate risk taking will now change the crime control equation in the suites and streets of America.

ACKNOWLEDGMENTS
||||||||||

I AM PLEASED TO ACKNOWLEDGE the assistance of a number of persons who played invaluable roles in the development of this book. I am grateful to Joseph Persico for allowing me to interview him about his ghostwriting role in the President's Secret Crime Report and his earlier work as Nelson Rockefeller's speechwriter. Joachim Savelsberg and Jonathan Simon commented on the complete manuscript and informed my thinking in numerous ways. Jeremy Hagan listened and responded patiently to my ideas about the financial crisis. Joshua Hagan consulted on cover design and assisted in its final composition. Wenona Rymond-Richmond was my co-author in our earlier book on Darfur and allowed me to import thoughts from that analysis into the current comparison of sexual violence in Darfur and Iraq. Eric Poehler contributed his superb mapmaking skills. Daniel Rothenberg allowed use of the extraordinary data he collected for the Iraq History Project and helped me to develop some of my thoughts about patterns in these data. Allison Lynch pulled the entire manuscript together and consulted on the cover concept. Linda Hagan listened to probably every idea in the book and provided unconditional love and support throughout.

REFERENCES
||||||||||

AFP. 2006. "Saddam Vows to Kill Prosecutor for Rape Charge." August 21.
———. 2008. "UN Denounces Rape as 'War Crime.'" June 19.
Akers, Ronald. 1977. *Deviant Behavior: A Social Learning Approach*. Belmont, CA: Wadsworth.
———. 1995. "Linking Sociology and Its Specialties: The Case of Criminology." *Social Forces* 71:1–16.
Akerlof, George, and Paul Romer. 1993. "Looting: The Economic Underworld of Bankruptcy for Profit." In *Brookings Papers on Economic Activity*, ed. William C. Brainard and George Perry, 2:1–73. Washington, DC: Brookings Institution Press.
Alvarez, Alexander. 1997. "Adjusting to Genocide: The Techniques of Neutralization and the Holocaust." *Social Science History* 21:139–78.
Ambos, Kai. 2009. "Prosecuting Guantanamo in Europe: Can and Should the Masterminds of the 'Torture Memos' Be Held Criminally Responsible on the Basis of Universal Jurisdiction?" *Case Western Reserve Journal of International Law* 42:405–48.
Andrews, Edmund. 2009. "Bernanke Concedes Fed Lapses." *New York Times*, December 4, B1.
Apuzzo, Matt, and Daniel Wagner. 2009. "Geithner Makes Time to Talk to Wall Street Bankers." Associated Press, October 8.
Askin, Kelly. 1997. *War Crimes Against Women: Prosecution in International War Crimes Tribunals*. The Hague, Netherlands: Kluwer Law International.
———. 2009. *War Crimes Against Women: Prosecution in International War Crimes Tribunals*. The Hague, Netherlands: Kluwer Law International.
Balbus, Isaac. 1973. *The Dialectics of Legal Repression*. New York: Russell Sage.
Banfield, Edward. 1968. *The Unheavenly City*. Boston: Little, Brown.
Barofsky, Neil. 2009. Factors Affecting Efforts to Limit Payments to AIG Counterparties (SITARP-10-03). Washington, DC: Office of Special Investigator for Toxic Assets Recovery Program, released November 17.
Bashir, Halima. 2009. *Tears of the Desert: A Memoir of Survival in Darfur*. New York: One World/Ballantine.
Bean, F., R. Chanove, R. Cushing, and R. de la Garza. 1994. *Illegal Mexican Immigration and the United States/Mexico Border: The Effects of Operation Hold*

the Line on the El Paso/Juarez Border. Washington, DC: U.S. Commission on Immigration Reform.

Beaumont, Gustave de, and Alexis de Tocqueville. 1833. *On the Penitentiary System in the United States and Its Application to France*. Reprt. Chicago: Vail-Ballou Press, 1964.

Becker, Howard. 1963. *Outsiders: Studies in the Sociology of Deviance*. New York: Free Press.

Beckett, Katherine. 1997. *Making Crime Pay: Law and Order in Contemporary American Politics*. New York: Oxford University Press.

Beinart, Peter. 2008. "The New Liberal Order." *Time*, November 13, 1.

Bellow, Saul. 1987. *More Die of Heartbreak*. New York: William Morrow.

Benford, Robert, and David Snow. 2000. "Framing Processes and Social Movements: A Review and Assessment." *Annual Review of Sociology* 26:611–39.

Bennett, Willam, John DiIulio, and John Walters. 1996. *Body Count: Moral Poverty . . . and How to Win America's War Against Crime and Drugs*. New York: Simon & Schuster.

Bernstein, Jared. 2007. "Updated CBO Data Reveal Unprecedented Increase in Inequality." Issue Brief no. 239. Boston: Economic Policy Institute.

Bernstein, Nina. 2010. "Officials Obscured Truth of Migrant Deaths in Jail." *New York Times*, January 10, A1.

Biderman, Albert. 1957. "Communist Attempts to Elicit False Confessions from Air Force Prisoners of War." *Bulletin of the New York Academy of Medicine* 39:616–25.

———. 1967. "Surveys of Population Samples for Estimating Crime Incidence." *Annals of the American Academy of Political and Social Science* 374: 16–33.

Blumstein, Alfred. 1993. "Making Rationality Relevant." *Criminology* 31:1–16.

Blumstein, Alfred, and Jacqueline Cohen. 1973. "A Theory of the Stability of Punishment." *Journal of Criminology, Criminal Law & Police Science* 63: 198–207.

———. 1987. "Characterizing Criminal Careers." *Science* 237:985–99.

Blumstein, Alfred, Jacqueline Cohen, and David Farrington. 1988. "Criminal Career Research: Its Value for Criminology." *Criminology* 26:1–36.

Blumstein, Alfred, Jacqueline Cohen, and Daniel Nagin. 1978. *Deterrence and Incapacitation: Estimating the Effects of Criminal Sanctions on Crime Rates*. Washington, DC: National Academy Press.

Blumstein, Alfred, Jacqueline Cohen, Jeffrey Roth, and Christy Visher. 1986. *Criminal Careers and "Career Criminals."* Vol. 1. Washington, DC: National Academy Press.

Blumstein, Alfred, and Joel Wallman. 2006. *The Crime Drop in America*. New York: Cambridge University Press.

Bonger, William. 1916. *Criminality and Economic Conditions*. Boston: Little, Brown.

Bonnie, Richard, and Charles Whitebread. 1974. *The Marihuana Conviction*. Charlottesville: University of Virginia Press.

Bourdieu, Pierre. 1989. "Social Space and Symbolic Power." *Sociological Theory* 7:1.

Boyne, Sean. 1997. "Inside Iraq's Security Network, Part One." *Jane's Intelligence Review* 7312–16.

Braithwaite, John. 1981. "The Myth of Social Class and Criminality Reconsidered." *American Sociological Review* 46:36–57.

Buck, Connie. 2009. "Angelo's Ashes: The Man Who Became the Face of the Financial Crisis." *New Yorker*, June 29, 46.

Buckley, William. 2009. "Goldman Settles Subprime Inquiry." *Wall Street Journal*, May 12, C3.

Burry, Michael. 2010. "I Saw the Crisis Coming: Why Didn't the Fed?" *New York Times*, April 4, WK10.

Bush, George W. 2004a. "Remarks on Efforts to Globally Promote Women's Human Rights," March 12. In *Public Papers of the Presidents—George W. Bush*. Washington, DC: Government Printing Office, 1:375–80.

———. 2004b. "Remarks in Des Moines, Iowa," April 15. In *Public Papers of the Presidents—George W. Bush*. Washington, DC: Government Printing Office, 1:580–91.

———. 2004c. "Interview with Al Arabiya Televion," May 5. In *Public Papers of the Presidents—George W. Bush*. Washington, DC: Government Printing Office, 1:770–73.

Calavita, Kitty, Henry Pontell, and Robert Tillman. 1997. *Big Money: Fraud and Politics in the Savings and Loan Crisis*. Berkeley and Los Angeles: University of California Press.

Cassidy, John. 2009. *How Markets Fail: The Logic of Economic Calamities*. New York: Farrar, Straus and Giroux.

Center for Global Justice. 2007. *The Anfal Decision: Breaking New Ground for Women's Rights in Iraq*. New York: Center for Global Justice.

Central Intelligence Agency. Inspector General. 1998. *Allegations of Connections Between CIA and the Contras in Cocaine Trafficking to the United States*. Vol. 1, *The California Story*. Vol. 2, *The Contra Story* (96–0143-IG). Washington, DC: Office of the Inspector General, Central Intelligence Agency.

Chambliss, William, and Robert Seidman. 1971. *Law, Order and Power*. Reading, MA: Addison-Wesley.

Chan, Sewell, and Eric Dash. 2010. "Financial Crisis Inquiry Wrestles with Setbacks." *New York Times*, April 6, B4.

Chernow, Ron. 1990. *The House of Morgan: An American Banking Dynasty and the Rise of Modern Finance*. New York: Grove Press.

Clark, Wesley. 2001. *Waging Modern War*. New York: Public Affairs.

Cloward, Richard, and Lloyd Ohlin. 1960. *Delinquency and Opportunity: A Theory of Delinquent Gangs*. New York: Free Press of Glencoe.

Cohan, William. 2009a. *House of Cards*. New York: Doubleday.

———. 2009b. "An Offer He Couldn't Refuse." *Atlantic*, September, 62.

Cohen, Albert. 1955. *Delinquent Boys*. New York: Free Press of Glencoe.

Cohen, Lawrence, and Marcus Felson. 1979. "Social Change and Crime Rate Trends: A Routine Activity Approach." *American Sociological Review* 44:588–608.

Cohen, Stanley. 2001. *States of Denial: Knowing about Atrocities and Suffering*. Cambridge: Polity Press.

Colvin, Mark, and John Pauly. 1983. "A Critique of Criminology: Toward an Integrated Theory of Delinquency Production." *American Journal of Sociology* 89:512–52.

Comfort, Megan. 2008. *Doing Time Together*. Berkeley and Los Angeles: University of California Press.

Committee on Foreign Relations, Subcommittee on Terrorism, Narcotics and International Operations. 1988. *Drugs, Law Enforcement and Foreign Policy*. Washington, DC: U.S. Government Printing Office.

CNBC. 2004. "Pentagon Officials to Answer Tough Questions from Senate Armed Services Committee Regarding Iraqi Prisoner Abuse." April 4.

Cressey, Donald. 1965. "The Respectable Criminal: Why Some of Our Best Friends Are Crooks." *Transaction* 2:12–15.

———. 1971. *Other People's Money: A Study of the Social Psychology of Embezzlement*. Glencoe, IL: Free Press.

———. 1979. *Theft of a Nation*. New York: Harper & Bros.

Cullen, Francis. 1988. "Were Cloward and Ohlin Strain Theorists? Delinquency and Opportunity Revisited." *Journal of Research in Crime and Delinquency* 25:214–41.

Currie, Elliott. 1999. "Radical Criminology or Just Criminology—Then and Now." *Crime and Social Justice* 26:16–18.

Dash, Eric. 2009. "U.S. Said to Rethink Sale of Citi Stake." *New York Times*, December 17, B5.

de Waal, Alex. 2004. "Counter-Insurgency on the Cheap." *London Review of Books* 25, no. 15:25–27.

———, ed. 2007. *War in Darfur and the Search for Peace*. Cambridge, MA: Harvard University Press.

Dillon, Sam. 1997. "U.S.-Mexico Study Sees Exaggeration in Migration Data." *New York Times*, August 31, A1, A6.

Durkheim, Émile. 1951 (1897). *Suicide*, trans. John Spaulding and George Simpson. Glencoe, IL: Free Press.

Duster, Troy. 1970. *The Legislation of Morality: Law, Drugs and Moral Judgment*. New York: Free Press.

Editors. 1976. "Editorial: Berkeley's School of Criminology, 1950–1976." *Crime and Social Justice* 6:1–3.

Elder, Glen. 1985. *Life Course Dynamics*. Ithaca, NY: Cornell University Press.

Elliott, Delbert, and Susan Ageton. 1980. "Reconciling Race and Class Differences in Self-Reported and Official Estimates of Delinquency." *American Sociological Review* 45:95–110.

Ennis, P. H. 1967. *Criminal Victimization in the United States: A Report of a National Survey*. Washington, DC: U.S. Government Printing Office.

Farberman, Harvey. 1975. "A Criminogenic Market Structure: The Automobile Industry." *Sociological Quarterly* 16:438–57.

Feeley, Malcolm. 2003. "Crime, Social Order and the Rise of the Neo Conservative Politics." *Theoretical Criminology* 7:111–30.

Feeley, Malcolm, and Austin Sarat. 1980. *The Policy Dilemma: Federal Crime Policy and the Law Enforcement Assistance Administration, 1968–1978*. Minneapolis: University of Minnesota Press.

Feeley, Malcolm, and Jonathan Simon. 1992. "The New Penology: Notes on the Emerging Strategy of Corrections and Its Implications." *Criminology* 30:449–74.

Fein, Helen. 1979. *Accounting for Genocide: National Responses and Jewish Victimization during the Holocaust*. New York: Free Press.

Feith, Douglas. 1985. "Law in the Service of Terror: The Strange Case of the Additional Protocol." *National Interest* 1:36–47.

Felson, Marcus. 1994. *Crime and Everyday Life: Insights and Implications for Society*. Thousand Oaks, CA: Pine Forge Press.

Flint, Julie, and Alex de Waal. 2005. *Darfur: A Short History of a Long War*. London: Zed Books.

Foster, Holly, and John Hagan. 2007. "Incarceration and Intergenerational Social Exclusion." *Social Problems* 54:399–433.

———. 2009. "The Mass Incarceration of Parents in America: Issues of Race/ Ethnicity, Collateral Damage to Children, and Prisoner Reentry." *Annals of the American Academy of Political and Social Science* 623:179–94.

Frankel, Marvin. 1972. *Criminal Sentences: Law Without Order*. New York: Hill and Wang.

Friend, Tad. 2009. "Cash for Keys: L.A.'s Go-To Guy on Foreclosures. *New Yorker*, April 6, 34.

Gamson, William. 1990. "Constructing Social Protest." In *Social Movements and Culture*, ed. H. Johnson and B. Klandermans. Minneapolis: University of Minnesota Press.

———. 1992. *Talking Politics*. New York: Cambridge University Press.

———. 1995. "Constructing Social Protest." In *Social Movements and Culture*, ed. H. Johnson and B. Klandermans. Minneapolis: University of Minneapolis Press.

Gardam, Judith, and Michelle Jarvis. 2001. *Women, Armed Conflict, and International Law*. Boston: Kluwer Law International.

Garfinkel, Harold. 1956. "Conditions of Successful Degradation Ceremonies." *American Journal of Sociology* 61:420–24.

Garland, David. 2001. *The Culture of Control: Crime and Social Order in Contemporary Society*. Chicago: University of Chicago Press.

Gawande, Atul. 2009. "Hellhole." *New Yorker*, March 30.

Geis, Gilbert. 1962. "Toward a Delineation of White-Collar Offenses." *Sociological Inquiry* 32:160–71.

Gillis, A. R. 1989. "Crime and State Surveillance in Nineteenth Century France." *American Journal of Sociology* 95:307–41.

Gilmore, Ruth. 2007. *Golden Gulag: Prisons, Surplus, Crisis and Opposition in Globalizing California*. Berkeley and Los Angeles: University of California Press.

Glueck, Sheldon, and Eleanor Glueck. 1950. *Unraveling Juvenile Delinquency*. New York: Commonwealth Fund.

———. 1968. *Delinquents and Non-Delinquents in Perspective*. Cambridge, MA: Harvard University Press.

Goffman, Erving. 1961. *Asylums*. Chicago: Aldine-Atherton.

———. 1963. *Stigma: Notes on the Management of Spoiled Identity*. Englewood Cliffs, NJ: Prentice-Hall.

———. 1974. *Frame Analysis: An Essay on the Organization of Experience*. New York: HarperCollins.

Goldsmith, Jack. 2007. *The Terror Presidency: Law and Judgment inside the Bush Administration*. New York: W. W. Norton.

Goodman, Peter. 2009. "Philadelphia Gives Struggling Homeowners a Chance to Stay Put." *New York Times*, November 18, 2009, A1, A26.

Gottfredson, Michael, and Travis Hirschi. 1986. "The True Value of Lambda Would Appear to Be Zero: An Essay on Career Criminals, Criminal Careers, Selective Incapacitation, Cohort Studies, and Related Topics." *Criminology* 24:213–33.

———. 1987. "Causes of White Collar Crime." *Criminology* 25:101–23.

———. 1988. "Science, Public Policy, and the Career Paradigm." *Criminology* 26:37–56.

———. 1990. *A General Theory of Crime*. Stanford, CA: Stanford University Press.

———. 1994. "National Crime Control Policies." *Society* 32:30–36.

———. 1995. "Control Theory and the Life-Course Perspective." *Studies on Crime and Crime Prevention* 4:1–13.

Gottschalk, Marie. 2006. *The Prison and the Gallows: The Politics of Mass Incarceration in America*. Cambridge: Cambridge University Press.

———. 2009. "The Long Reach of the Carceral State: The Politics of Crime, Mass Imprisonment, and Penal Reform in the United State and Abroad." *Law & Social Inquiry* 34:439–72.

Gourevitch, Philip, and Errol Morris. 2008. *Standard Operating Procedure.* New York: Penguin Press.

Government Accounting Office. 1994. *Financial Derivatives: Actions Needed to Protect the Financial System,* 19, c. 6. Washington, DC: U.S. Government Accounting Office.

Greenberg, David. 1981. *Crime and Capitalism.* Palo Alto, CA: Mayfield.

Grogger, Jeffrey, and Michael Willis. 2000. "The Emergence of Crack Cocaine and the Rise in Urban Crime Rates." *Review of Economics and Statistics* 82:519–29.

Gurr, Ted R. 1979. "On the History of Violent Crime in Europe and America." In *Violence in America: Historical and Comparative Perspectives,* ed. Hugh P. Graham and Ted R. Gurr. Newbury Park, CA: Sage.

———. 1981. "Historical Trends in Violent Crimes: A Critical Review of the Evidence." In *Crime and Justice: Annual Review of Research,* ed. M. Tonry and N. Morris, 3:295–353. Chicago: University of Chicago Press.

Gusfield, Joseph. 1963. *Symbolic Crusade: Status Politics and the American Temperance Movement.* Urbana: University of Illinois Press.

Hagan, John. 1991. "Destiny and Drift: Subcultural Preferences, Status Attainments and the Risks and Rewards of Youth." *American Sociological Review* 56:567–82.

———. 1993. "The Social Embeddedness of Crime and Unemployment." *Criminology* 31, no. 4: 465–91.

———. 2003. *Justice in the Balkans: Prosecuting War Crimes at The Hague Tribunal.* Chicago: University of Chicago Press.

Hagan, John, and Celesta Albonetti. 1982. "Race, Class and the Perception of Criminal Injustice in America." *American Journal of Sociology* 88:329–55.

Hagan, John, and Ilene Bernstein. 1979. "Conflict in Context: The Sanctioning of Draft Resisters, 1963–76." *Social Problems* 27, no. 1: 109–22.

Hagan, John, and Ronit Dinovitzer. 1999. "Children of the Prison Generation: Collateral Consequences of Imprisonment for Children and Communities" *Crime and Justice* 26:121–62.

Hagan, John, Gabrielle Ferrales, and Guillermina Jasso. 2008. "How Law Rules: An Iraqi Judicial Sentencing Experiment" *Law & Society Review* 42:605–44.

———. 2010. "Collaboration and Resistance in the Punishment of Torture in Iraq." *Wisconsin Journal of International Law,* in press.

Hagan, John, and Bill McCarthy. 1997. *Mean Streets: Youth Crime and Homelessness.* New York: Cambridge University Press.

Hagan, John, and Alberto Palloni. 1988. "Crimes as Social Events in the Life Course. Reconceiving a Criminology Controversy." *Criminology* 26:87–100.

———. 1990. "The Social Reproduction of a Criminal Class in Working Class London, circa 1950–80." *American Journal of Sociology* 96:265–99.

Hagan, John, and Wenona Rymond-Richmond. 2009. *Darfur and the Crime of Genocide*. New York: Cambridge University Press.

Hagan, John, Wenona Rymond-Richmond, and Alberto Palloni. 2009. "Racial Targeting of Rape in Darfur." *American Journal of Public Health*, in press.

Hagan, John, Carla Shedd, and Monique Payne. 2005. "Race, Ethnicity and Youth Perceptions of Criminal Injustice." *American Sociological Review* 70:381–407.

Harir, Sharif. 1992. "Militarization of Conflict: Displacement and the Legitimacy of the State: A Case from Darfur, Western Sudan." In *Conflicts in the Horn of Africa: Human and Ecological Consequences of Warfare*, ed. T. Tvedt. Uppsala, Norway: Uppsala University.

Hashim, Ahmed. 2006. *Insurgency and Counter-Insurgency in Iraq*. London: Hurst and Co.

Hatfield, Michael. 2006. "Fear, Legal Determinacy and the American Lawyering Culture." *Lewis & Clark Law Review* 10:511–29.

Hawkins, Darnel. 1986. *Homicide among Black Americans*. Lanham, MD: University Press of America.

Herbert, Bob. 2010. "Jim Crow Policing." *New York Times*, January 2, A27.

Hernandez, Raymond. 2009. "Dodd to Have Surgery for Prostrate Cancer but Vows to Seek Re-election." *New York Times*, August 1, A12.

Hersh, Seymour. 2004. *Chain of Command: The Road from 9/11 to Abu Ghraib*. New York: HarperCollins.

Herszenhorn, David. 2009. "Ethics Committee Clears 2 Senators Over Loans." *New York Times*, August 8, A9.

Hickman, Laura, and Marika Suttorp. 2008. "Are Deportable Aliens a Unique Threat to Public Safety? Comparing the Recidivism of Deportable and Nondeportable Aliens." *Crime & Public Policy* 7:59–82.

Hilberg, Raul. 1985. The *Destruction of the European Jews*. New York: Holmes and Meier.

Hindelang, Michael. 1974. "The Uniform Crime Reports Revisited." *Journal of Criminal Justice* 2, no. 1: 1–17.

Hindelang, Michael, Michael Gottfredson, and James Garofallo. 1978. *Victims of Personal Crime: An Empirical Foundation for a Theory of Personal Victimization*. Cambridge: Ballinger.

Hindelang, Michael, Travis Hirschi, and Joseph Weis. 1981. *Measuring Delinquency*. Beverly Hills, CA: Sage.

Hinton, S. E. 1967. *Outsiders*. New York: Viking Press.

Hirschi, Travis. 1969. *Causes of Delinquency*. Berkeley and Los Angeles: University of California Press.

Hirschi, Travis, and Michael Gottfredson. 2002. "The Generality of Deviance." In Travis Hirschi, *The Craft of Criminology: Selected Papers*, ed. John Laub. New Brunswick, NJ: Transaction Publishers.

Holder, Eric. 2009. "Attorney General Eric Holder at the Department of Justice African American History Month Program." Washington, DC: U.S. Department of Justice, February 18.

Horowitz, Irving Louis. 1980. *Taking Lives: Genocide and State Power*. New Brunswick, NJ: Transaction Books.

Hunt, S. A., and R. Benford. 1994. "Identity Talk in the Peace and Justice Movement." *Journal of Contemporary Ethnography* 22:488–517.

Ianni, Francis. 1972. *A Family Business*. New York: Sage.

———. 1974. *Black Mafia*. New York: Simon & Schuster.

Immigration Commission. 1911. *Report of the Immigration Commission*. U.S. Congress, Senate, 61st Congr., S. Doc. 750, vol. 36. Washington, DC: U.S. Government Printing Office.

Industrial Commission. 1901. "Special Report on General Statistics of Immigration and the Foreign Born Population." Washington, DC: U.S. Government Printing Office.

Johnson, Richard. 1980. "Social Class and Delinquent Behavior: A New Test." *Criminology* 18:86–93.

Johnson, Simon. 2009. "The Quiet Coup." *Atlantic*, May.

Johnson, Simon and James Kwak. 2010. *13 Bankers: The Wall Street Takeover and the Next Financial Meltdown*. New York: Pantheon Books.

Kaufman, Henry. 2009. *The Road to Financial Reformation: Warnings, Consequences, Reforms*. New York: Wiley.

Kennedy, Robert. 1960. *The Enemy Within: The McClellan Committee's Crusade Against Jimmy Hoffa and Corrupt Labor Unions*. New York: Harper & Row.

Keynes, John Maynard. 1936. *The General Theory of Employment, Interest and Money*. Cambridge: Macmillan/Cambridge University Press.

Klinker, Philip, and Rogers Smith. 1999. *The Unsteady March: The Rise and Decline of Racial Equality in America*. Chicago: University of Chicago Press.

Kornhauser, Ruth. 1978. *Social Sources of Delinquency*. Chicago: University of Chicago Press.

Kouwe, Zachary. 2009a. "Judge Rejects a Settlement Over Bonuses." *New York Times*, September 15, A1.

———. 2009b. "Civil Suit Says Lender Ignored Own Warnings. *New York Times*, December 8, B1, B4.

LaFree, Gary. 1998. *Losing Legitimacy: Street Crime and the Decline of Social Institutions in America*. Boulder, CO: Westview Press.

Lanchester, John. 2009. "Outsmarted: High Finance vs. Human Nature." *New Yorker*, June 1, 83.

Lane, Roger. 1980. "Urban Police and Crime in Nineteenth Century America." In *Crime and Justice: An Annual Review of Research*, ed. N. Morris and M. Tonry, 2:1–44. Chicago: University of Chicago Press.

Laub, John. 2003. "The Life Course of Criminology in the United States." *Criminology* 42:1–26.

Laub, John, Daniel S. Nagin, and Robert J. Sampson. 1988. "Trajectories of Change in Criminal Offending: Good Marriages and the Desistance Process." *American Sociological Review* 63:225–38.

Laub, John, and Robert J. Sampson. 2003. *Shared Beginnings, Divergent Lives: Delinquent Boys to Age 70*. Cambridge, MA: Harvard University Press.

Lemert, Edwin. 1951. *Social Pathology*. New York: McGraw-Hill.

———. 1967. *Human Deviance, Social Problems and Social Control*. Englewood Cliffs, NJ: Prentice-Hall.

Leonhardt, David. 2006. "What Statistics on Home Sales Aren't Saying." *New York Times*, December 6.

Levine, Harry. 2007. Testimony at Hearings of New York State Assembly Committees on Codes and on Corrections, Albany, New York, May 31.

Levitt, Steven, and Sudir Venkatesh. 2001. "The Financial Activities of Urban Street Gangs." *Quarterly Journal of Economics* 115:755–89.

Lewis, Michael. 2008. "The End." *Portfolio.com*, November 11.

———. *The Big Short: Inside the Doomsday Machine*. New York: Norton.

Light, Ivan. 1977. "The Ethnic Vice Industry, 1880–1944." *American Sociological Review* 42:464–79.

Lowenstein, Roger. 2000. *When Genius Fails: The Rise and Fall of Long-Term Capital Management*. New York: Random House.

Lowy, Martin. 1991. *High Rollers: Inside the Savings and Loan Debacle*. New York: Praeger.

Lynch, James, and William Sabol. 2004. "Effects of Incarceration on Informal Social Control in Communities." In *Imprisoning America: The Social Effects of Mass Incarceration*, ed. Mary Patillo, David Weiman, and Bruce Western, 135–64. New York: Russell Sage Foundation.

Makiya, Kanan (Samir al-Khalil). 1989. *Republic of Fear: The Politics of Modern Iraq*. Berkeley and Los Angeles: University of California Press.

Mandl, Sabine. 2001. "Krieg gegen die Frauen." In *Frauenrechte*, ed. Elizabeth Gabriel. Vienna: Neuer Wissenschaftlicher Verlag.

Al-Marashi, Ibrahim. 2002. "Iraq's Security and Intelligence Network: A Guide and Analysis." *Middle-East Review of International Affairs Journal* 6, no. 3:1–13.

Matsueda, Ross. 2006. "Differential Social Organization, Collective Action, and Crime." *Crime, Law & Social Change* 46:3–33.

Matsueda, Ross L., and Ronald L. Akers. 2005. "Donald R. Cressey." In *Encyclopedia of Criminology*, ed. Richard A. Wright and J. Mitchell Miller. New York: Routledge.

Matza, David. 1964. *Delinquency and Drift*. New York: Wiley.

Matza, David, and Gresham Sykes. 1961. "Juvenile Delinquency and Subterranean Values." *American Sociological Review* 26:712–20.

McIntire, Mike. 2009. "Murky Middlemen: Tracking Loans Through a Firm That Holds Millions." *New York Times*, April 24, B1.

McClellan, Scott. 2003. Press briefing. White House, December 3. http://georgewbush-whitehouse.archives.gov/news/releases/2003/12/2003 1203-6.html.

McCord, Joan. 1995. "Crime in the Shadow of History." In *Current Perspectives on Aging and the Life Cycle*, vol. 4, *Delinquency and Disrepute in the Life Course*, ed. John Hagan, 105–18. Greenwich, CT: JAI Press.

Meese, Edwin. 1992. *With Reagan: The Inside Story*. Washington, DC: Regnery Publishing.

Merton, Robert. 1938. "Social Structure and Anomie." *American Sociological Review* 3:672–82.

Messner, S., G. Deane, L. Anselin, and B. Pearson-Nelson. 2005. "Locating the Vanguard in Rising and Falling Homicide Rates Across U.S. Cities." *Criminology* 43:661–96.

Miller, Walter. 1958. "Lower Class Culture as a Generating Milieu of Gang Delinquency." *Journal of Social Issues* 14:5–19.

Mills, C. Wright. 1956. *The Power Elite*. New York: Oxford University Press.

Moffitt, Terrie. 1993. "Adolescence-Limited and Life-Course Persistent Antisocial Behavior: A Developmental Taxonomy." *Psychological Review* 100:674–701.

Monkkonen, Eric. 1981. *Police in Urban America, 1860–1920*. New York: Cambridge University Press.

———. 2006. "AHR Forum: Homicide: Explaining America's Exceptionalism." *American Historical Review* 3, no. 1 (February).

Moore, Joan. 1991. *Going Down to the Barrio: Homeboys and Homegirls in Change*. Philadelphia: Temple University Press.

Moore, Solomon. 2009. "Hispanics Are Largest Ethnic Group in Federal Prisons, Study Shows." *New York Times*, February 10, 2009, A16.

Morgenson, Gretchen. 2009a. "Ex-Chief Accused of Stock Fraud at a Big Lender." *New York Times*, June 5, A1.

———. 2009b. "Looking for Lenders' Little Helpers." *New York Times*, July 12, B2.

———. 2009c. "Revisiting a Fed Waltz with AIG." *New York Times*, November 22, B1, B6.

———. 2009d. "Get Ready, Get Set, Point Fingers." *New York Times*, December 13, B1.

Morgenson, Gretchen. 2010. "The Swaps That Swallowed Your Town." *New York Times*, March 7, B1, B4.

Morgenson, Gretchen, and Louise Story. 2009. "Banks Bundled Debt, Bet Against It and Won." *New York Times*, December 24, A1.

Morgenson, Gretchen, and Don Van Natta. 2009. "Paulson's Calls to Goldman Tested Ethics During Crisis." *New York Times*, August 9, A1.

Morris, Norval, and Gordon Hawkins. 1972. *Honest Politicians' Guide to Crime Control*. Chicago: University of Chicago Press.

Moynihan, Daniel Patrick. 1965. *The Negro Family: The Case for National Action*. Washington, DC: U.S. Department of Labor, Office of Policy and Planning.

———. 1969. *Maximum Feasible Misunderstanding: Community Action in the War on Poverty*. New York: Free Press.

Mumola, Christopher. 2000. *Incarcerated Parents and Their Children*. Bureau of Justice Statistics Report no. NCJ 182335. Washington, DC: U.S. Department of Justice.

Murakawa, Naomi. 2006. "The Racial Antecedents to Federal Sentencing Guidelines." *Roger Williams University Law Review* 11, no. 2: 473–94.

Musto, David. 1973. *The American Disease: Origins of Narcotic Control*. New Haven, CT: Yale University Press.

Nagel, Ilene. 1990. "Foreword: Structuring Sentencing Discretion: The New Federal Sentencing Guidelines." *Journal of Criminal Law & Criminology* 80: 883–943.

Nagin, Daniel. 1998. "Criminal Deterrence Research: A Review of the Evidence and a Research Agenda for the Outset of the 21st Century." *Crime and Justice* 23:1–42.

National Council on Crime and Delinquency. 2006. "U.S. Rates of Incarceration: A Global Perspective." Fact sheet prepared by Christopher Hartney. Oakland, CA: National Council on Crime and Delinquency.

National Institute of Justice. 1984. "Too Much Crime . . . Too Little Justice: The Police, Court, and Correctional Officials Who Administer America's Criminal Justice System Speak Out for Change." Report of the President's Advisory Board. Unpublished. Papers of Joe Persico, State University of New York, Albany.

National Opinion Research Center. 2000. *General Social Survey*. Chicago: National Opinion Research Council at the University of Chicago.

Newman, Gramae. 1976. *Comparative Deviance*. New York: Elsevier.

New York Times. 1970. "Moynihan Memorandum on the Status of Negroes." March 1, 69.

———. 2009. "Editorial: Predatory Brokers." April 10, A18.

———. 2010. "Editorial: AIG, Greece, and Who's Next?" March 5, A20.

Nocera, Joe. 2009. "On Deals, Two Judges Just Say No." *New York Times*, August 15, B2.

Norris, Floyd. 2009. "A Lack of Rigor Has a Price." *New York Times*, November 13, B1, B8.

———. 2010. "Fortunate Timing Seals a Deal." *New York Times*, April 23, B1, B4.

Nye, F. Ivan, and James F. Short. 1957. "Scaling Delinquent Behavior." *American Sociological Review* 22:326–32.

Oberschall, Anthony. 2000. "The Manipulation of Ethnicity: From Ethnic Co-operation to Violence and War in Yugoslavia." *Ethnic and Racial Studies* 23:982–1001.

Office of the Prosecutor. 2007. "Situation in Darfur: The Sudan. Prosecutor's Application under Article 58(7)." No. ICC-02/05. International Criminal Court, February 27, The Hague.

———. 2008. "Situation in Darfur: Prosecutor's Application for Warrant of Arrest Under Article 58 Against Omar Hassan Ahmad AL BASHIR." No. III-OPT-20080714. International Criminal Court, July 14, The Hague.

O'Neill, Tip. 1994. *All Politics Is Local: And Other Rules of the Gang*. Boston: Bob Adams.

Overbye, Dennis. 2009. "Mathematical Models and the Mortgage Mess." *New York Times*, March 10, D4.

Pager, Devah. 2003. "The Mark of a Criminal Record." *American Journal of Sociology* 108:937–75.

———. 2007. *Marked: Race, Crime, and Finding Work in an Era of Mass Incarceration*. Chicago: University of Chicago Press.

Persico, Joseph. 1982. *The Imperial Rockefeller: A Biography of Nelson A. Rockefeller*. New York: Washington Square Press.

Peterson, Ruth, and Lauren Krivo. 2009. "Race, Residence, and Violent Crime: A Structure of Inequality." *Kansas Law Review* 57:903–33.

Pettit, Becky, and Bruce Western. 2004. "Mass Imprisonment and the Life Course: Race and Class Inequality in U.S. Incarceration." *American Sociological Review* 69:151–69.

Pew Center on the States. 2010. *Prison Count 2010: State Population Declines for the First Time in 38 Years*. March. http://www.pewcenteronthestates.org/report_detail.aspx?id=57653.

Philippon, Thomas, and Ariell Reshef. 2009. "Wages and Human Capital in the U.S. Financial Industry: 1909–2006." NBER Working Paper no. 14644. Cambridge, MA: National Bureau of Economic Research.

Pillay, Navi. 2009. "Sexual Violence: Standing By the Victim." Address to The Hague Colloquium on Sexual Violence as an International Crime, Dutch Ministry of Foreign Affairs, June 17.

Platt, Anthony. 1969. *The Child Savers: The Invention of Delinquency*. Chicago: University of Chicago Press.

Portes, A., and J. Sensenbrenner. 1993. "Embeddedness and Immigration: Notes on the Social Determinants of Economic Action." *American Journal of Sociology* 98:1320–50.

Powell, Michael. 2009a. "Blacks and Latinos Are Hit Hardest as New York Foreclosures Rise." *New York Times*, May 16, A14.

———. 2009b. "Suit Accuses Wells Fargo of Steering Blacks to Sub-Prime Mortgages in Baltimore." *New York Times*, June 7, 15.

———. 2009c. "Memphis Accuses Wells Fargo of Discriminating Against Blacks." *New York Times*, December 31, A15.

———. 2010. "Federal Judge Rejects Suit by Baltimore Against Bank." *New York Times*, January 9, A11.

Power, Samantha. 2004. "Dying in Darfur." *New Yorker*, August 30, 58.

Pritchard, J., and S. Zaide. 1981. *The Tokyo War Crimes Trial*. New York: Garland Press.

Quinney, Richard. 1970. *The Social Reality of Crime*. Boston: Little, Brown.

Radlet, Michael. 1989. *Facing the Death Penalty: Essays on a Cruel and Unusual Punishment*. Philadelphia: Temple University Press.

Reagan, Ronald. 1964. "A Time for Choosing: An Address on Behalf of Barry Goldwater." October 27. Ronald Reagan Presidential Library. http://www.reagan.utexas.edu/archives/reference/timechoosing.html.

———. 1981. "Remarks at the Annual Meeting of the International Association of Chiefs of Police in New Orleans, Louisiana." September 28. In *Public Papers of the President, Ronald Reagan, 1981–1989*. Ronald Reagan Presidential Library. http://www.reagan.utexas.edu/archives/speeches/1981/92881a.htm.

———. 1985. "Address before a Joint Session of the Congress on the State of the Union," February 6. In *Public Papers of the President, Ronald Reagan, 1981–1989*. Ronald Reagan Presidential Library. http://www.reagan.utexas.edu/archives/speeches/1985/20685e.htm

Reasons, Charles. 1974. "The Politics of Drugs: An Inquiry in the Sociology of Social Problems." *Sociological Quarterly* 15:381–404.

Reinhart, Carmen M., and Kenneth S. Rogoff. 2009. *This Time Is Different: Eight Centuries of Financial Folly*. Princeton, NJ: Princeton University Press.

Rivera, Amaed, B. Cotto-Escalera, A. Desai, J. Huezo, and D. Muhammad. 2008. *Foreclosed*. Boston: Institute for Policy Studies, United for a Fair Economy.

Robinson, W. S. 1950. "Ecological Correlation and the Behavior of Individuals." *American Sociological Review* 15:351–57.

Roosevelt, President Franklin. 1934. "Address." In *Proceedings of the Attorney General's Conference on Crime*. Washington, DC. http://www.archives.gov/research/guide-fed-records/groups/060.html.

Rose, Dina, and Todd Clear. 1998. "Incarceration, Social Capital, and Crime: Implications for Social Disorganization Theory." *Criminology* 36:441–80.

Rose, H., and P. McClain. 1990. *Race, Place and Risk: Black Homicide in Urban America*. Albany: New York University Press.

Rossi, Peter, Emily Waite, Christine Bose, and Richard Berk. 1974. "The Seriousness of Crimes: Normative Structure and Individual Differences." *American Sociological Review* 39:224–37.

Rothenberg, Daniel. 2008. The Iraq History Project. Institute of Human Rights, DePaul University College of Law, Chicago.

Rumbaut, Ruben. 1997. "Assimilation and Its Discontents: Between Rhetoric and Reality." *International Migration Review* 31:923–60.

Rumbaut, Ruben, and Walter Ewing. 2007. "The Myth of Immigrant Criminality." http://norderbattles.ssrc.org/Rumbaut_Ewing/index.html.

Rusche, George, and Otto Kirchheimer. 1939. *Punishment and Social Structure*. New York: Columbia University Press.

Russell, Richard B. 1960. "Remarks." *Congressional Record*, March 16, 5721.

Sampson, Robert. 1993. "Linking Place and Time: Dynamic Contextualism and the Future of Criminological Inquiry." *Journal of Research in Crime and Delinquency* 4:426–44.

———. 2006. "Open Doors Don't Invite Criminals: Is Increased Immigration Behind the Drop in Crime?" *New York Times*, March 11, A2.

Sampson, Robert, and John H. Laub. 1990. "Stability and Change: Crime and Deviance over the Life Course: The Salience of Adult Social Bonds." *American Sociological Review* 55:609–27.

———. 1992. "Crime and Deviance in the Life Course." *Annual Review of Sociology* 18:63–84.

———. 1993. *Crime in the Making*. Cambridge, MA: Harvard University Press.

———. 2005. "Seductions of Method: Rejoinder to Nagin and Tremblay's 'Developmental Trajectory Groups: Fact or Fiction?'" *Criminology* 43:905–13.

Sampson, Robert, Jeffrey Morenoff, and Felton Earls. 1999. "Beyond Social Capital: Spatial Dynamics of Collective Efficacy for Children." *American Sociological Review* 64:633–60.

Sampson, Robert, Steven Raudenbush, and Felton Earls. 1997. "Neighborhoods and Violent Crime: A Multilevel Study of Collective Efficacy." *Science* 277:918–24.

Sampson, Robert, and P.O. Wikstrom. 2009. "The Social Order of Violence in Chicago and Stockholm Neighborhoods: A Comparative Inquiry." In *Order, Conflict and Violence*, ed. Stathis Kalyvas, Ian Shapiro, and Tarek Masoud. Cambridge: Cambridge University Press.

Sampson, Robert, and William Julius Wilson. 1994. "Toward and Theory of Race, Crime and Urban Inequality." In *Crime and Inequality*, ed. John Hagan and Ruth Peterson. Stanford, CA: Stanford University Press.

Sands, Philippe. 2008. *Torture Team: Rumsfeld's Memo and the Betrayal of American Values*. New York: Macmillan.

Sassen, Saskia. 1999. *Globalization and Its Discontents*. New York: New Press.

Satter, Beryl. 2009. *Family Properties: Race, Real Estate, and the Exploitation of Black Urban America*. New York: Metropolitan Books.

Savelsberg, Joachim J. 1992. "Law That Does Not Fit Society: Sentencing Guidelines as a Neoclassical Reaction to the Dilemmas of Substantivized Law." *American Journal of Sociology* 97:1346–81.

———. 1994. "Knowledge, Domination, and Criminal Punishment." *American Journal of Sociology* 99:911–43.

———. 2010. *Crimes Against Humanity*. In press. Thousnad Oaks, CA: Sage.

Savelsberg, Joachim, Lara Cleveland, and Ryan King. 2004. "Institutional Environments and Scholarly Work: American Criminology, 1951–1993." *Social Forces* 82:1275–1302.

Savelsberg, Joachim, and S. Flood. 2004. "Criminological Knowledge: Period and Cohort Effects in Scholarship." *Criminology* 42, no. 4: 1009–41.

Savelsberg, Joachim, Ryan King, and Lara Cleveland. 2002. "Politicized Scholarship? Science on Crime and the State." *Social Problems* 49:327–48.

Savelsberg, Joachim, and Robert Sampson. 2002. "Introduction: Mutual Engagement: Criminology and Sociology?" *Crime, Law, and Social Change* 37:99–105.

Sayad, Abdelmalek. 2004. *The Suffering of the Immigrant*. Cambridge, MA: Polity Press.

Scheingold, Stuart. 1984. *The Politics of Law and Order: Street Crime and Public Policy*. New York: Longman.

Schoenfeld, Heather. 2009. "The Politics of Prison Growth: From Chain Gangs to Work Release Centers and Supermax Prisons, Florida, 1955–2000." Ph.D. diss., Northwestern University, Evanston, Ill.

Schrager, Laura, and James Short. 1978. "Toward a Sociology of Organizational Crime." *Social Problems* 25:407–19.

Scott, Peter, and Jonathan Marshall. 1998. *Cocaine Politics: Drugs, Armies, and the CIA in Central America*. Berkeley and Los Angeles: University of California Press.

Segal, David. 2009a. "Ohio Sues Ratings Firms For Losses in Funds." *New York Times*, November 21, B1, B6.

———. 2009b. "Despite Crisis, Raters of Debt Skirt Overhaul." *New York Times*, December 8, A1, A20.

Sellin, Thorsten. 1938. *Culture Conflict and Crime*. New York: Social Science Research Council.

Sellin, Thorsten, and Marvin Wolfgang. 1964. *The Measurement of Delinquency*. New York: Wiley.

Shane, Scott. 2008. "China Inspired Interrogations at Guantanamo." *New York Times*, July 2.

Shank, Gregory. 2008. "Paul Takagi Honored." *Crime and Social Justice* 35:2.

Shapiro, Susan. 1984. *The Wayward Capitalists*. New Haven, CT: Yale University Press.

Shaw, Clifford, and Henry McKay. 1931. *Social Factors in Juvenile Delinquency*. Washington, DC: National Commission of Law Observance and Enforcement.

Simon, Jonathan. 1998. "Refugees in a Carceral Age: The Rebirth of Immigration Prisons in the United States." *Public Culture* 10:577–606.

———. 2007. *Governing Through Crime*. New York: Oxford University Press.

Simon, William, and John Gagnon. 1976. "The Anomie of Affluence: A Post-Mertonian Conception." *American Journal of Sociology* 82:356–78.

Shaw, Clifford, and Henry McKay. 1931. *Social Factors in Juvenile Delinquency*. Washington, DC: National Commission of Law Observance and Enforcement.

Skogan, Wesley. 1986. "Methodological Issues in the Study of Victimization." In *Crime Policy to Victim Policy*, ed. Ezat Fattah. New York: St. Martin's Press.

Smith, Adam. 1937. *Wealth of Nations*, ed. Edwin Canann. New York: Random House.

Smith, William French. 1991. *Law and Justice in the Reagan Administration: The Memoirs of an Attorney General*. Stanford, CA: Hoover Institution Press.

Snow, David, and Pamela Oliver. 1995. "Social Movements and Collective Behavior: Social Psychological Dimensions and Considerations." In *Sociological Perspectives on Social Psychology*, ed. Karen Cook, Gary Fine, and James House. Boston: Allyn & Bacon.

Snow, David, E. Rochford, S. Worden, and S. Benford. 1986. "Frame Alignment Processes, Micromobilization, and Movement Participation." *American Sociological Review* 51:464–81.

Sorkin, Andrew. 2009. *Too Big to Fail: The Inside Story of How Wall Street and Washington Fought to Save the Financial System from Crisis—and Themselves*. New York: Viking.

———. 2010. "At Lehman, Watchdogs Were in Place." *New York Times*, March 15, B1, B8.

Spitzer, Steven. 1975. "Toward a Marxian Theory of Deviance." *Social Problems* 22:638–51.

Stewart, James. 1991. *Den of Thieves*. New York: Simon & Schuster.

Steffensmeier, D., E. A. Allan, M. Harer, and C. Streifel. 1989. "Age and the Distribution of Crime." *American Journal of Sociology* 94:803–31.

Steffensmeier, Darrell, and Jeffrey Ulmer. 2006. "Black and White Control of Numbers Banking in Black Communities, 1970–2000." *American Sociological Review* 71:123–56.

Stith, Kate, and Steve Koh. 1993. "The Politics of Sentencing Reform: The Legislative History of the Federal Sentencing Guidelines." *Wake Forest Law Review* 28:223–90.

Story, Louise, and Andrew Dash. 2009. "E-Mail Shows Concerns Over Merrill Deal." *New York Times*, October 14, B1.

Story, Louise, and Landon Thomas. 2009. "Tales from Lehman's Crypt." *New
York Times*, September 13, B1, B7.

Story, Louise, Landon Thomas, and Nelson Schwartz. 2010. "Wall St. Helped
Mask Debt Shaking Europe." *New York Times*, February 14, A1, A16.

Streitfeld, David, and John Collins Rudolf. 2009. "States Are Pondering
Fraud Suits Against Banks." *New York Times*, November 3, B1.

Sullivan, Andrew. 2009. "Dear President Bush." *Atlantic*, October, 78.

Sullivan, Mercer. 1989. *Getting Paid: Youth Crime and Work in the Inner City.*
Ithaca, NY: Cornell University Press.

Surowiecki, James. 2009. "Ratings Downgrade." *New Yorker*, September 28, 25.

Sutherland, Edwin. 1924. *Criminology*. Philadelphia: Lippincott.

———. 1943. "Development of the Theory." In *Edwin H. Sutherland on Analyzing
Crime*, ed. Karl Schuessler, 13–29. Chicago: University of Chicago Press.

———. 1949. *White Collar Crime*. New York: Dryden Press.

Sutton, John. 2000. "Imprisonment and Social Classification in Five Common-
Law Democracies, 1955–1985." *American Journal of Sociology* 2:350–86.

Swigert, Victoria Lynn, and Ronald Farrell. 1980. "Corporate Homicide: Definitional Processes in the Creation of Deviance." *Law & Society Review*
125:161–82.

Sykes, Gresham, and David Matza. 1957. "Techniques of Neutralization: A
Theory of Delinquency." *American Sociological Review* 22:664–70.

Taguba, Major General Antonio. 2004. "Treatment of Abu Ghraib Prisoners
in Iraq, Article 15–6 Investigation of the 800th Military Police Brigade,
March." http://news.findlaw.com (April 4, 2004).

Tanenhaus, Sam. 2009. *The Death of Conservatism*. New York: Random House.

Tannenbaum, Franklin. 1938. *Crime and the Community*. Boston: Ginn.

Taylor, Stuart. 1984. "New Crime Act a Vast Change, Officials Assert." *New
York Times*, October 15, A1.

Taylor, Ian, Paul Walton, and Jock Young. 1973. *The New Criminology: For a
Social Theory of Deviance*. London: Routledge.

Tett, Gillian. 2009. *Fool's Gold*. New York: Simon & Schuster.

Thomas, Michael. 1991. "The Greatest American Shambles." *New York Review of Books*, January 31, 30–35.

Thompson, Hunter. 1967. *Hell's Angels*. New York: Ballantine.

Thornberry, Terrence, and Margaret Farnsworth. 1982. "Social Correlates of
Criminal Involvement: Further Evidence on the Relationship between Social Status and Criminal Behavior." *American Sociological Review* 47:505–18.

Tilly, Charles. 1985. "War Making and State Making as Organized Crime." In
Bringing the State Back In, ed. Peter Evans, Dietrich Rueschemeyer, and
Theda Skocpol, 169–91. Cambridge: Cambridge University Press.

Timberlake, James. 1963. *Prohibition and the Progressive Movement: 1900–1920*. Cambridge, MA: Harvard University Press.

Tittle, Charles, and Robert Meier. 1990. "Specifying the SES Delinquency Relationship." *Criminology* 28:271–99.

Tittle, Charles, W. J. Villemez, and Douglas Smith. 1978. "The Myth of Social Class and Criminality: An Empirical Assessment of the Empirical Evidence." *American Sociological Review* 47:505–18.

Tonry, Michael. 1995. *Malign Neglect: Race, Crime, and Punishment in America*. New York: Oxford University Press.

———. 1996. *Sentencing Matters*. New York: Oxford University Press.

Tracy, Paul, Marvin Wolfgang, and Robert Figlio. 1985. *Delinquency Careers in Two Birth Cohorts*. New York: Putnam Press.

Tripp, Charles. 2002. *History of Iraq*. New York, Cambridge University Press.

Turk, Austin. 1969. *Criminality and the Legal Order*. Chicago: Rand McNally.

———. 1976. "Law, Conflict and Order: From Theorizing Toward Theories." *Canadian Review of Sociology and Anthropology* 13:282–94.

United Nations (UN). 1998. Judgment: The Prosecutor v. Jean-Paul Akayesu. International Criminal Tribunal for Rwanda, Case No. IT-96–4-T. http://www.ictr.org.

———. 1999a. Judgment: The Prosecutor v. Goran Jelisi. International Criminal Tribunal for the former Yugoslavia, Case No. IT-95-T. http://www.icty.org.

———. 1999b. Judgment: The Prosecutor v. Goran Jelisi. International Criminal Tribunal for the former Yugoslavia, Case No. IT-95-T. U.S. Department of State, 2004. http://www.icty.org.

———. 2004. *Documenting Atrocities in Darfur*. Washington, DC: Bureau of Democracy, Human Rights, and Labor and Bureau of Intelligence and Research.

U.S. Department of State. 2004. *Documenting Atrocities in Darfur*. Washington, DC: Bureau of Democracy, Human Rights and Labor and Bureau of Intelligence and Research.

U.S. Sentencing Commission. 1991. *The Federal Sentencing Guidelines*. Washington, DC: United States Sentencing Commission.

U.S. Sentencing Commission. 1995. *Special Report to the Congress: Cocaine and Federal Sentencing*. Washington, DC: U.S. Sentencing Commission, March.

van der Wilt, Harmen. 2009. "The Continuous Quest for Proper Modes of Criminal Responsibility." *Journal of International Criminal Justice* 7:307–14.

Vasagar, Jeevan. 2004. "Militia Chief Scorns Slaughter Charge." *Guardian*, July 16.

Veblen, Thorstein. 1899. *The Theory of the Leisure Class*. New York: Viking Press.

Visher, Christy. 1986. "The Rand Inmate Survey: A Reanalysis." In *Criminal Careers and "Career Criminals,"* vol. 1, ed. Alfred Blumstein et al. Washington, DC: National Academy Press.

Vold, George. 1958. *Theoretical Criminology*. New York: Oxford University Press.

Wacquant, Loic. 1999. "'Suitable Enemies': Foreigners and Immigrants in the Prisons of Europe." *Punishment and Society* 1:215–23.

———. 2001. "Deadly Symbiosis: When Ghetto and Prison Meet and Mesh." *Punishment and Society* 3:95–133.

Warren, H. 2007. "Measure Against Rape Fails at the U.N." *New York Times*, November 17, A10.

Wax, Emily. 2004. "In Sudan: A 'Big Sheik' Roams Free." *Washington Post*, July 18.

Wayne, Leslie. 2009. "Goldman Pays to End State Inquiry Into Loans." *New York Times*, May 12, B3.

Weaver, Vesla. 2007. "Frontlash: Race and the Development of Punitive Crime Policy." *Studies in American Political Development* 21:230–65.

Webb, James. 2009. "The National Criminal Justice Act of 2009. Introduced in the Senate March 26, 2009." http://webb.senate.gov/issuesandlegislation/criminaljusticeandlawenforcement/Criminal_Justice_Banner.cfm.

West, Donald, and David Farrington. 1977. *The Delinquent Way of Life*. London: Heinemann.

Western, Bruce. 2006. *Punishment and Inequality in America*. New York: Russell Sage Foundation.

Western, Bruce, and Becky Pettit. 2005. "Black-White Wage Inequality, Employment Rates, and Incarceration." *American Journal of Sociology* 111: 553–78.

Western, Bruce, Becky Pettit, and Josh Guetzkow. 2002. "Black Economic Progress in the Era of Mass Imprisonment." In *Collateral Damage: The Social Cost of Mass Incarceration*, ed. Meda Chesney-Lind and Marc Maurer. New York: Free Press.

Wheeler, Stanton, and Michael Rothman. 1982. "The Organization as Weapon in White Collar Crime." *Michigan Law Review* 80, no. 7: 1403–26.

Wildeman, Christopher. 2009. "Parental Imprisonment, the Prison Boom, and the Concentration of Childhood Disadvantage." *Demography* 46:265–80.

Wilentz, Sean. 2008. *The Age of Reagan: A History, 1974–2008*. New York: Harper Collins.

Wilkins, Leslie. 1964. *Social Deviance*. London: Tavistock.

Wilson, James Q. 1975. *Thinking About Crime*. New York: Basic Books.

———. 1993. "Crime and Public Policy." In *Crime*, ed. James Q. Wilson and Joan Petersilia. Ithaca, NY: ICS Press.

———. 1994. "Prisons in a Free Society." *Public Interest* 11:37–40.

Wilson, James Q., and Richard Herrenstein. 1986. *Crime and Human Nature*. New York: Simon & Schuster.

Wolfgang, Marvin. 1972. *Delinquency in a Birth Cohort*. Chicago: University of Chicago Press.

———. 1995. "Transitions of Crime in the Aging Process." In *Delinquency and Disrepute in the Life Course*, ed. John Hagan. Greenwich, CT: JAI Press.

Wood, Elizabeth. 2006. "Variation in Sexual Violence During War." *Politics & Society* 34:307–41.

Zanetti, Veronique. 2007. "Women, War, and International Law." In *Civilian Immunity in War*, ed. Igor Primorate. Oxford: Oxford University Press.

Zatz, Marjorie, and William Chambliss. 1993. *Making Law: Law, the State and Structural Contradictions*. Bloomington: Indiana University Press.

Zawati, Hilmi. 2007. "Impunity or Immunity: Wartime Male Rape and Sexual Torture as a Crime Against Humanity." *Torture* 17:27–47.

Zubaida, Sami. 2003. "The Rise and Fall of Civil Society in Iraq." http://www.Opendemocracy.net/debates/article-2–88–953.jsp.

Zuckerman, Gregory. 2009. *The Greatest Trade Ever: The Behind-the-Scenes Story of How John Paulson Defied Wall Street and Made Financial History*. New York: Broadway Books.

INDEX
||||||||||